The Transnational Crime of Human Trafficking

Human trafficking is a multi-faceted crime. It suffers from definitional and implementation problems. One facet, the focus of this book, is the transnational nature of much of the crime, and the need for practitioners to operate across borders to combat it.

Europe has taken a distinctive approach to cross border law enforcement and judicial cooperation, which could be used as a model in other areas of the world. This publication examines these problems from a Council of Europe and European Union perspective, including the now post-Brexit UK. The UK has adopted a distinctive approach to legislating and operationalising its trafficking in human beings (THB) legal frameworks, also legislating for "slavery, servitude, forced and compulsory labour", resulting in distinctive results in internal UK law enforcement. It is argued here that this approach and the results should inform THB legislative and operational developments more widely. Further action in legal and operational frameworks is, however, clearly needed and the book advocates the adoption of a human security "freedom from fear" approach. Ultimately, the interaction of different legal frameworks, and different jurisdictions requires transnational practitioners to adopt a constructivist approach, as was adopted for the development of the internal EU area of freedom, security and justice.

The book will be of interest to academics, researchers and policy-makers working in the areas of transnational law, migration law, criminology and international relations.

Maria O'Neill is senior lecturer in law, University of Abertay, UK.

Transnational Criminal Justice

The concept of 'transnational criminal justice' has frequently been interpreted in the academic literature as 'international criminal justice' or 'global criminal justice'. Many publications that use the term 'transnational' therefore discuss international criminal justice and international legal frameworks. Another form of studies that has developed under the umbrella of transnationality in the field of criminal law is comparative. There has hence been a move from the terminology of 'international', 'global' and 'comparative' criminal justice towards 'transnational' criminal justice.

This series considers these developments, but focuses primarily on publications that adhere to a more literal interpretation of the term 'transnational'. The aim of the series is to provide a forum for discussion of bilateral and multilateral relationships between nations in the field of criminal justice. International law influences these relationships, but is not the focus here. Equally, to explain transnational relationships, comparative analyses are required. While incorporating comparative studies in this series, their aim is the explanation of challenges to criminal justice cooperation in bilateral or multilateral relationships.

Series Editor
Saskia Hufnagel, Queen Mary University of London, UK

Titles in this series:

Terrorism, Criminal Law and Politics
The Decline of the Political Offence Exception to Extradition
Julia Jansson

Assets, Crimes and the State
Innovations in 21st Century Legal Responses
Edited by Katie Benson, Colin King and Clive Walker

Policing Transnational Crime
Law Enforcement of Criminal Flows
Edited by Saskia Hufnagel and Anton Moiseienko

Confinement, Punishment and Prisons in Africa
Edited by Marie Morelle, Frédéric Le Marcis and Julia Hornberger

Global Perspectives on Cultural Property Crime
Edited by Michelle D. Fabiani, Kate Melody Burmon and Saskia Hufnagel

For more information about this series, please visit: https://www.routledge.com/Transnational-Criminal-Justice/book-series/TRANSCJ

The Transnational Crime of Human Trafficking

A Human Security Approach

Maria O'Neill

Routledge
Taylor & Francis Group
LONDON AND NEW YORK

First published 2024
by Routledge
4 Park Square, Milton Park, Abingdon, Oxon OX14 4RN

and by Routledge
605 Third Avenue, New York, NY 10158

Routledge is an imprint of the Taylor & Francis Group, an informa business

British Library Cataloguing-in-Publication Data
A catalogue record for this book is available from the British Library

Library of Congress Cataloging-in-Publication Data
Names: O'Neill, Maria, author.
Title: The transnational crime of human trafficking / Maria O'Neill.
Description: Abingdon, Oxon [UK] ; New York, NY : Routledge, 2023. | Series: Transnational criminal justice | Includes bibliographical references and index. | Summary Provided by publisher.
Identifiers: LCCN 2023023360 (print) | LCCN 2023023361 (ebook) | ISBN 9781032552613 (hardback) | ISBN 9781032552620 (paperback) | ISBN 9781003429791 (ebook)
Subjects: LCSH: Human trafficking (International law) | Human trafficking--Law and legislation--Grat Britain. | Human trafficking--Law and legislation--European Union countries.
Classification: LCC KZ7155 .O54 2023 (print) | LCC KZ7155 (ebook) | DDC 345/.02551--dc23/eng/20230802
LC record available at https://lccn.loc.gov/2023023360
LC ebook record available at https://lccn.loc.gov/2023023361

ISBN: 978-1-032-55261-3 (hbk)
ISBN: 978-1-032-55262-0 (pbk)
ISBN: 978-1-003-42979-1 (ebk)

DOI: 10.4324/9781003429791

Typeset in Galliard
by Taylor & Francis Books

Contents

Table

Acknowledgements

This book started with a small research grant from the Society of Legal Scholars, which, along with consultancy fee income, together with research leave from the University of Abertay, enabled a period of stay at the Institute of Advanced Legal Studies, London, as a visiting research fellow. Brexit and Covid-19 contributed to a delay in completing this project. My thanks to all those who supported the development of this book.

1 Introduction

Introduction

The crime of trafficking in human beings (THB) is gaining a renewed focus within the European Union (EU), and the member states of the EU. This is a complex crime, which is difficult to distinguish from other closely related crimes, both legally and in the practice of law enforcement. By its very nature it regularly crosses jurisdictional boundaries, with jurisdictions being either source, transit, or destination countries. Clear countries of origin have been identified by the EU, with bi-lateral law enforcement arrangements having been developed in a number of these cases. The European Commission reports that Nigeria, Albania, Vietnam, China, and Sudan all featured prominently as countries of origin.[1] Many of these countries are also significant countries of origin for the now post Brexit United Kingdom (UK).

While it is difficult to come up with definitive numbers as to the extent of THB, the European Commission in their 2020 report,[2] using 2017–2018 data, were reporting 14,145 victims of trafficking in the then EU 27 member states, and when the pre-Brexit United Kingdom (UK) numbers were added, 26,268 victims. Is should be noted that reported does not mean actual victims, as many go unreported. The European Commission found that 60% of the recorded victims were trafficked for sexual exploitation, with 15% bring trafficked for labour exploitation in the EU 27, with the numbers being 46% and 22% when the pre-Brexit UK was added. The EU 2020 report stated that 72% female victims and 23% male for the EU 27, becoming 58% and 39% with pre-Brexit UK numbers.[3] The UK has been reporting much higher than EU average male and forced labour numbers for some years.[4] Forty-nine per cent of the EU 27 victims in the 2020 report were

1 European Commission, Data collection on trafficking in human beings in the EU, Publications Office of the European Union, 2020, p 27.
2 Ibid.
3 Ibid., p 6.
4 E.g. Official Statistics, Modern Slavery: National Referral Mechanism and Duty to Notify statistics UK, Quarter 1 2021 – January to March second edition, updated 27 January 2022, published 3 June 2021 (online) which was reporting 75% male to 25% female potential victims of trafficking.

DOI: 10.4324/9781003429791-1

EU nationals, with that number being 41% when UK numbers were added, with 34% of the EU 27 victims having been trafficked in their own state, and 27% with the pre-Brexit UK added. Of these victims 22% were children in the EU 27, with 32% with the UK.[5] The 2021–2022 annual report of the UK's Independent Ant-slavery Commissioner, was reporting that 12,727 referrals had been made in 2021 to the UK's National Referral Mechanism (NRM), up 20% on 2020, with a further 3,190 potential victims having been identified, but who did not want to enter the NRM.[6] 5,465 potential child victims were identified in the UK in 2021–2022 annual report.[7]

As evidenced by the above numbers, THB may happen within one country, thereby making it a purely domestic crime, but more often it is a transnational crime. Related crimes are also listed as international law crimes, becoming subject to the jurisdiction of the International Criminal Court. When sufficiently serious, enslavement, sexual slavery and enforced prostitution are all listed as crimes against humanity under Article 7 of the Rome Statute of the International Criminal Court. The Rome Statute also provides at Article 8 for war crimes, which includes sexual slavery and enforced prostitution. War crimes and crimes against humanity, as international crimes, occur less frequently than transnational crimes, and are outside the focus of this book.

The current global framework to combat THB is the Protocol to Prevent, Suppress and Punish Trafficking in Persons, Especially Women and Children (THB Protocol), supplementing the United Nations Convention against Transnational Organized Crime 2000 (Palermo Convention), which came into force in 2003. The THB Protocol, taking the "3Ps" approach of prosecuting the act, prevention, and protection of victims of trafficking has, at the time of writing, 117 signatories and 181 parties, with countries still joining in 2023. Putting the global consensus underpinning the THB Protocol effectively into force is now the current challenge, in all countries, and not just the protocol's most recent signatories. The basic legal framework in Europe comprises the Council of Europe (CoE) Convention against Trafficking in Human Beings 2005 (the Warsaw Convention),[8] and the EU Directive 2011/36/EU on THB (THB directive).[9]

It should be noted that the crime of THB has been legislated for by the UN in the context of organised crime, together with its allied, but different crime of human smuggling. THB has been disaggregated from organised crime in other legal documents and jurisdictions. The THB definition in other fora now includes other crimes which have been previously and differently legislated for by a variety of international organisations, as well as in individual states domestic laws, to

5 European Commission, op. cit., p 6.
6 Independent Anti-Slavery Commissioner, Annual Report 2021–2022, HMSO, 2022, p 7.
7 Ibid., p 20.
8 CETS No. 197.
9 Directive 2011/36/EU of the European Parliament and of the Council of 5 April 2011 on preventing and combating trafficking in human beings and protecting its victims, and replacing Council Framework Decision 2002/629/JHA, OJ L 101/1.

include slavery, forced labour, forced prostitution, forced begging, child sexual exploitation, and the forced removal of human organs. Pinning down exactly what is the definition of the crime of THB, to facilitate effective and efficient interactions between states, is a challenge. This challenge will be taken up in Chapter 2.

As stated by Stoyanova,[10] THB can be examined either through the human rights prism, or through the criminal law prism. Much academic legal scholarship to date has focused on the rights debate, and the obligations on states to properly legislate to combat THB. The distinctive criminal law prism can then be divided into international, transnational and national criminal law. The "multifaceted nature of the trafficking phenomenon"[11] also provides much space for criminal legal argument, with many focusing on the boundaries between THB and prostitution (to include child sexual exploitation) and THB and migration.[12] Neglected in academic debate to date has been the legal obligation to develop, operationalise and deepen existing transnational criminal law provisions in order to combat THB along the trafficking supply chains. While there is merit is saying that the outer edges of THB is legally problematic,[13] the issue of legal definitions also impacts on the development and operationalisation of the transnational legal framework to combat THB, law enforcement, particularly in Europe, are finding that the volume of serious THB is such that law enforcement is only going over the lowest hanging fruit.[14] In addition, the approach to legislating for THB the UK (examined in Chapter 7), having taken a much broader approach than is adopted under its international and European legal obligations, to also include the crimes of "slavery, servitude, forced and compulsory labour", is also instructive. This contribution argues that the Canadian human security approach, of freedom from fear, advocated by Glasius and Kaldor,[15] should be adopted to deal with THB. This would require further development of International and European THB law and practice, to include using several other legal provisions, many of which already exist. Practitioners tasked with operationalisation of, what is for them, multi-layered legal frameworks transnationally would need to adopt Onuf-style constructivism[16] in order to develop the necessary transnational law enforcement and prosecution frameworks, and thereby both better protect victims of THB and

10 V. Stoyanova, *Human Trafficking and Slavery Reconsidered: Conceptual Limits and States' Positive Obligations in European Law*, Cambridge University Press, 2017, p 427.
11 E. Herlin-Karnell, 'Understanding Trafficking in Human Beings as Mixed Migration', in R. Haverkamp, E. Herlin-Karnell and C. Lernestedt, *What is Wrong with Human Trafficking? Critical Perspectives on the Law*, Hart Publishing, 2018, p 101.
12 Stoyanova, op. cit.
13 R. Haverkamp, E. Herlin-Karnell and C. Lernested, 'Introduction', in R. Haverkamp, E. Herlin-Karnell and C. Lernestedt, *What is Wrong with Human Trafficking? Critical Perspectives on the Law*, Hart Publishing, 2018, p 4.
14 Europol presentation at the IALS, London on the 3 October 2017.
15 M. Glasius, and M. Kaldor, *A Human Security Doctrine for Europe: Project, Principles, Practicalities*, Routledge, 2006.
16 N. Onuf, *World of Our Making*, University of South Carolina Press, 1989.

related exploitation, and better combat transnational crime, a requirement of state security.

Human Security

In this era of globalisation, a new security paradigm needs to emerge. Both new technology and increased mobility "have infused the transnationalisation of criminal activity".[17] As we are all living in a transnational world, not only does "national society" and the "international legal order … [require us] to ensure the legal equality of all individuals",[18] but so too does the emerging transnational legal framework. As has been recognised by many commentators, we can no longer secure inside the state by isolating it from the outside. Kaldor has stated that "the outside is increasingly perceived as a world where individuals as well as state rights apply", and where states "no longer have the same autonomy to pursue their interests".[19] Security in this context is "in fact very broad, and demands a broad and well-equilibrated, multi-agency approach", with the "blurring of the lines between global and domestic" already having an impact.[20] Is worth noting that Kaldor, among others, refers to the blurring of boundaries between inside and outside the state. She does not discuss the disappearing of boundaries.[21] The negotiation of that blurring of boundaries requires constructivism, not just by states, and diplomats, but by all those involved in the cross-border justice or law enforcement operation, both as individuals and as agencies of their own state. Illicit markets, such as the THB market, "pits governments against agile, stateless and resourceful networks empowered by globalisation",[22] with the "weakness of states [being] often exploited (and sometimes caused) by criminal elements".[23]

Generally, but also in the context of THB, there is a need to focus on human beings, in a transnational context, and not just on the concept of "state security", with the UN's Human Development Report calling for a move away "from an exclusive stress on territorial security to a much greater stress on people's security".[24] The right to personal security is seen as not just protection from "agents of the state" but also "safety against physical assault by private actors".[25] States have

17 M. den Boer, 'Governing Transnational Law Enforcement in the EU: Accountability after Fusing Internal and External Security', in M. den Boer and J. de Wilde, *The Viability of Human Security*, Amsterdam University Press, 2008, p 71.
18 W. Bruggeman, 'Failing Global Justice and Human Security', in M. den Boer and J. de Wilde, *The Viability of Human Security*, Amsterdam University Press, 2008, p 66.
19 M. Kaldor, 'From Just War to Just Peace', in M. den Boer and J. de Wilde, *The Viability of Human Security, Amsterdam University Press*, 2008, p 24.
20 Bruggeman, op. cit., p 60.
21 Kaldor, op. cit., p 36.
22 Bruggeman, op. cit., p 57.
23 Ibid., p 57.
24 *Human Development Report 1994*, UNDP, New York, 1994, p 24.
25 J. Donnelly, *Universal Human Rights in Theory and Practice*, Cornell University Press, 2013, p 35.

"tended to privilege state security through an emphasis on enhanced border control and law enforcement", in their responses to human trafficking,[26] which has led to clear problems in their approach. The concept of "human security" is emerging to occupy this space. A human security approach provides that "all lives ought to weigh the same".[27] The concept of human security, as pointed out by Friman and Reich, "originates from the policy community", rather than the academic or legal community, resulting in a "relative lack of theoretical and analytical precision".[28] Rather it has emerged to address a particular security challenge.

The concept of human security was "first coined in the 1994 Human Development Report" of the UN Development Programme, and further developed into a broad ranging policy agenda by the Commission on Human Security.[29] While human security is "peopled centred"[30] two diverging dominant themes have emerged from this debate, the concept of "freedom from want" championed by Japan, and "freedom from fear", advocated by Canada. While both themes feed into the broader trafficking in human beings' discourse, this book will follow the "freedom from fear" approach. For Canada, the freedom from fear approach to human security has identified five policy priorities; "protection of civilians, peace support operations, conflict prevention, governance and accountability, and public safety".[31] These all form the backdrop to issues relating to human trafficking, in particular the protection of civilians and public safety themes.

THB often arises in the context of failed states or states in conflict, where individuals are no longer benefiting from the protection of their state of origin, or they have become effectively stateless. The challenges of protecting individuals where there is a lack of a state counterpart to interact with are large. Nevertheless, there are enough effectively operating states which can cooperate to combat THB along the trafficking supply chain. A focus needs to be taken on human beings, with all human beings being of equal worth, and not just a state's own citizens. It should be possible to substantially reduce the gaps of protection of the individual arising from the lack of protection being given to the failed state or state in conflict.

The concept of "human security" is closely connected with the concept of "human rights". However is should be noted that "distinctions of nationality are deeply embedded in international human rights regimes",[32] with the right to claim human rights being "only against governments of which they are nationals"

26 H. R. Friman and S. Reich, 'Human Trafficking and Human Security', in H. R. Friman and S. Reich, *Human Trafficking, Human Security and the Balkans*, Pittsburgh Press, 2007, p 136/7.

27 J. de Wilde, 'Speaking or Doing Human Security?', in M. den Boer and J. de Wilde, *The Viability of Human Security*, Amsterdam University Press, 2008, p 237.

28 Friman and Reich, op. cit., p 138.

29 Kaldor, op. cit., p 35.

30 Human Development Report, op. cit., p 23.

31 Bruggeman, op. cit., p 59.

32 Donnelly, op. cit., p 274.

or are otherwise resident.[33] However internationally recognised human rights, to include the right to be free from slavery or slave like practices, are, as stated by Donnelly, "minimal standards of decency, not luxuries of the West".[34] The concept of "human security" requires that "nation-states can no longer privilege the lives of their own nationals",[35] requiring states to intervene to protect those individuals that come within their sphere of influence, and who are not being adequately protected, whether it is due to war, or in the case of failed or weak states, by their own states.[36] Human security thinking is often deployed in the context of military operations, arguing for the means to be used to be "based on law enforcement rather than war-fighting", with its premise in a zone of conflict being "the equal value of all human lives" rather than traditionally, in the context of war, "privileging one side",[37] as in the case of transnational crime, and in particular in THB situations. The same argument needs to be deployed in non-war like security situations, when both nationals and non-nationals within a particular states' sphere of influence needs to be protected, such as the willingness to investigate and prosecute across state boundaries transnational serious and organised crime, an issue which will be examined in Chapter 4. Yet the "human security approach remains underutilised and its potential unrealized".[38] It is this author's view, supporting Friman and Reich, that the human security approach best meets the needs of tackling transnational crime of THB.

Human security, while now a very broad concept, includes issues related to transnational crime. In addition, the UN Millennium Declaration of the General Assembly, of 8 September 2000, takes a human security approach, referring, *inter alia*, to the need to "intensify our efforts to fight transnational crime in all its dimensions, including trafficking as well as smuggling in human beings and money laundering".[39] Another important document in this area, the Helsinki Final Act of the Conference on Security and Cooperation in Europe (CSCE), the predecessor to the Organisation for Security and Cooperation in Europe (OSCE), set out the cold war view of security cooperation in Europe, along with a very broad range of other policy areas that East and West were to cooperate on. Donnelly argues that the "most important elements of the Helsinki process" were its human rights provisions, with human rights "not merely addressed in a major security agreement between the superpowers" but "were treated as a security measure".[40] They were used as a point of argument between East and West for many years after the conclusion of the agreement.

33 Ibid.
34 Ibid., p 213.
35 M. Glasius and M. Kaldor, 'A Human Security Vision for Europe and Beyond', in M. Glasius and M. Kaldor, *A Human Security Doctrine for Europe: Project, Principles, Practicalities*, London, Routledge, 2006, p 15.
36 Ibid.
37 Ibid., p 17.
38 Friman and Reich, op. cit., p 153/4.
39 UN Millennium Declaration of the General Assembly, of 8 September 2000, II. Peace Security and Disarmament, 9. 7th indent.
40 Donnelly, op. cit., p 261.

Following the "freedom from fear" analysis, the EU's Barcelona Report has called for "coordination between intelligence, foreign policy, trade policy, development policy and security policy initiatives" of the EU member states and the EU's institutions. This was to be done along with "other multilateral actors, including the United Nations, the World Bank, the IMF and regional institutions", in order to develop an effective human security approach.[41] Again this is a very broad canvas, with only some of these themes being developed further in this book, with the focus being on the EU supranational legal framework, where any EU law conflicting with national law over rides that national law, and its interaction with global regulatory actors in tackling a number of the issues which arise. Friman and Reich point out that "human trafficking is a multifaceted challenge to human security that requires a multifaceted, integrated response".[42] Only some of these facets will be addressed in this book. The response of individual member states located along specific THB routes will also be important in developing capacity to respond to this social and criminal phenomenon as it arises in practice.

Writers in human security see it as being "a subset of human rights" with a second subset being "human development".[43] Article 8 of the International Covenant on Civil and Political Rights 1966[44] expressly provides that "no one shall be held in slavery; slavery and the slave-trade in all their forms shall be prohibited". It goes on to state that "no one shall be held in servitude", and "no one shall be required to perform forced or compulsory labour". The provisions in this treaty, which has, at the time of writing, 173 state parties and a further 6 signatories, are deemed to be "universal in the sense that they have been accepted by almost all states".[45] Several countries which have not acted on this treaty on civil and political rights profess the Islamic religion. Donnelly argues that Islam requires its followers "to treat others with respect and dignity", and to "pursue both personal well-being and social justice". These are "divine commands that establish duties" rather than rights.[46] It is worth noting at this point that of the non-parties listed (18 countries) 10 of those countries, including many of the missing Islamic countries from the International Covenant on Civil and Political Rights list, have acceded to the THB Protocol, making at least, the slavery, servitude and forced labour provisions even more "universal". These rights not to be treated as a slave or be kept in slavery like conditions are therefore "binding in international law".[47] The impact of this "universality" will be examined in more

41 The Barcelona Report of the Study Group on Europe's Security Capabilities, A Human Security Doctrine for Europe, Barcelona, 15 September 2004, p 16.

42 Friman and Reich, op. cit., p 142.

43 A. Tanaka, 'Toward a Theory of Human Security' (2015), *JICA-RI Working Paper*, No. 91, JICA Research Institute, p 3.

44 Adopted and opened for signature, ratification, and accession by General Assembly resolution 2200A (XXI) of 16 December 1966 entry into force 23 March 1976, in accordance with Article 49.

45 Donnelly, op. cit., p 94.

46 Ibid., p 79.

47 Ibid., p 94.

depth in Chapter 2, in the context of *ius cogens*, and the provisions of Articles 53 and 64 of the Vienna Convention on the Law of Treaties, 1969. The effect of this universality is that any challenges to their provisions "are simply not seriously engaged" with at the global political level.[48] The universal human rights discourse therefore "has resulted in an agenda that does not distinguish North from South or East from West".[49]

The "primacy of human rights" is the key difference in approach between human security and the traditional concept of state security, which would prioritise the state, and the citizens of that state over all other individuals, thereby leaving some individuals without protection.[50] It is those individuals without protection, or without adequate protection, who most often fall victim to traffickers. It is for this reason that the human security approach is a most appropriate lens with which to examine the issue of the transnational crime of THB. As it is no longer possible to isolate one population from another in the context of globalisation, and its ancillary risks, the human security approach recognises "the interdependence and interlinkages among the world's people".[51] The human security approach seeks to "forge alliances that can yield much greater force together than alone",[52] an issue which will be revisited in Chapters 3 and 4. The Commission on Human Security expressly referred to the need to formulate "strategies to combat human trafficking and smuggling, and implementing relevant international and regional conventions, while protecting the rights of victims".[53]

The human security approach does not deny the need for state security, but runs parallel with it, and recognises that failing to tackle human security issues will have an adverse effect on state security. Human security, as an approach, "holds out a potential path to address human trafficking without necessarily becoming paralyzed by the debate over prostitution"[54] with trafficking related to prostitution being only one part of the complex crime that is now THB.

The failure to tackle THB and related exploitation will have a seriously adverse effect on the individuals and populations which fall victim to traffickers, but so too will the societies in which THB victims are exploited, leading to the development of an underclass to be exploited, with all the consequences that means for the "host" society, with the considerable proceeds of the crime of THB being recycled by the criminal gangs into other areas of organised crime, such as drugs or weapons crime, or being used to fund terrorist activities. The European Security Strategy 2003[55] has identified "organised crime, which includes cross-border trafficking in women, illegal migrants and children, with the effect that state

48 Ibid., p 95.
49 de Wilde, op. cit., p 236.
50 The Barcelona Report, op. cit., p 14.
51 Commission on Human Security, *Human Security Now*, The Commission, 2003, p 130.
52 Ibid.
53 Ibid., p 135.
54 Friman and Reich, op. cit., p 153.
55 European Security Strategy, Brussels, 12 December 2003, fifth threat, p 4.

authority and state institutions run the risk of being undermined".[56] This undermining of state authority and state institutions will happen all along the THB chain, from country of origin of the victims, through countries of transit to country or countries of destination. The allied crimes of bribery and corruption, not the focus of this book, will also strongly feature in developing and maintaining the transnational THB chain.

There is therefore a need to develop an "integrated security policy"[57] to advance this human security framework, not just between different agencies within states, but across states, to tackle the threat of THB. These law enforcement and justice networks need to follow the THB routes, from state of origin, through state of transit and to state or states of destination. It will not be sufficient to have states of one geo-political block or another work among themselves on this issue. This transnational crime challenge requires "the transnationalisation of law enforcement – whether by police, customs, immigration or national security officials", and not just among those countries, such as within the EU, who have developed joint working practices.[58] Taking the EU as example, while many THB victims found within the EU are from the EU, many others are from third countries. The countries from which those victims originated, and through which they transited, on their way to the EU, need to work together to combat that THB. How this issue is tackled, and who is allocated the responsibility to coordinate these developments will be determined by how that jurisdiction is structured, to include at the political, law enforcement and justice levels. This may well differ from the approach taken in adjoining states with whom officials must work. These issues of internal state structure and differences in approach have all been addressed within the EU, with mechanisms having been put in place to deal with structural differences from one country to another. Bridges need to be built, recognising that the internal structure of different jurisdictions is not going to change. Nevertheless, justice and human and due process rights need to be safeguarded to ensure safe convictions of the criminals, and effective protection and rehabilitation of the victims.

In addition, the EU countries are also countries of transit, as victims enter and leave the EU through key air-transport hubs, and countries of origin of victims. The same can be said of every country of the world. These law enforcement structures that either have been, or need to be developed, tend "to be both vertically organised along formal 'top-down' levels of governance, as well as horizontally, along more informally organised networks and exchange of information and intelligence".[59] Where these developments have occurred, as stated by den Boer, "at the intersection between vertical and horizontal forms of transnational policing, new structures can be found", as has happened in the EU with joint

56 den Boer, op. cit., p 73.

57 C. Fijnaut, 'The Lack of Coherence between Internal and External Security Policies of the European Union', in M. den Boer and J. de Wilde, *The Viability of Human Security*, Amsterdam University Press, 2008, p 106.

58 den Boer, op. cit., p 71.

59 Ibid.

investigation teams,[60] discussed further in Chapter 4. These developments will give rise to new inter-cultural and inter-legal challenges, and to tensions in law enforcement governance.[61]

THB therefore is a global phenomenon, which requires a transnational response. As stated by Hough, "increasingly … governments are coming to recognize their own limitations and see the Canute-like futility of a sovereign resisting the waves of globalization".[62] The *modus operandi* of the various criminal organisations involved in THB will differ from one region of the globe to another. Vulnerabilities of individuals will also differ from one social structure to another. Several different possible models arise. Approaches adopted in other areas of transnational legal interest, such as commercial law, include the traditional approach of comity, or the more enhanced approach of positive comity, which is normally treaty based, either this is using bi-lateral or multi-lateral legal arrangements. Comity as a workable concept, however, "is far more complex than it might appear". It locates "under this label a diverse set of practices".[63] These could develop either inside the myriad of regional integration associations (RIAs) that exist globally, using the terminology of the World Trade Organisation, or outside pre-existing RIA agreements, responding to actual and well-established THB routes as they exist on the ground. As pointed out by D'Alterio,[64] this can be quite a complex area, leading to: "*(a)* the recognition of the jurisdiction and implementation of decisions by judges belonging to supranational systems" (for example, the EU); "*(b)* the dialogue between courts for solving transnational cases"; "*(c)* the resort to foreign or global law" (presumably where this exists); and "*(d)* in cross-citation between courts belonging to different judicial systems". She goes on to say that "comity is, indeed, a polysemic expression, utilized in diverse ambits", and having "heterogeneous meanings".[65] When examined from the perspective of judicial activity, it still "appears as an open-ended term, hardly referable to a precise institution or legal principle".[66] Rather it "reveals the existence of a variety of fairly distinct judicial techniques, associated with the general phenomenon of judicial comity according to its various modalities".[67]

Examined in a different way, there is a need to negotiate the differences between legal jurisdictions with national judiciaries doing all within their powers to negotiate these gaps, where possible, while still operating within their own legal frameworks. It could be argued that a variety of national judiciaries have developed their own construction of mutual meaning making, or constructivism, in

60 Ibid.
61 Ibid., p 72.
62 P. Hough, 'Global Steps towards Human Security' (2008) 19 *Security and Human Rights*, 1, p 23.
63 E. D'Alterio, 'From Judicial Comity to Legal Comity: A Judicial Solution to Global Disorder?' (2001), 9 *I CON* 2, p 395.
64 Ibid.
65 Ibid., p 399.
66 Ibid.
67 Ibid.

tacking the need to bridge gaps between jurisdictions. Constructivism at a method of analysis adopted by this book will be discussed further below. The judicial responses have differed from one context or jurisdiction to another. As jurisdictions begin or further develop their approach to the transnational crime of THB, national judiciaries will be aware of the need to start bridging the judicial gaps between jurisdictions, to be able to safely apprehend and convict the organised crime gangs running THB networks, and to rescue and rehabilitate victims. The detail of how exactly this will be facilitated or develop will differ from one jurisdiction, or group of jurisdictions, to another.

The approach taken by the EU in negotiating jurisdictional gaps between its member states is known as "mutual recognition" which is an advanced form of cooperation between states, occurring as it does within a well-developed RIA. Mutual recognition within the EU, in the context of law enforcement and security measures, in the EU, is itself problematic, attracting the attention of academics from a range of discipline areas.[68] This issue, as addressed within the EU, will be taken up in Chapter 6.

While counties with shared interests and shared levels of development have traditionally found their collaborators among their own type, the movement of victims, and their organised crime abusers are moving from one type of country to another, from countries of victim supply to victim demand, typically from poorer countries to wealthier countries, leading to the need for jurisdictions to work together, not on the basis of the same ideology, or similar approaches to law enforcement or victim support, but in order to address a particular crime problem, for as long as that crime problem persists, in order to protect their own citizens and society.

Constructivism

Kaldor's blurring of the boundaries, together with the requirement for new arrangements to develop between states located along THB supply routes, in ways that have not been seen before, is going to be challenging for all involved. New structures will have to be developed, by diplomats negotiating on behalf of their states, and by those who then must implement those agreements or arrangements once they have been concluded. Some very high levels of trust will have to be developed between states, with the levels of trust required for law enforcement and justice issues being of a much higher level than those traditionally developed for economic or commercial issues. How exactly these arrangements will develop will differ from region to region of the globe, and possibly from country to country, if no consensus already exists for groups of countries in RIAs on transnational crime. The EU's approach to the issue is best understood following Onuf's approach to constructivism.[69] Constructivism is an approach to understanding which has developed in both sociology and international

68 E.g. S. Lavenex 'Mutual Recognition and the Monopoly of Force: Limits of the Single Market Analogy' (2007) 14 *Journal of Public Policy*, 5; C. Janssens, *The Principle of Mutual Recognition in EU law*, Oxford University Press, 2013.

69 Onuf, op. cit.

relations (IR), in the 1990s, and is now emerging in legal scholarship. Usually, constructivism at the IR level focuses on the relationship between states. However, Onuf, taking an IR approach, looks more to the individuals within the structures that are being developed. Here agents, such as in the context of THB, justice and law enforcement personnel, and the structures in which they operate, whether that be law enforcement or national prosecution authorities, interact with each other, in a transnational setting, in developing mutual understandings in ways which have assisted the development of the European Union's Area of Freedom Security and Justice (AFSJ), to date.

Constructivism examines the meaning attributed to objects, with social constructs or understandings informing how meaning is attributed to those objects.[70] Constructivism has been classified as "an approach to social inquiry". It is based on two premises, "the environment in which agents take action is social as well as material", and that the setting which provides the actors "with understandings of their interests ([it] 'constitutes' them)".[71] There is therefore "a process of interaction" between the structures and the individuals which are operating within those structures,[72] that interaction leading to the further development of those structures and understandings as to how they are to operate in future. As this approach to constructivism was developed in the field of IR it examined the meanings that societies, or states, attributed to international treaties or other arrangements. These meanings and the drafting of those treaties, will differ in style from one region to another, reflecting the legal make up and context of the societies which they represent. Those who interpret the resulting treaties will also differ in cultural background from one region of the world to another, based as they are in differently constructed legal jurisdictions, some with quite differing approaches to law, leading to different meanings being constructed. Equally different professionals in each jurisdiction will take a different approach, bringing their own levels of professionalism, to the interpretation and implementation of these treaties.

If the focus of the treaty writers and implementers is kept on combatting the transnational criminality behind THB then the drafters of these treaties, and those implementing them, will attempt to negotiate the differences in legal and social make up of their societies, legal systems, and frameworks, to lead to the development of effective transnational mechanisms. Within each (fully developed) legal jurisdiction a balance has been struck between the interests of the state in prosecuting criminals, and the interests of the courts and the legal professions in providing adequate legal defence to the accused, and ensuring that due process is followed, and all rights, to include human and due process rights being available to be exercised by the defendant and the victim. This balance must also operate in

70 J. Cristol, 'Constructivism', Oxford Bibliographies, retrieved from www.oxfordbibliographies.com/view/document/obo-9780199743292/obo-9780199743292-0061.xml.

71 J. Jupille, J.A. Caporaso, J.T. Checkel, 'Integrating Institutions: Rationalism, Constructivism, and the Study of the European Union' (2003) 36 *Comparative Political Studies* 1, p 14.

72 Ibid.

the transnational context, as by the time an individual is brought before a court after a transnational law enforcement operation, justice must not only be done, but be seen to be done, in all relevant jurisdictions. It is important that both justice and law enforcement professionals are involved in this process, as not just the interests of the state but also those of effective criminal defence, and human and due process rights, under which ever code or international agreement applies to the various relevant jurisdictions to the international agreement, are effectively addressed. Equally less developed criminal legal jurisdictions will have to provide the necessary checks and balances, at least for transnational law enforcement and justice operations, if the envisaged transnational structures are to operate effectively. This is necessary to ensure safe convictions of the criminals engaged in THB, and thereby successfully tackle the underlying transnational criminality. This will be a complex task, with the solutions arrived at in one bi-lateral or multi-lateral agreement not necessarily being workable in another, even with some of the same participating states or legal jurisdictions. A global response would therefore not be appropriate in this context.

A web of networked agreements should prove to be more effective than a global response, with countries with similar legal systems and similar law enforcement and justice structures being more able to easily come to these agreements. In this context state security, while continuing to exist as an issue more generally, is taking a back seat to the need to provide human security, both to individuals and to members of communities affected by this crime. In the EU, in developing the legal framework, and implementing the legal framework once it was enacted, the individual justice and law enforcement official has had a major impact in designing what were essentially ground up initiatives, which only later were adopted by the member states, and legislated for in a top-down fashion. The development of the resulting AFSJ is neither perfect not complete. There is an accepted argument within the EU legal framework that the security provisions are more fully developed that the freedom or justice provisions, something that all interested parties are currently working on. In addition, the question arises as to what type of security has been developed by the EU to address the issue of THB.

Onuf developed a strand of constructivism which advocated that "constructivism is a universal experience"[73] and one that we cannot avoid, as we are located within one type of society or another. Therefore Onuf's constructivism applies "not simply to the level of states, but to humans in any dimension of their social activity, international relations being merely one, albeit an extremely important one, among many".[74] Whether this mutual construction of understanding has happened at the level of either the individual, following Onuf's

73 V. Kubáklová, 'The Twenty Years' Catharsis: E. H. Carr and IR', in V. Kubáklová, N. Onuf and P. Kowert, *International Relations in a Constructed World*, Routledge, 1998, p 72.

74 Ibid.

approach,[75] or the institution, both are highly relevant in the construction of a completely new law and practice framework for cross-border law enforcement.

Cardwell, writing from a legal perspective has stated that "constructivists claim that social realities only exist by human agreement through intersubjective understanding, and are therefore susceptible to change".[76] This is a problem when it comes to the interpretation of law enforcement and justice provisions in a transnational setting. In areas where there was no pre-existing legal and practice framework, such as in former EU Police and Judicial Cooperation in Criminal Matters (PJCCM), when practitioners were asked to build a new legal and practice jurisdiction, they necessarily brought their own socialised understandings of how to, for example, conduct law enforcement operations, and through interaction with their counterparts from other jurisdictions, negotiate a shared understanding as to how a transnational law enforcement operation was to work. It is the human being at the interface between the relevant jurisdictions who has "constructed", with his (or her) counterparts, a new social reality. The activities of the Police Working Group on Terrorism (established 1979) and TREVI (established 1976) were cases in point, as was the original construction of the Europol Drugs Unit (1995–1999), which started operating before its underpinning legislation was enacted, and which eventually developed into today's Europol. It took some time, therefore, for the EU to reach its current level of development in combatting transnational crime.

Within the EU the susceptibility to change which arises from constructivism,[77] however, referred to in the above quote from Cardwell, is a key issue when it comes to the issue of fundamental and human rights, as set out in the EU Charter of Fundamental Rights, and the European Convention on Human Rights (ECHR), both of which inform the operation of both the EU and its member states, particularly in the context of justice and law enforcement. The traditional constructivist approach to the development of EU law enforcement and security strategies is now encountering an increasing constitutionalism within the EU legal framework, highlighting significant legal tensions. Less constructivist, and more grounded in individual member states norms, has been judicial cooperation in criminal matters. Judicial co-operation, and justice issues generally, have lagged behind the development of cross border law enforcement provisions in the EU, leading to the acknowledged imbalance in the AFSJ. The EU member states have, however, developed a shared understanding of the role of "the rule of law, democracy and fundamental freedoms and human rights".[78] A constructivist approach can be also traced through these developments, with Walker and Tierney

75 Ibid.

76 P. J. Cardwell, *EU External Relations and System of Governance The CFSP, Euro-Mediterranean Partnership and Migration*, Routledge, 2009, p 75.

77 Ibid.

78 Lord Neuberger at a conference at the Supreme Court of Victoria, Melbourne, The role of judges in human rights jurisprudence: a comparison of the Australian and UK experience, 8 August 2014, retrieved from www.supremecourt.uk/docs/speech-140808.pdf.

referring to "the infiltration of criminal law into the European transnational constitutional mosaic" as being "gradual and 'bottom up'".[79]

As stated by Wiener, "the context in which norms evolve matters in a significant way".[80] The creation and development of a shared identity is the key to the development of these norms. While EU member states have developed a shared understanding of the role of "the rule of law, democracy and fundamental freedoms and human rights",[81] the law enforcement communities, in particular, being task orientated, have, at least at the transnational level, developed a shared understanding of the tasks to be undertaken. Focusing on the need to tackle transnational serious and organised crime, they have developed a shared identity and community. They have negotiated their own member states structural and operational differences, while still complying with their own legal systems and operating procedures, in order to achieve their objectives. The same approach will continue to be needed to fully develop an effective policy and legal framework to combat THB. EU member states domestically focused prosecutors and judges are also adjusting to these developments, with "interaction … taking place within the legal realm",[82] with a number of transnational norms being adopted into the legal structures, such as the effect that can be clearly seen of the THB directive,[83] a process that Wiener refers to as "interaction, interpretation, internalization".[84] She goes on to hypothesise that legal rules are "embedded in a set of beliefs which is created through the rule of law *as* a social practice", a process which should lead to high levels of compliance with those laws.[85]

Chapter Outlines

Recognising that not just norms, but also legal terminology, the use of that terminology, and how it evolves is significant, and acknowledging that the EU is subject to external legal, and to a lesser extent policy, influences in the area of THB, this book focuses on the legal terms used to construct the crime of THB, and its overlapping and ancillary crimes. Through this process the gaps in the legal framework are identified, and supplementary legal provisions examined to further develop the human security picture. The EU, while being a unique supranational legal jurisdiction with competence to legislate for transnational crime for the benefit of its member states under its AFSJ, post the Lisbon Treaty 2009, is being influenced by external forces, not just from its own member states, but also by a

79 N. Walker and S. Tierney, 'Introduction', in N. Walker and S. Tierney, *A Constitutional Mosaic? Exploring the New Frontiers of Europe's Constitutionalism*, Hart Publishing, 2011, p 17.
80 A. Wiener, 'Contested Compliance: Interventions on the Normative Structure of World Politics' (2004) 10 *European Journal of International Relations*, 195.
81 Neuberger, op. cit.
82 Ibid.
83 Directive 2011/36/EU op. cit.
84 Wiener, op. cit., p 197.
85 Ibid., p 197.

variety of global regulatory actors. The EU has been influenced by those of both regional (the CoE) and international norms and legal provisions. Given the multi-level structure of governance in the EU, as it affects EU member states, Krisch speaks about "the Enmeshment of Laws".[86] This then gives rise to the issue of how to construct and navigate what he also refers to as the "pluralist web of legal orders"[87] as it affects and influences the EU in this area.

An example of the enmeshment of laws can be seen in the THB directive, Article 2.3.[88] This provision defining the crime of THB for internal EU use the European Parliament and the Council have used several legal terms which have already been legislated for or adjudicated upon in other *forae* when developing its own definition of THB. Article 2.3 provides that:

> Exploitation shall include, as a minimum, the exploitation of the prostitution of others or other forms of sexual exploitation, forced labour or services, including begging, slavery or practices similar to slavery, servitude, or the exploitation of criminal activities, or the removal of organs.

Many individual words and phrases in this provision have already had a lengthy and well-developed historical background, at an international as well as a national level. This legal history needs to be examined to pin down exactly what this particular provision means, particularly when building up a shared mutual understanding of the crime of THB in a transnational context. Nevertheless, a lack of clarity remains. Building on this legal historical background, across several legal jurisdictions will be crucial to the development of the mutual meaning making with the EU in developing this area of law and practice. It has also to be acknowledged that the individual EU member states may decide to over-implement, or "gold plate" the provisions of the THB directive, to complete their THB framework, both under influence from the same external legal obligations on the EU, but also based on internal member state political pressure and initiative. For example, the pre-Brexit UK has, pursuant to its requirements to enact the provisions of the THB directive,[89] gone further than was required in that piece of legislation, and, have implemented legislation, at least for England and Wales (E&W), for what it has classified as "modern slavery", leading to possible life imprisonment.[90] This term "modern slavery" has also appeared in non-legal academic writing on THB, and unless it is defined at a supra-national level, may well muddy the waters in defining and delimiting the parameters of the THB crime from a transnational context. There is therefore a complexity which arises when examining the definitions being adopted at the EU level, in its response to the

86 N. Krisch, *Beyond Constitutionalism: The Pluralist Structure of Postnational Law*, Oxford University Press, 2010, p 160.
87 Ibid., p 165.
88 Directive 2011/36/EU op. cit.
89 Ibid.
90 Modern Slavery Act 2015, c.30, section 5.3, "where the offence is committed by kidnapping or false imprisonment".

positive obligation placed on states, or in its own case, international organisations to respond to this crime, and the need to protect the human rights of the victims of THB. This examination will be undertaken in Chapter 2.

While the EU operates based on the supranationality of its legal provisions, which have direct effect within the legal jurisdictions of its member states, the same cannot be said of the other regulatory actors in this area. The regulatory frameworks which have enacted laws in this area, which range from the United Nations to the International Labour Organisation, to the CoE, all operate in the international law and policy arenas. In addition, the non-law based OSCE or the Financial Action Task Force recommendations have led to legal provisions globally, also have important contributions to make to tackling this crime area.

The dominant method of exploitation of THB victims is through sexual exploitation. There is little consensus at either the EU or international level on how to tackle sexual exploitation generally, with many jurisdictions taking radically diverging views on the issue. The responses of individual jurisdictions to these issues are required to be considered to complete the picture of the legal framework for combatting THB of individual EU member states. The examination of the separate jurisdictions of the EU in this area is however an enormous task and is outside the scope of this book. There are, however, substantial legal provisions on several other sub-themes which derive from the THB legal framework. These include the issue of forced labour and child protection. Chapter 5 will focus on the specific rights and vulnerabilities of children in the context of transnational THB and allied crimes.

The variety of global regulatory and policy actors making a significant contribution to the development of the EU's regulatory and practice framework to combat THB will be examined in the context of various themes which emerge when this issue is examined in detail. The issue of how to negotiate the interlegality between these different actors remains for those states which are not members of the EU supranational legal framework. The networked governance approach adopted by Krisch for developing a "bridge between different supremacy"[91] may be one approach. Krisch examines constitutionalism and pluralism as competing prisms in the context of global integration, both assuming that there is a "clear separation between domestic and international law",[92] the focus of his work, rather than the supranational law of the EU. There is no such clear separation in the context of member state/EU/ECHR relations, which lie at the core of the EU's AFSJ debate. Krisch does however point out that pluralism "remains vulnerable to exploitation in certain circumstances". He argues that a "constitutionalist model [might prove to be] a stronger bulwark against abuse by the powerful".[93] Krisch's networked governance approach may not, therefore, be suitable when dealing with issues going to the core of fundamental rights issues, such as arrest and detention, nor is it likely that he envisaged its use in this way. This

91 Krisch, op. cit., p 228.
92 Ibid., p 235.
93 Ibid., p 259.

will be an issue for theorists based outside the EU. While the political conditions might prove very challenging for the development of a constitutionalist model at the global level, or non-EU RIA level, the conditions for its development within the EU, an issue which Krisch does not address directly, are much more favourable. This is an issue which will be examined in the Chapter 6, which will take an overview to the EU's response to its external legal obligations, and the initiatives by its member states which have led to developments in the EU legal and policy structure in combatting THB. The CoE provisions on THB will also be examined in Chapter 6.

While the UK has now left the EU, its gold plating of the provisions of the THB directive, and the differing response to its implementation in the three sub-national jurisdictions of the UK, Northern Ireland, Scotland, and E&W merits examination. The differing approach to the defining and operationalisation of THB, or in E&W, modern slavery provisions, may also be the reason that the UK has been reporting a much higher number of potential victims, and a different balance across the male-female and forced labour-sexual exploitation divide. The UK's approach to implementing the THB directive will be examined in Chapter 7.

In addition, as many issues intersect with the issue of THB which cannot be addressed in one volume, such as the crimes of bribery and corruption, referred to above, as well as the crime of human smuggling, with which THB is often confused. It will have to be left to other scholars to examine these further issues in greater depth. Many issues also arise from THB which do not require a legal response, but are issues for society or authority more broadly, such as information and education campaigns, the provision of appropriate health and psychiatric care for victims, etc. The reader will have to understand that a legal analysis of this issue is only one approach which needs to be examined in order to effectively tackle THB. The fuller picture of how to combat this crime requires a broader understanding of the human security debate, to include both the issues of "freedom from want" and "freedom from fear", introduced earlier in this chapter. This book will conclude however, looking at the gaps in the legal framework as they affect and are adopted by the EU and the post Brexit UK, making recommendations where the discipline of law can contribute to the construction of an effective legal and policy framework to combat THB as a transnational crime. It is impossible to take a comprehensive approach to the crime of THB, as the issue is too large. However, it is hoped that the selection of legal issues examined in this book will prompt further discussion and analysis by both academics and practitioners, assisting in moving the analysis of the relevant issues forward, and improving the knowledge and understanding of at least some of the legal issues which arise. This will be reflected in the concluding chapter.

Bibliography

Barcelona Report of the Study Group on Europe's Security Capabilities, A Human Security Doctrine for Europe, Barcelona, 15 September 2004.

Cardwell, P. J., *EU External Relations and System of Governance The CFSP, Euro-Mediterranean Partnership and Migration*, Routledge, 2009.

Commission on Human Security, *Human Security Now*, The Commission, 2003.

Cristol, J., 'Constructivism', Oxford Bibliographies, retrieved from www.oxfordbibliographies.com/view/document/obo-9780199743292/obo-9780199743292-0061.xml.

D'Alterio, E., 'From Judicial Comity to Legal Comity: A Judicial Solution to Global Disorder?' (2001) 9 *I CON* 2, 394–424.

Donnelly, J., *Universal Human Rights in Theory and Practice*, Cornell University Press, 2013.

European Commission, Data Collection on Trafficking in Human Beings in the EU, Publications Office of the European Union, 2020.

European Security Strategy, Brussels, 12 December 2003.

Friman, H. R. and Reich, S., *Human Trafficking, Human Security and the Balkans*, Pittsburgh Press, 2007.

Glasius, M., and M. Kaldor, M., *A Human Security Doctrine for Europe: Project, Principles, Practicalities*, Routledge, 2006.

Haverkamp, R., Herlin-Karnell, E., and Lernestedt, C., *What is Wrong with Human Trafficking? Critical Perspectives on the Law*, Hart Publishing, 2018.

Hough, P., 'Global Steps towards Human Security' (2008) 19 *Security and Human Rights* 1, 15–23.

Independent Anti-Slavery Commissioner, *Annual Report 2021–2022*, HMSO, 2022.

Janssens, C., *The Principle of Mutual Recognition in EU Law*, Oxford University Press, 2013.

Jupille, J., Caporaso, J. A., and Checkel, J. T., 'Integrating Institutions: Rationalism, Constructivism, and the Study of the European Union' (2003) 36 *Comparative Political Studies* 1, 7–14.

Krisch, N., *Beyond Constitutionalism: The Pluralist Structure of Postnational Law*, Oxford University Press, 2010.

Kubáklová, V., 'The Twenty Years' Catharsis: E. H. Carr and IR', in Kubáklová, V., Onuf, N. and Kowert, P., *International Relations in a Constructed World*, Routledge, 1998, 41–73.

Walker, N. and Tierney, S., 'Introduction', in Walker, N. and Tierney, S., *A Constitutional Mosaic? Exploring the New Frontiers of Europe's Constitutionalism*, Hart Publishing, 2011, 1–16.

Lavenex, S., 'Mutual Recognition and the Monopoly of Force: Limits of the Single Market Analogy' (2007) 14 *Journal of Public Policy* 5, 762–779.

Neuberger, L., at a conference at the Supreme Court of Victoria, Melbourne, The Role of Judges in Human Rights Jurisprudence: A Comparison of the Australian and UK Experience, 8 August 2014, retrieved from www.supremecourt.uk/docs/speech-140808.pdf.

Onuf, N., *World of Our Making*, University of South Carolina Press, 1989.

den Boer, M. and de Wilde, J., *The Viability of Human Security*, Amsterdam University Press, 2008.

Stoyanova, V., *Human Trafficking and Slavery Reconsidered: Conceptual Limits and States' Positive Obligations in European law*, Cambridge University Press, 2017.

Tanaka, A., *Toward a Theory of Human Security*, JICA-RI Working Paper, No. 91, JICA Research Institute, 2015.

UNDP, *Human Development Report 1994*, UNDP, New York, 1994.

UN Millennium Declaration of the General Assembly, 8 September 2000.

Wiener, A., 'Contested Compliance: Interventions on the Normative Structure of World Politics' (2004) 10 *European Journal of International Relations*, 189–234.

Legislation

Directive 2011/36/EU of the European Parliament and of the Council of 5 April 2011 on preventing and combating trafficking in human beings and protecting its victims, and replacing Council Framework Decision 2002/629/JHA, OJ L 101/1.

2 Definitions and Negotiating the Interlegality

Introduction

Human trafficking is a global criminal phenomenon. A web of global contacts and networks will be required to properly address this crime. However, this book will take as its focus Europe, and in particular the regional integration organisation of the European Union (EU), and the approach that it is taking to tackle this crime for the benefit of its residents and citizens, which may well prove to be a model for other networks and organisations around the world. Additionally, the individual member states of the EU may be taking further measures in this area. For example, the now post-Brexit UK has, pursuant to its requirements to enact the provisions of Directive 2011/36/EU[1] on THB, while it was still a member of the EU, gone further than was required, and, has implemented legislation for what it has classified, for the sub-national jurisdiction of England & Wales (E&W), as "modern slavery", leading to possible life imprisonment. The UK will be the focus of Chapter 7. This chapter will focus on the complexity resulting from the definitions being adopted by the EU, its response to the positive obligation placed on states, or international organisations to respond to THB, and the need to protect the human rights of victims. Further complexity arises with the additional enactment of THB provisions in individual EU member states, leading to diversity in approaches, and academic criticism, given that the EU has only adopted minimum rules in defining the criminal offence.[2] This diversity in national implementation, could give rise to issues for transnational cooperation,[3] both inside the EU, where the European Arrest Warrant does not always require the double criminality test to be met,[4] but also in the EU's surrender provisions with third countries, to include the post Brexit UK, where the double criminality test may need to be met.[5]

1 Directive 2011/36/EU of the European Parliament and of the Council of 5 April 2011 on preventing and combating trafficking in human beings and protecting its victims, and replacing Council Framework Decision 2002/629/JHA, OJ L 101/1.
2 Ibid., Article 2.3.
3 V. Stoyanova, *Human Trafficking and Slavery Reconsidered: Conceptual Limits and States' Positive Obligations in European Law*, Cambridge University Press, 2017, p 32.
4 Council Framework Decision 2002/584/JHA on the European Arrest Warrant, OJ L 190, 18/07/2002, p 1, Article 2.2.
5 UK EU Trade and Cooperation Agreement, Articles 599.4.

DOI: 10.4324/9781003429791-2

Adopting a policy approach of human security, there is a need to focus on human beings and the security threats that they face, as discussed in Chapter 1. This "people centred" approach requires a discussion at to how the different layers of law interact to affect the legal status of those at the centre of the transnational crime of trafficking in human beings (THB).

The EU, while being a unique supranational legal jurisdiction with competence to legislate for transnational crime for the benefit of its member states under its Area of Freedom, Security and Justice (AFSJ), post the Lisbon Treaty 2009, is influenced by external forces. These are not just from its own member states, but also by a variety of global regulatory frameworks. How the EU has reacted to these external forces, as well as to initiatives of its own member states, will be examined in Chapter 6. Outside the EU (and the EU's pre-Brexit influence on the UK), are a variety of legal and policy actors which operate directly on their individual contracting parties or member states. The EU's own member states have a direct influence on the EU, complimenting the EU's own obligations to comply with international legal obligations.[6] In examining international law and its impact on both the supranational legal framework of the EU, and on individual member states, further complexity arises. Negotiating the resulting interlegality resulting in the various layers of law from global and regional actors requires an examination of the Vienna Convention on the Law of Treaties 1969.

THB is an area that has been legislated for by different international treaties, in several different ways. There have been long standing legislative efforts at a global level to combat the crime of slavery, such as the 1926 Slavery Convention. More recently the key international piece of legislation is the Protocol to Prevent, Suppress and Punish Trafficking in Persons, Especially Women and Children (THB Protocol), which is attached to the UN Convention on Transnational Organised Crime 2000 (Palermo Convention). The UN, the ILO and in particular the Council of Europe (CoE), all based on international law, are key drivers in the development of EU law on THB. They determine not only the definition of the crime, but also the positive obligations on states to respond to this crime area, and the protection that needs to be provided to victims of this crime. These external drivers have taken slightly diverging approaches to these issues, all of which need to be examined, particularly as the EU's own court, the Court of Justice (CJEU), and the court of the CoE, the ECtHR, expressly refer to and rely on these external provisions in developing their own law. The International Labour Organisation (ILO) for its part has legislated several times on forced labour, starting with the 1930 Forced Labour Convention (No. 29), which was followed up, *inter alia*, with the 1957 Abolition of Forced Labour Convention (No. 105) and more recently by the 2014 Protocol to the Forced Labour Convention 1930 and the Forced Labour (Supplementary Measures) Recommendation,

6 E.g. Case 149/96, *Portugal v Council*, [1999] ECR I-8395, relying on Case 70/87 *Fediol v Commission* [1989] ECR 1219 and Case C-69/89 *Nakajima v Council* [1991] ECR I-2069.

2014 (No. 203). At the CoE level there is also the Convention on Action against Trafficking in Human Beings 2015 (THB Convention), known as the Warsaw Convention.[7]

In addition, there are a wide variety of specialised pieces of legislation covering child protection, such as the CoE Convention on the Protection of Children against Sexual Exploitation and Sexual Abuse 2007[8] and the CoE Convention against Trafficking in Human Organs 2015,[9] all jostling for position within the international legal sphere, before the specialised supranational legal provisions of the EU in this area are examined. The issue of how to navigate competing international legal orders and their international treaties needs first to be examined before the content of their provisions can be approached. Examining how these provisions interact brings the Vienna Convention on the Law of Treaties 1969 into play, and in particular Article 30 dealing with "successive treaties relating to the same subject matter", which at the time of writing has 116 parties. Article 30 of the Vienna Convention needs to be interpreted in the context of customary law, which "continues to exist independently alongside Article 30".[10]

Returning to the discussion in Chapter 1 on the need for new arrangements to develop between states located along THB supply routes, and the need for new structures to be developed, it is necessary for all involved to be clear what legal provisions are already in place, at a global and regional level, to combat THB and its allied crime areas. Adopting Onuf style constructivism, the meaning attributed to objects, or even legal provisions and structures, is a necessary starting point for agents (diplomats, lawyers, and law enforcement) interactions to further develop the structures in which these agents operate. It is only from this starting point that the mutual construction of understanding, following Onuf's approach[11] can be developed. Law enforcement practitioners and prosecutors operating transnationally will take their guidance on the international, and transnational legal provisions from domestically based lawyers. However, there is already a lack of clarity about the exact meaning of the basic international legal building blocks in this area, with Haverkamp *et al.* pointing out that legal definitions "differ remarkably between jurisdictions",[12] with some jurisdictions copying verbatim the international legal definitions on THB, importing into their own jurisdictions "all the uncertainties implanted in the international law definition", leading to negative consequences for the operationalisation of those legal provisions.[13]

7 CETS No. 197.
8 CETS No. 201.
9 CETS No. 216.
10 M. E. Villiger, *Commentary on the 1969 Vienna Convention on the Law of Treaties*, Martinus Nijhoff Publishers, 2009, p 409.
11 V. Kubálková, 'The Twenty Years' Catharsis: E. H. Carr and IR' in V. Kubálková, N. Onuf and P. Kowert, *International Relations in a Constructed World*, Routledge, 1998, p 72.
12 R. Haverkamp, E. Herlin-Karnell and C. Lernested, 'Chapter 1' in R. Haverkamp, E. Herlin-Karnell and C. Lernestedt, *What is Wrong with Human Trafficking? Critical Perspectives on the Law Hart Publishing*, 2018, p 4.
13 Stoyanova (2017), op. cit., p 181.

The construction of mutual understanding as understood by Onuf style constructivists needs to start with the development of a mutual understanding of the meaning of the actual words being used to define THB. In addition, an individual's, or a state's understanding of those individual words will be affected by how those words are used in other international legal documents, and within their own legal systems. In addition, and as acknowledged in Chapter 1, there is a need to negotiate the interlegality between the various actors who legislate for combating THB, and allied crime areas, before one addresses the supranationality which is inherent within the EU legal framework.

As pointed out by Stoyanova, the definition of the crime in the THB protocol was "crafted in a legal context, namely transnational organised crime" which has goals "distinct form the precepts of national substantive criminal law and it is rife with ambiguities".[14] In addition, "states cannot simply reproduce in their domestic criminal laws the definitions of slavery, servitude and forced labour used in [another body of law,] human rights law".[15] Stoyanova goes on to state that human rights law, to include the case law emanating from the European Court of Human Rights (ECtHR), to be discussed below, "are applied for the purpose of establishing state responsibility". National criminal law, in contrast, to include the provisions of the EU directive on THB, as it is required to be implemented, "is applied for the purpose of establishing individual criminal responsibility".[16] The drafting of the international legal provisions, the terminology used, and the further provisions of international legal documents and human rights case law are not easily transposed into national criminal legal, and police practice, provisions. For example, the judicial activism seen[17] in the ECtHR case of *Rantsev v Cyprus and Russia* in expanding the provisions of Article 4 European Convention on Human Rights (ECHR) to include THB, discussed below, would not be tolerated in the interpretation of a piece of domestic criminal law before national criminal courts. As stated by Stoyanova, "human rights interpretative techniques can conflict with the principles underlying the contemporary criminal justice systems".[18] For example, an unattributed commentary on the *Rantsev* case[19] speaks about the ECHR as being "a living instrument which must be interpreted in light of present-day conditions",[20] thereby allowing Article 4 ECHR to also include the previously unspecified crime of THB. National and EU criminal legal provisions, however, operate within different legal frameworks. National criminal law is premised on the

14 V. Stoyanova, 'Article 4 of the ECHR and the Obligation of Criminalising Slavery, Servitude, Forced Labour and Human Trafficking' (2014) 3 *Cambridge Journal of International and Comparative Law*, 2, p 442.

15 Ibid.

16 Ibid.

17 European Court of Human Rights, Guide to Article 4 – Prohibition of Slavery and Forced Labour, Council of Europe, updated on 31 December 2018, paragraph 9.

18 Stoyanova (2014), op. cit., p 422.

19 *Rantsev v Cyprus and Russia*, Application no. 25965/04, ECtHR, 7 January 2010.

20 Case comment, 'Rantsev v Cyprus and Russia (App. No.25965/04): Trafficking in Human Beings – Sexual Exploitation – "Artiste" Visa Regime in Cyprus' (2010) 3 *European Human Rights Law Review*, p 327.

principle of *nulle crimen sin lege* (no crime without law), which does not permit the expansive interpretation of national criminal laws and does not permit national criminal laws to be treated as living instruments. Any updates need to be by way of legislation, if the crime is legislatively based, or by strict rules on judicial activism if we are discussing (often older crimes in predominantly) common law jurisdictions. Not only is the EU, as a supranational legal jurisdiction, influenced by the provisions of Article 7 ECHR (No punishment without law), but the EU also has its own, more detailed, provisions in Article 49 EU CFR (Principle of legality and proportionality of criminal sanctions and penalties). An analysis of the EU's approach to the principle of legality will be undertaken in Chapter 6.

However, a starting point for an analysis of the multi-layered approach required while negotiating the interlegality of the various actors who legislate to combat THB beings can reasonably be taken to be Article 2.3 of Directive 2011/36/EU,[21] as referred to in Chapter 1 which provides that:

> Exploitation shall include, as a minimum, the exploitation of the prostitution of others or other forms of sexual exploitation, forced labour or services, including begging, slavery or practices similar to slavery, servitude, or the exploitation of criminal activities, or the removal of organs.

A development of a shared understanding of the meaning of each of the key words in this sentence would greatly assist in moving the legal analysis of the crime of THB forward. Fortunately, while the EU and its court, the Court of Justice of the EU (CJEU) are new to this area of law, the ECtHR has a history of grappling with many of the key concepts used by the EU in this definition for THB. It should be noted that the jurisprudence of the ECtHR mainly developed in the absence of the CoE Convention on Action against Trafficking in Human Beings 2015,[22] with its judicial activism focus being rather on the Article 4 ECHR. Article 4 has been "one of the least invoked provisions of the otherwise widely explored ECHR".[23] Cameron has pointed out that Article 4 "has lived something of a 'twilight existence'" with "few violations having been found" to Article 4 provisions "during the first fifty years that the Convention has been in force".[24] As stated by Stoyanova, Article 4 "contains a cluster of different concepts" many of which are building on pre-existing international legal provisions, relying on "instruments which pre-date the birth of the instruments and mechanisms of human rights law", the context in which they are deployed by the ECtHR.[25]

21 Directive 2011/36/EU, op. cit.

22 CETS No. 197.

23 V. Mantouvalou, 'Servitude and Forced Labour in the 21st Century: The Human Rights of Domestic Workers' (2006) 35 *Industrial Law Journal* 4, p 406.

24 I. Cameron, 'European Court of Human Rights January 2005 – March 2006' (2007) 13 *European Public Law*, 1, p 11.

25 N. L. McGeehan, 'Misunderstood and Neglected: The Marginalisation of Slavery in International Law' (2011) 16 *The International Journal of Human Rights* 3, p 437.

The Article 4 ECHR terms for slavery, servitude and forced labour are highly relevant to the EU definition of THB. In addition, the jurisprudence of the ECtHR has developed to encompass what is now understood to be the crime of THB, with greater clarity having been brought to the ECtHR's understanding of THB in the 2021 Grand Chamber case of *SM v Croatia*.[26] In addition, the case law of the ECtHR has "introduced another concept"[27] that of "exploitation" which also needs to be examined, as discussed later in this chapter.

Vienna Convention on the Law of Treaties

International law contains "four principles serving to resolve conflicts between successive treaties".[28] There must be a real incompatibility between the treaties for these to apply. If "apparent conflicts … can be resolved by interpretation" then that approach "is the first to be chosen".[29] The highest ranking law is known as *jus cogens*, and any treaty, such as the UN treaty, "incorporating *jus cogens* – shall prevail over a treaty of lower rank".[30] Article 103 UN Charter itself provides that it "shall prevail over all conflicting treaty obligations of the Member States".[31] *Jus cogens* is a peremptory norm of general international law, which features in Articles 53 and 64 of the Vienna Convention, of which more later, in the context of slavery and THB. The second rule of international law is *rule lex posterior derogate legi priori*, which means that a later treaty overrides an earlier treaty. However, the third rule, *lex prior in tempore, potior in jure,* "grants priority to the earlier treaty" when conflicting treaties have diverging membership.[32] The fourth rule in this sequence is *lex specialis derogate legi generali*, stating that specialised laws override general laws. In establishing dates for treaties, the majority consensus is that the date should be the date of adoption of the treaty "since the adoption of the treaty always constitutes a new legislative intention".[33] Nevertheless the obligations only "have effect for State Parties" from the "date of entry into force of the treaty in question".[34]

For its part Article 30 Vienna Convention has been referred to as being "particularly obscure", and being "among the most debated provisions".[35] Its provisions are "residuary rules" only applying if a treaty does not itself address issues of

26 *SM v Croatia*, Application no. 60561/14, ECtHR, 25 June 2020.
27 V. Stoyanova, 'Dancing on the Borders of Article 4: Human Trafficking and the European Court of Human Rights in the *Rantsev* Case' (2012) 30 *Netherlands Institute of Human Rights* 2, p 180.
28 Villiger, op. cit., p 399.
29 K. Odendahl, 'Article 30 Application of Successive Treaties Relating to the Same Subject Matter', in O. Dörr and K. Schmalenback, *Vienna Convention on the Law of Treaties A Commentary*, Springer, 2018, p 511.
30 Villiger, op. cit., p 399.
31 Op cit., footnote no. 28, p 511.
32 Villiger, op. cit., p 399.
33 Odendahl, op. cit., p 509/10.
34 Ibid., p 510.
35 Ibid., p 507.

conflict.[36] While providing for a hierarchy mechanism for treaties, it does not regulate all the situations that may arise referring "***inter alia*** to rules of State responsibility",[37] leading to "the possible fragmentation of a treaty between the parties, offering flexible, tailor-made treaty relations".[38] It also recognises that conflict of law clauses may also be incorporated into treaties. Either a treaty may claim priority for itself, a matter which "lies outside the Convention",[39] or a conflict of law clause in a treaty may cede priority to another treaty, which is covered by Article 30 paragraph 2. If there are, however, "colliding conflict clauses" in two interrelated treaties, then they are both treated as "non-existent", cancelling each other out, and leading to the application of the provisions of Article 30 of the Vienna Convention.[40]

Issues of hierarchy are also addressed in Articles 53 and 64 of the Vienna Convention. Article 53 covers recognised *ius cogens* (peremptory norms, which override or influence the interpretation of other provisions) at the time of that treaty's conclusion,[41] with Article 64 covering emerging *ius cogens.* If a treaty conflicts with recognised *ius cogens*, then it is void under Article 53. Article 53 does not, however, have retroactive effect.[42] If the treaty in question preceded the Vienna Convention, then "it becomes void, not retroactively and *ab initio*, but as soon as the general peremptory rule has emerged".[43] If however the treaty is found, later, to conflict with an emerging *ius cogens*, or *ius cogens superveniens*[44] which is new *vis-à-vis* any existing treaty,[45] then under Article 64 the treaty was originally valid, and then it either, in whole or in part, "becomes void and terminates".[46] This situation will forbid "the continued existence and performance of the treaty", with the parties released from any obligation to perform the treaty further, although "any rights, obligations or situations having previously arisen may be maintained".[47] However, if only "individual treaty provisions" conflict with *jus cogens*, then "only these provisions will become void and terminate", with all other treaty provisions remaining in force.[48] This new peremptory norm would have to have emerged before the Convention entered into force, which was on the 29 January 1980, to be covered by Article 53. If the norm emerged after that date, then it

36 Ibid., p 512.
37 Villiger, op. cit., p 411.
38 Ibid.
39 Ibid., p 405.
40 Odendahl, op. cit., p 513.
41 K. Schmalenback, 'Article 53 Treaties Conflicting with a Preemptory Norm of General International Law "*Jus Cogens*"', in O. Dörr and K. Schmalenback, *Vienna Convention on the Law of Treaties A Commentary*, Springer, 2012.
42 Villiger, op. cit., p 669.
43 Ibid.
44 Ibid., p 795.
45 Ibid., p 793.
46 Ibid.
47 Ibid., p 793/4.
48 Ibid., p 793.

would be covered by Article 64.[49] Both Article 53 and 64 have led to more academic commentary than invocation in practice, with both provisions, and Article 64, being seen as "exceptional in practice".[50] Nevertheless, Article 53 does, and Article 64 could potentially, address issues of relevance to this book.

Top of the international legal hierarchy is *ius cogens*, which has been developed from Roman civil law,[51] through a few different legal theories. It is arguable that *ius cogens* represents an "academic desire to constitutionalize the somewhat anarchic international legal order".[52] *Ius cogens*, or peremptory norms are generally accepted standards, which are rarely invoked in practice. While *ius cogens* has never been fully defined, there was a general understanding at the time of drafting the convention that the "trade in slavery, piracy and genocide" were included.[53] The ruling against slavery at this level included, at the time of the signing of the convention, a ban on sexual slavery.[54] The recognition of the ban on slavery arose from the "signature in Brussels, on 2 July 1890, of the General Act condemning the slave trade".[55] Lagerwall is of the view that while the act itself "cannot be considered as a source of a new *ius cogens* norm prohibiting slavery" it can however been seen as "the expression of an agreement reinforcing the progressively established adherence to this ban and to its 'non-derogatory' character".[56] She goes on to say that "only norms that enjoy a more generalized agreement should be considered to have a peremptory character, namely the ban on the save trade as such. As a result, that ban could be considered an example of a norm".[57]

For a norm to achieve the standard of *ius cogens*, it is not necessary for all states to subscribe to the norm. Rather "it is enough if a very large majority" of states subscribes to the norm,[58] with the "international community of States as a whole" being the bodies interested in "the existence and observance of the customary rule".[59] It is arguable, therefore, that while slavery, to include sexual slavery, may be recognised under Article 53 that international norms dealing

49 K. Schmalenback, 'Article 64 Emergence of New Peremptory Norm of General International Law ("Jus Cogens")', in O. Dörr and K. Schmalenback, *Vienna Convention on the Law of Treaties: A Commentary*, Springer, 2012, p 1122.

50 A. Lagerwall, 'Article 64 Emergence of a New Peremptory Norm of General International Law ("Jus Cogens")', in O. Corten and P. Klein, *The Vienna Conventions on the Law of Treaties: A Commentary*, Oxford University Press, 2011, Volume II, p 1459.

51 Schmalenback, Article 53, op. cit., p 899.

52 Ibid.

53 Ibid., p 903.

54 Ibid., p 938, relying on, for sexual slavery the ruling in the Special Court for Sierra Leone *Prosecutor v Sesay, Lallon and Gbao* (Trial Chamber) SCSL-04–15-T, 2 March 2009, para 157, and for slavery, inter alia, US Court of Appeal for the 9th Circuit, *United States v Matta-Ballesteros* 71 F3d 754, 764 n 5 (1995).

55 Lagerwall, op. cit., p 1459.

56 Ibid.

57 Ibid.

58 Schmalenback, Article 53, op. cit., p 911.

59 Ibid., p 913.

with THB more broadly may have to rely on the provisions of Article 64 of the Convention, as an emerging norm. This may well be arguable as the THB Protocol (signed and ratified after the Article 53 cut-off date, of 29 January 1980) now has at the time of writing, 117 country signatories and 181 parties, with countries falling into one or other of these two lists. It is recognised, however, that these norms have a dynamic nature.[60] Unethical treaties, should they arise in this area, are not in breach of the norms, and are "not per se invalid, but unenforceable".[61]

The Definitions as They Affect the EU

Once the issue of how to navigate between competing international legal orders has been addressed, then the actual content of the provisions need to be examined. This needs to start with the terms used to define the relevant crimes, and how these have been interpreted in differing legal jurisdictions. Here it needs to be recognised that THB is a much more recently defined crime, while underlying crimes such as slavery, servitude etc. are comparatively well established, and recognised and adjudicated on in more international legal forums. For example, the EU is more focused on the crime of THB than its counterparts the CoE and the ECtHR, with express provisions in the EU's Charter of Fundamental Rights on the topic. Despite the fact that there is no express reference to THB in the ECHR, the CoE does have an international treaty, the CoE THB Convention.[62] In addition, the ECtHR has had a longer period of time to examine some of the key issues which arise than the CJEU, particularly in developing an understanding of the terms slavery, servitude, forced and compulsory labour in the case law of the ECtHR. The case law of the ECtHR, on Article 4 ECHR, which prohibits slavery and forced labour, is therefore a better starting point for examining the EU legal response in this area. Once this has been done then the other terms used in Article 3.2 of Directive 2011/36/EU, such as prostitution, sexual exploitation and the forced removal of organs will need to be examined. Beyond the narrow focus on the definition of THB in the EU directive, the transnational crime of smuggling of migrants needs to be distinguished from THB, with the overarching transnational offence of organised crime being required to complete the picture. There was some "initial confusion" between smuggling and THB in EU documents, which has since, at a legal definition level, been "cleared up",[63] although practitioners often have a real challenge in distinguishing the two crimes when they occur in practice. A distinction needs to be maintained between these two serious and organised crimes at all levels, however, to have rational debates and effective responses to these crimes.

60 Villiger, op. cit., p 674.
61 Schmalenback, Article 53, op. cit., p 902.
62 CETS No. 197.
63 M. Vinkovic, 'The "Unbroken Marriage" – Trafficking and Child Labour in Europe' (2010) 13 *Journal of Money Laundering Control* 2, p 98.

Slavery, Servitude, and Forced and Compulsory Labour

Four distinct but overlapping crimes underpin the modern crime of THB. These are slavery, servitude, forced labour and compulsory labour. These terms were developed much earlier than the definition of THB, within the context of different legal systems, and "prior to the birth of human rights law".[64] The different sources and uses of these definitions becomes an issue, particularly in the context of their use by the EU to underpin its definition of THB. For example, the ICTY ruling in *Kunarac*, in the context of international criminal law, in referring to the "'apparently' distinct definitions of slavery, servitude and forced labour", considered that "the distinctions drawn in human rights law are irrelevant for the purposes of international criminal law".[65]

The ECtHR's two key cases in European human rights law, the earlier case of *Siliadin*,[66] and the subsequent case of *Rantsev*,[67] take diverging approaches to the interpretation of the four components of Article 4 ECHR. *Rantsev* explicitly brought THB within the Article 4 framework, while also, implicitly criticised the earlier "*Siliadin* judgement and, by extension, the human rights law framework on slavery, servitude and forced labour."[68] The issue of the definition of THB at the ECtHR gained some clarity with the Grand Chamber case of *SM* v *Croatia*,[69] which requires the three constituent elements (action, means and exploitative purpose) of the international definition of THB to be present in cases of adult victims for the crime to be recognised as such by the ECtHR.[70] Stoyanov points out that individual member states, in implementing their domestic THB legislation, have left out one or other of these three constituent elements of the THB crime,[71] leading to substantial differences in domestic legislation. The ECtHR would recognise THB either as occurring both internal to a jurisdiction and transnationally, regardless of any connection with organised crime.[72] Nevertheless, it is worth pointing out that neither the THB Protocol nor the EU THB directive are human rights texts. Rather they are transnational criminal law provisions, one based in international law, the other in supranational law, both requiring correct transposition into domestic criminal law. Precision of definition is a requirement in domestic criminal law. It is necessary to examine, therefore, where precision may be found for these different crimes, which all form part of the definition provided for in the EU directive on THB.

64 McGeehan, op. cit., p 437.
65 Ibid., p 441.
66 *Siliadin v France*, Application no. 73316/01, ECtHR, 26 October 2005.
67 *Rantsev v Cyprus and Russia*, op. cit.
68 McGeehan, op. cit., p 441.
69 *SM v Croatia*, op. cit.
70 Ibid., p 2 of the judgment.
71 R. Haverkamp, E. Herlin-Karnell and C. Lernested, 'Introduction', in R. Haverkamp, E. Herlin-Karnell and C. Lernestedt, *What is Wrong with Human Trafficking? Critical Perspectives on the Law*, Hart Publishing, 2018, p 5.
72 *SM v Croatia*, op. cit., p 2 of the judgment.

At a global level the Universal Declaration of Human Rights "prohibits slavery and servitude" at Article 4, while forced and compulsory labour are, in addition to slavery and servitude, prohibited by the International Covenant on Civil and Political Rights at Article 8.[73] Some would argue that "enslavement is an umbrella term" covering all four categories, and that while "separate practices do exist in international law" any distinction between slavery, servitude, and forced and compulsory labour "is irrelevant in the sphere of international criminal law".[74] However, the sphere of international criminal law is not the focus of this book. Rather, the focus is on the implementation and operation of transnational law in Europe in combatting THB, as influenced by its regional, as well as global actors in grappling with the crimes of slavery, servitude, forced and compulsory labour. With this particular focus clear differences have emerged, at least in the use of the different terms; slavery, servitude, forced and compulsory labour, as will be examined further in this chapter. A debate has also emerged as to whether slavery, servitude, forced and compulsory labour "converges"[75] with the THB, or whether, while overlapping in places, they are in fact different crimes. Stoyanova points out that exploitation by itself is sufficient for slavery, servitude and forced labour, but that further elements need to be proven for THB.[76] There is a need therefore for each jurisdiction to legislate to combat both THB and "slavery, servitude, forced and compulsory labour". Stoyanova reports that this is not the case outside the context of THB in many CoE member states, with other states only criminalising slavery as a crime against humanity, and not as a standard domestic crime.[77] She points out that while states are not required to define slavery, servitude, forced or compulsory labour in any particular way under Article 4 ECHR, they are obliged to criminalise them in their domestic legal systems.[78] In addition, the offence of THB can occur in anticipation of exploitation, while slavery, servitude, forced and compulsory labour requires the exploitation to have occurred.[79] If the THB is to occur in anticipation of exploitation, then the *mens rea* of "recruitment, transportation, transfer, harbouring or receipt" becomes more difficult to establish for investigators and prosecutors.[80]

The ECtHR for its part also looks outwards, to international law to determine the meaning of words that it needs to interpret. The CoE is of the view that as an international treaty, the ECHR must be interpreted in accordance with the provisions of the Vienna Convention of the 23rd May 1969 on the Law of Treaties, discussed above, which required that "the ordinary meaning to be given to the words in their context and in the light of the object and purpose of the provision

73 Mantouvalou, op. cit., p 398.
74 McGeehan, op. cit., p 441.
75 Stoyanova (2017), op. cit., p 292.
76 Ibid.
77 Ibid., p 343/4.
78 Ibid., p 438.
79 Ibid., p 292.
80 Ibid., p 293.

from which they are drawn".[81] The ordinary meaning of words have often been developed based on other international treaties, such as the Article 4 ECHR prohibition on forced and compulsory labour, which echoes the provisions of the earlier 1930 ILO Forced Labour Convention.[82] However, under the case law of the ECtHR, slavery, servitude, forced and compulsory labour, and THB, have all been given different, if overlapping meanings, something which may be at variance with other international bodies, such as the Nuremberg Tribunal (war crimes) ruling in *US v Oswald Pohl and Others.*[83] This needs to be taken into consideration when interpreting the same words in EU law, while we await definitive rulings from the CJEU.

Slavery

One of the oldest of the crimes underpinning the modern definition of THB is the crime of slavery. It was the "first human right to be protected by international treaty" the Berlin Treaty 1885.[84] For its interpretation of slavery the ECtHR relies on the provisions of the League of Nations' 1926 Slavery Convention for the "classic" definition of slavery "as it was practised for centuries".[85] In addition, under the UN regime, slavery was also covered by the 1948 Universal Declaration of Human Rights, at Article 4, which more broadly states that "No one shall be held in slavery or servitude; slavery and the slave trade shall be prohibited in all their forms". This was supplemented by the UN Supplementary Convention on the Abolition of Slavery, the Slave Trade, and Institutions and Practices Similar to Slavery, 1956. There is, however, "no specific reference to forced labour" in the Slavery Convention.[86] Article 1 of the 1926 Slavery Convention defines slavery as "the status or condition of a person over whom any or all of the powers attaching to the right of ownership are exercised". This issue of the "right of ownership" has cause problems for both ECtHR case law and academic commentators, with McGeehan referring to "the fallacious notion that slavery relates to ownership".[87] Article 1.2 goes on to define the slave trade as including "all acts involved in the capture, acquisition or disposal of a person with intent to reduce him to slavery; all acts involved in the acquisition of a slave with a view to exchanging him; all acts or disposal by sale or exchange of a slave acquired with a view to being sold or exchanged, and, in general, every act of trade or transport in slaves". Slavery was also referred to as "chattel slavery" in the International Criminal Tribunal for the

81 European Court of Human Rights, Guide to Article 4, op. cit., paragraphs 5.
82 ILO Forced Labour Convention, 1930 (No. 29), UNTS, 39(612).
83 *US v Oswald Pohl and Others*, judgment of 3 November 1947, US Military Tribunal Nuremberg, p 15, available online at http://werle.rewi.hu-berlin.de/POHL-Case.pdf.
84 S. Drew, 'Human Trafficking: A Modern Form of Slavery?' (2002), 4 *European Human Rights Law Review*, p 481.
85 *Siliadin v France*, op. cit., p 33, paragraph 122.
86 Mantouvalou, op. cit., p 398.
87 McGeehan, op. cit., p 455.

Yugoslavia case of *Prosecutor v Kunarac, Vukovic and Kovac*,[88] a point which was relied on in the ECtHR case of *Rantsev v Cyprus and Russia*.[89] However, an issue also arises as to whether this 1926 definition of slavery is overly restrictive, and the focus should be, as stated by the Appeal Chamber in *Kunarac* that "slavery has evolved to the point where it related exclusively to a condition, not a legal status".[90] Worth noting here, is that the definition of slavery in the 1926 Slavery Convention does not include "the phrase 'all its forms'",[91] a phrase which is used in the 1948 Universal Declaration of Human Rights, Article 4. There is therefore a lack of a precise definition of slavery in the key slavery convention, the 1956 Supplementary Convention, with reliance being made on the 1926 Slavery Convention for the meaning of the word "slavery".

Examples of slavery have been provided in international legal texts and case law, but "as yet, no systematic attention has been directed to the question of what would constitute exercise of such powers against a human being".[92] It is also a term that is frequently used in non-slavery contexts to provide rhetorical emphasis. Case law has added to the confusion in the interpretation of this term. For example, at the ECtHR in *Siliadin v France*, the court speaks about a "genuine rights of legal ownership",[93] which conflicts with the ruling of the Appeal Chamber in *Kunarac*, and ECtHR's subsequent ruling in *Rantsev v Cyprus and Russia*[94] which endorsed the *Kunarac* approach to the definition of slavery,[95] discussed below.

The "prohibition on slavery and servitude" cannot be derogated from by member state pursuant to Article 15.2 ECHR.[96] This condition of slavery was distinguished by the ECtHR from the concept of servitude in the *Siliadin* case, an approach with differs from that taken in the international military tribunal cases. In *Siliadin* the victim was "clearly deprived of her personal autonomy", however she was not "reduced to the status of an 'object'".[97] The appeals chamber of the tribunal in *Prosecutor v Kunarac, Vukovic and Kovac*,[98] a 2002 military tribunal ruling, went on to say that there are "various contemporary forms of slavery", with the more extreme being "chattel slavery". There are, however, other examples, which resulted in "the exercise of any or all of the powers attaching to the right of ownership" resulting in "some destruction of

88 *Prosecutor v Kunarac, Vukovic and Kovac*, 12 June 2002, *Appeals Chamber, International Tribunal for the Former Yugoslavia*, Case No. IT-96–23 & TI-96–23/1-A, paragraph 117.
89 *Rantsev v Cyprus and Russia*, op. cit., paragraph 142.
90 McGeehan, op. cit., p 440.
91 J. Allain and R. Hickey, 'Property and the Definition of Slavery' (2012), 61 *International and Comparative Law Quarterly* 4, p 919.
92 Ibid., p 933.
93 *Siliadin v France*, op. cit., p 33, paragraph 122.
94 *Rantsev v Cyprus and Russia*, op. cit., p 27, paragraph 141.
95 McGeehan, op. cit., p 436.
96 Drew, op. cit., p 482.
97 *Siliadin v France*, op. cit., p 33, paragraph 122.
98 *Prosecutor v Kunarac, Vukovic and Kovac*, op. cit., paragraph 117.

the juridical personality", with the greater such destruction happening in the case of "chattel slavery", with the difference being "one of degree".[99] The appeals chamber of the tribunal in *Prosecutor v Kunarac, Vukovic and Kovac*,[100] went on to say that while exercising a "right of ownership over a person" was now too narrow a definition for the word slavery and that the approach take in the 1926 Slavery Convention, of exercising "any or all of the powers attaching to the right of ownership" was more appropriate when addressing the issue of modern day slavery. The court was unprepared to "comprehensively enumerate all the forms of such a complex socio-economic relationship as slavery"[101] as to do so would "only serve to quasi-legitimise new forms of slavery" that would "inevitably arise".[102]

Servitude

Servitude is less clearly defined in international law, with only the 1956 Supplementary Slavery Convention, Article 1, enumerating "practices and institutions which confer servile status on victims".[103] These include "debt bondage", "serfdom", practices involving forced marriage, or ownership over a woman, and the transfer of children for the purposes of exploitation. The ECtHR in *Siliadin* did provide a definition for servitude, being "an obligation to provide one's services that is imposed by the use of coercion, and is to be linked with the concept of 'slavery'".[104] However, as pointed out by Stoyanova "the Court did not make it explicitly clear what actually the link between slavery and servitude was", however the understanding being that slavery "is graver than servitude".[105] While "distinct from slavery" it is still lacking a precise definition.[106]

The crime of servitude, for its part, has been found to be "an obligation to provide one's services that is imposed by the use of coercion" in the ECtHR case of *CN and V v France*.[107] This is despite the fact that the, all be it much older ruling of the Trial Chamber (US Military Tribunal, Nuremberg) in *US v Oswald Pohl and Others*,[108] (which was referred to in the more recent case of *Prosecutor v Kunarac, Vukovic and Kovac*),[109] stated, in 1947, that "involuntary servitude, even if tempered by humane treatment, is still slavery".[110] Consent cannot,

99 Ibid.
100 Ibid.
101 McGeehan, op. cit., p 454.
102 Ibid., p 454/5.
103 Ibid., p 437.
104 *Siliadin v France*, op. cit., p 33, paragraph 124.
105 Stoyanova (2012), op. cit., p 182.
106 Ibid. p 455.
107 *CN and V v France*, Application no. 67724/09, ECtHR, 11 October 2012, paragraph 89.
108 *US v Oswald Pohl and Others*, op. cit., p 15.
109 *Prosecutor v Kunarac, Vukovic and Kovac*, op. cit., paragraph 123.
110 *US v Oswald Pohl and Others*, op. cit., p 15.

however, "legitimise [either] slavery or servitude".[111] Consent may however be relevant in the context of forced or compulsory labour.[112]

Servitude is seen by the ECtHR as being linked to the concept of slavery but is not slavery itself. "Institutions similar to slavery and practices similar to slavery" has been recognised by the ECtHR in the case of *CN and V v France*,[113] relying on the UN Supplementary Convention on the Abolition of Slavery, the Slave Trade, and Institutions and Practices Similar to Slavery 1956 for its definition. The court in that case used the definition of a "serf" to mean the obligation "to live in another person's property and the impossibility of altering his condition", relying on the *Van Droogenbroeck* case.[114] The 1956 Convention itself defines practices similar to slavery as being debt bondage, serfdom, and "any institution or practice" involving the marriage of a woman "without her right to refuse", and "any institution or practice" whereby someone under the age of 18 "is delivered by either or both of his natural parents or by his guardian to another person, whether for reward or not, with a view to the exploitation of the child or young person or of his labour". This latter scenario was found by the ECtHR to most closely match the facts in *Siliadin*.

Servitude was stated in *Rantsev v Cyprus and Russia*[115] to "entail an obligation, under coercion, to provide one's services", something which is linked to, but is not the same as slavery (relying on *Seguin v France*,[116] and *Salidain* para 124). The *Siliadin*[117] case also stated that servitude was a "particularly serious form of denial of freedom". In *Siliadin* the individual was referred to as a being "serf" if he is obliged to "live on another's property" and for whom it is impossible to change his conditions.[118] Also relevant was the "impossibility of altering his/her condition".[119] Stoyanova is of the view that the ruling in *Siliadin* means that one set of circumstances can be classified as "both forced labour and servitude".[120]

Servitude, or "practices similar to slavery", while being distinguished from slavery itself, is also distinguished from forced and compulsory labour. The ECtHR in *CN and V v France*[121] observed that servitude corresponds to a special type of forced or compulsory labour, or in other words "aggravated" forced or compulsory labour, with the victim believing that "their condition is permanent and that the situation is unlikely to change". Article 4 ECHR covered the issue of slavery and servitude in part 1, and forced and compulsory labour in part 2. The ECtHR

111 Mantouvalou, op. cit., p 410.
112 Ibid., p 410.
113 *CN and V v France*, op. cit., p 19 paragraph 90.
114 *Van Droogenbroeck v Belgium*, Application no. 7906/77, Commission's report of 9 July 1980, Series B no. 44, p 30, paragraphs 78–80.
115 *Rantsev v Cyprus and Russia*, op. cit., p 58, paragraph 275.
116 *Seguin v France*, Application no. 42400/98, 43722/98, 50331/99, ECtHR, 16 April 2002, 7 January 2003, and 8 July 2003.
117 *Siliadin v France*, op. cit., p 33, paragraph 123.
118 European Court of Human Rights, Guide to Article 4, op. cit., paragraph 17.
119 Stoyanova (2012), op. cit., p 182.
120 Ibid., p 182.
121 *CN and V v France*, op. cit., paragraph 91.

has confirmed this distinction between the two classifications, stating that it sees "servitude" as a specific form of the more broadly defined concept of "forced or compulsory labour".[122] This was also at issue in the military service case of *W, X, Y, and Z v the United Kingdom*[123] (Commission decision), where the Commission held that while the clause exempting military service from the provisions on "forced or compulsory labour", there was no such military service exemption for "slavery or servitude".[124] These are therefore clearly different categories for the ECtHR. For its part, the Slavery Convention 1925, Article 5 refers to forced and compulsory labour, it does not define it, so recourse must be made to other sources to develop the ECtHR's understanding of these terms.

Forced or Compulsory Labour

The ECtHR has pointed out that there is a lack of guidance within its legal framework as to what is meant by the terms "forced or compulsory labour" in *Van der Mussele v Belgium*,[125] despite it being clearly prohibited in Article 4.2 ECHR. The court gave Article 4.2 ECHR a broad meaning, in that "labour" did not just mean manual work, but "includes other work as well as services".[126] The court in that case went on to use the ILO Convention No. 29 (Forced Labour Convention), with the ECtHR using this definition "as a starting point" for interpreting this term for the purposes of ECHR law. A central principle of the ILO is that "labour is not a commodity", which is "enshrined in its Constitution".[127] However, also according to the ILO Constitution, "authentic interpretation" of any of the ILO Conventions "can be given only by the International Court of Justice".[128] There is therefore a lack of authentic interpretation of the provisions "forced or compulsory labour", to cover all of the relevant issues at the ILO level.

The ECtHR in *Van der Mussele* pointed out that the ILO treaties "bind almost all ECHR member States".[129] The 1930 Forced Labour Convention has defined forced and compulsory labour at Article 2.1 as "all work or service which is exacted from any person under the menace of any penalty and for which the said person has not offered himself voluntarily". The ECtHR also found that the forced or compulsory labour provisions Article 4 ECHR should be similarly

122 Ibid., paragraph 91.

123 Case of *W, X, Y, and Z v United Kingdom*, Applications nos. 2435–8/67. Commission ruling of the 19 July 1968 (unnumbered paragraphs).

124 Ibid.

125 *Van der Mussele v Belgium*, Application no. 8919/80, ECtHR, 23 November 1983, paragraph 32.

126 P. H. Van Kempen and S. Lestrade, 'Limiting the Criminalisation of Human Trafficking; Protection Against Exploitative Labour versus Individual Liberty and Economic Development', in R. Haverkamp, E. Herlin-Karnell and C. Lernestedt, *What is Wrong with Human Trafficking? Critical Perspectives on the Law*, Hart Publishing, 2018, p 229.

127 Mantouvalou, op. cit., p 412.

128 Vinkovic, op. cit., p 90.

129 Mantouvalou, op. cit., p 403.

interpreted for ECHR law.[130] However the ECtHR in that case went on to say that "sight should not be lost of [the ECHR's] special features or the fact that it is a living instrument to be read 'in light of the notions currently prevailing in democratic states'". The ECtHR's definition of forced and compulsory labour will therefore be expected to evolve from the original ILO's definition over time, and as working conditions and standards change.[131] This will be a challenge for domestic criminal law.

The words "forced" and "compulsory" were examined by the ECtHR in *Van der Mussele*, with "forced" being recognised as involving "physical or mental constraint".[132] *CN and V v France*[133] examined the phrase "cost of coercion" used by the International Labour Conference in 1999, acknowledging not only "physical violence or restraint" but also "subtler forms, of a psychological nature, such as threats to denounce victims to the police or immigration authorities when their employment status is illegal". *Siliadin* also referred to "physical or mental constraint"[134] when discussing forced or compulsory labour. This would include the *Van der Mussele* discussion of "work 'exacted … under the menace of any penalty' and also performed against the will of the person concerned, that is work for which he 'has not offered himself voluntarily'".[135] *Chowdury and Others v Greece*[136] has held that a victims prior consent "is not sufficient to exclude the characterisation of work as forced labour", and that the facts need to be examined in each case.[137]

In addition, a further legal document of the CoE, the European Social Charter (ESC) has provisions on social and labour rights. This is interpreted by the European Committee of Social Rights. Its Article 1 paragraph 2 provides the need of contracting state parties "to protect effectively the right of the worker to earn his living in an occupation freely entered into". The phrase "freely entered into" has been interpreted by the European Committee of Social Rights, the "former committee of Independent Experts, the monitoring body of the ESC", "as prohibiting forced labour", with any work carried out against the worker's wishes being "contrary to the Charter".[138] For her part, Stoyanova echoes concerns expressed earlier in this chapter about transposing this time "the ILO forced labour definition in a criminal law statute [and whether this] establishes an effective basis [for] … crimes so that they can be effectively applied", with the "rights of the accused" being "also an important consideration in this context".[139] The positive obligation

130 *Van der Mussele v Belgium*, op. cit., paragraph 32.
131 Ibid., paragraph 32.
132 Ibid., paragraph 34.
133 *CN and V v France*, op. cit., paragraph 77.
134 *Siliadin v France*, op. cit., p 32, paragraph 117.
135 *Van der Mussele v Belgium*, op. cit., paragraph 34.
136 *Chowdury and Others v Greece*, Application no. 21884/15, ECtHR, 30 March 2017.
137 Ibid., paragraph 96.
138 Mantouvalou, op. cit., p 400.
139 Stoyanova (2014), op. cit., p 436.

of states to effectively implement and enforce legislation will be addressed later in Chapter 4.

As a consequence of the above rulings Mantouvalou has stated that international labour law and international human rights law "should no longer be regarded as competitive", given the "overlap and convergence" when it comes to the "protection of labour rights".[140] The above "judicial cross-fertilisation and dialogue", discussed by Mantouvalou in the context of forced and compulsory labour,[141] can be seen throughout the development of the jurisprudence for slavery, servitude, forced and compulsory labour, and for THB. However, it would be a mistake to assume that given the substantial overlaps and cross fertilisation, that the terminology is being used in the same way in each of the jurisdictions, and for both rights, and transnational law enforcement purposes.

Two issues arise, however, further to the above discussion, that of non-criminalisation of the key crimes underlying THB in national law, and ineffective or unclear criminalisation in national law. There is a need for national provisions to have high quality and clear definitions in place to cover these key crimes,[142] with any ambiguity in their enactment, or "their restrictive interpretation" being likely to give rise to problems such as were encountered in *Siliadin* and *CN and V v France.*[143] In addition many ILO states, according to ILO reports, have "not provided for the specific offence of forced labour in their criminal law".[144] Also there is academic, and practitioner debate, about the outer edges of THB for forced and compulsory labour, given the lack of precision in the legal definitions, both internationally and domestically. Firstly, jurisdictions need to legislate for both THB and "slavery, servitude, forced and compulsory labour". Then an understanding needs to develop that there is a continuum of exploitation, from the standard contract law issues, to be resolved at domestic employment law tribunals, through the state legal provisions on abusive labour law practices, which are the concern of labour inspectors, who normally issue administrative penalties, but there may also be provision for criminal penalties, through then to the more severe offences entailing, depending on the facts of the case, either the THB provisions or the slavery, servitude, forced or compulsory labour provisions. If any of the required legal provisions, or relevant law enforcement capacity is missing from national legislative provisions, or lacking in some way, then people will continue to be exploited without an effective response.

The ILO has called for increased workplace inspections and closer cooperation between labour inspectors and the police.[145] The ILO is of the view that the UN protocol gives "rather wide latitude to States … in the treatment of victims of

140 Mantouvalou, op. cit., p 408.
141 Ibid., p 407.
142 Stoyanova (2014), op. cit., p 430.
143 Ibid., p 424.
144 Ibid., p 428.
145 ILO, Human Trafficking and Forced Labour Exploitation – Guidelines for Legislation and Law Enforcement Special Action Programme to Combat Forced Labour, ILO, 2005, p 61.

trafficking". It points to Article 14 of the UN protocol which provides that law makers should consult "other international instruments",[146] stating that the ILO has already set out in its own conventions "standards for the protection of migrant workers, including trafficking victims",[147] and that these should inform states when implementing laws under the THB Protocol. The ILO provides requirements for labour inspection regimes, *inter alia*, under the Labour Inspection Convention, 1947 (No. 81), its 1995 Protocol,[148] and the Labour Inspection (Agriculture) Convention, 1969 (No. 129). Other specialised ILO conventions focusing on specific sectors (such as agriculture, mining, and transport) are also relevant.[149] However, even in countries where labour inspectors take their work seriously, "the low status of labour inspectors [in some countries] weakens their determination to press for enforcement measures",[150] something required to be addressed by the 2014 Protocol to the Forced Labour Convention 1930 (Article 2.c.ii). The ILO has also, in its policy documents, called for coordination in the enforcement activities of labour inspectors and police, and immigration if the worker is a migrant, in forced and compulsory labour.[151]

Once all these provisions are in place in each jurisdiction, there should no longer the attempt to broaden one definition in order to cover situations which are not otherwise covered in that legal jurisdiction, thereby avoiding the scenario of THB laws trying to cover "consensual, mutual advantageous, exploitative labour and non-exploitative labour", as described by Van Kempen and Lestrade.[152] This book takes a human security approach to THB, being a freedom from fear approach,[153] which if adopted, would sharpen the definitions of THB, and this situation would be avoided. Other laws are, or should be, on national statute books to address exploitative situations short of either THB or slavery, servitude, forced or compulsory labour.

Exploitation

What is clear from the above analysis is that "a clear gradation among the abuse practices of slavery, servitude and forced labour" in the case of *Siliadin v France*,[154] an analysis which has been carried forward in subsequent ECtHR case law. These terms appear to reflect different levels of severity of exploitation. It is less clear if there is a gradation between these categories and THB in the context of exploitation, and the facts of each case would need to be examined. The term

146 Ibid., p 2.
147 ILO, op. cit., p 46.
148 P081 – Protocol of 1995 to the Labour Inspection Convention, 1947.
149 ILO, op. cit., p 49.
150 Ibid., p 51.
151 Ibid., p 28.
152 Van Kempen and Lestrade, op. cit., p 236.
153 M. Glasius and M. Kaldor, *A Human Security Doctrine for Europe: Project, Principles, Practicalities*, Routledge, 2006.
154 Stoyanova (2012), op. cit., p 181.

"exploitation" itself merits examination. Viganò points out that the term "exploitation" is not defined in any supranational THB instrument,[155] with exemplars only being provided. For example, the THB Protocol provides that its provisions include "at a minimum, the exploitation of the prostitution of others or other forms of sexual exploitation, forced labour or services, slavery or practices similar to slavery, servitude or the removal of organs". It was intended that states could "exercise their discretion and determine themselves what should be meant by 'exploitation' in their respective legal systems".[156] While domestic contexts can effectively establish the current or anticipated types of exploitation being encountered in their jurisdiction, the level of exploitation being proscribed under THB laws now varies distinctly from one jurisdiction to another. Thorburn argues that the term "exploitation" is "simply too broad and too eclectic"[157] when examined across jurisdictions, posing a problem for, not just those jurisdictions, but also transnational law enforcement and the double criminality tests than need to be met for extradition. Thorbun argues that a narrower definition of exploitation, focusing on the most severe types, would merit a more severe punitive response to THB.[158] A freedom from fear approach would point in that direction, and would lead to situations, such as in the UK, where the maximum possible penalty for THB, along with slavery, servitude, forced and compulsory labour, is life imprisonment.[159]

While the 1926 Slavery Convention sets the benchmarks for the current definition of slavery, "subsequent interpretation of its provisions" trying to "bring modern forms of exploitation within" it definitions, "have lacked consistency and resulted in large measures of confusion".[160] Stoyanova is of the view that the term "exploitation" when used by itself "is a form of abuse [with] a lower threshold as opposed to slavery, servitude and forced labour".[161] The approach of the UK legislation, with the possibility of life for both offences, would indicate otherwise for those UK jurisdictions. Stoyanova points out that the THB Protocol does not require the criminalisation of exploitation, but rather "the 'recruitment, transportation, transfer or receipt of persons' by certain means 'for the purpose of exploitation'".[162] She argues that there is no overlap between THB and the provisions

155 F. Viganò, 'Introduction: An Unfortunate State of the Law', in R. Haverkamp, E. Herlin-Karnell and C. Lernestedt, *What is Wrong with Human Trafficking? Critical Perspectives on the Law*, Hart Publishing, 2018, p 241.

156 Viganò, op. cit., p 241.

157 M. Thorburn, 'Human Trafficking: Supplying the Market for Human Exploitation', in R. Haverkamp, E. Herlin-Karnell and C. Lernestedt, *What is Wrong with Human Trafficking? Critical Perspectives on the Law*, Hart Publishing, 2018, p 175.

158 Ibid., p 163.

159 Modern Slavery Act 2015, section 5.1.a, Human Trafficking and Exploitation (Scotland) Act 2015, section 1.6 and section 4.5, Human Trafficking and Exploitation (Criminal Justice and Support for Victims) Act (Northern Ireland) 2015, section 1.6 and section 2.9.

160 Allain and Hickey, op. cit., p 938.

161 Stoyanova (2012), op. cit., p 183.

162 Ibid., p 184.

of Article 4 ECHR.[163] However, this analysis does not work when the provisions of the EU directive on THB are examined. The provisions of Article 4 ECHR, all be it in the context of human rights law, is clearly connected with the provisions of the transnational criminal law of the EU, and they assist in defining THB as provided for in the EU directive, and as required to be implemented by EU member states (to include at the time of its enactment, the UK). Hathaway makes a similar point.[164] However, as Stoyanova goes on to say, "a meaningful legal debate on this issue is, however impeded" due not just to the lack of certainty of the meaning of "exploitation" but also "the lack of the ECtHR's jurisprudence on Article 4".[165] Both ECtHR and CJEU jurisprudence may further develop this point in the years to come.

The term "exploitation" is not used in Article 4 ECHR. Stoyanova argues that if the ECtHR is to expand the provisions of the ECHR to cover the term exploitation, that this judicial activism will be to develop "exploitation" only as a term "linked with recruitment, transportation, transfer, harbouring or receipt of persons, by means of coercion or deception" in the context of THB, and not as a stand-alone concept.[166] As pointed out by Stoyanova,[167] there is some debate between Hathaway and Gallagher as to the exact role of the term "exploitation" in the context of THB, with Hathaway arguing that the THB Protocol does not place an obligation on states to "do anything about the conditions of being exploited".[168] Gallagher, examining the THB Protocol, argues that it might be possible to argue that exploitation *per se* could bring an action into the ambit of THB, without the need for the processes of recruitment, transportation and transfer, however "a close reading of the *travaux préparatoires* provides no evidence to support a contention that this is what the drafters had in mind".[169] Gallagher argues that an expansion of the term "harbouring" to "include all situations in which individuals are coercively or forcibly exploited (for example, all cases of forded labor) would render redundant that three part definition" of action, means and purpose in the THB Protocol.[170] In the absence of the independent use of the term "exploitation" in the legal definitions there is a high probability that individuals in extreme vulnerable situations will still fall outside the current definitions of THB and must rely on possibly less robust legal provisions to gain protection from law enforcement agencies or to otherwise gain redress. This issue was expressly addressed in the UK's provisions in the UK Modern Slavery Act 2015, of which more below. As pointed out by Stoyanova, the issue of

163 Ibid.
164 J. Hathaway, 'The Human Rights Quagmire of Human Trafficking' (2008), 49 *Virginia Journal of International Law* 1, p 49.
165 Stoyanova (2012), op. cit., p 180.
166 Ibid., p 172.
167 Ibid., p 34.
168 Hathaway, op. cit., p 9.
169 A. Gallagher, *The International Law of Human Trafficking*, Cambridge University Press, 2010, p 31.
170 Ibid.

how to "conceptualize exploitation" needs to be addressed in domestic criminal law,[171] and in such a way as facilitates transnational criminal law.

Human Trafficking

Defining what is THB requires a thorough understanding of what is understood by the crimes of slavery, servitude, forced and compulsory labour. The crime of THB also needs to be distinguished then from the above crimes, even at the same time as it also encompasses elements of them. Equally it needs to be understood that some of the above definitions have been developed in the context of international human rights law, or even international labour law, and not in the context of either transnational, supranational or even national criminal law, with their varying nuances and emphases.

The ECtHR has acknowledged that Article 4 ECHR does not expressly refer to THB in the case of *Rantsev v Cyprus and Russia*.[172] However, the court gets over this point by stating, that at least for ECHR law, there is an obligation on states to "penalise and prosecute effectively" any act which leads to "a situation of slavery, servitude or forced or compulsory labour",[173] which in itself is sufficient to bring THB within the ambit of Article 4 ECHR. The court then went on to use the THB Protocol and the CoE THB Convention,[174] which define what the ECtHR itself means by THB in the context of Article 4 ECHR.[175] It considers that THB within the meaning of Article 3(a) of the Palermo Protocol and Article 4(a) of the CoE THB Convention, falls within the scope of Article 4 of the Convention.[176] The court, accounting for the lack of an express reference to THB in the drafting of the ECHR, has acknowledged that the international legal order has developed since its initial drafting, bringing the crime of THB to the fore. It went on to say in *Rantsev* that "trafficking ran 'counter to the spirit' of art.4, and could not be considered compatible with a democratic society and the values expounded in the Convention".[177] This therefore allowed the court to expand the remit of Article 4 ECHR to include THB, taking what has been referred to by Stoyanova,[178] as the "broader meaning of norms" approach to interpretation of the ECHR.

However, as pointed out by Kirchner and Frese, the "court has shied away from stating explicitly that trafficking amounts to enslavement".[179] *SM v Croatia*[180] then expressly addresses ECtHR's understanding of THB, as discussed above.

171 Stoyanova (2017), op. cit., p 68.
172 European Court of Human Rights, Guide to Article 4, op. cit., paragraph 9.
173 *Rantsev v Cyprus and Russia*, op. cit., p 60, paragraph 284.
174 CoE Convention on Action against Trafficking in Human Beings, Warsaw, 16. V.2005, CETS No. 197.
175 European Court of Human Rights, Guide to Article 4, op. cit., paragraph 6.
176 *Rantsev v Cyprus and Russia*, op. cit., paragraph 284.
177 Case comment, 'Rantsev v Cyprus and Russia', op. cit., p 330.
178 Stoyanova (2014), op. cit., p 422.
179 S. Kirchner and V. M. Frese, 'Slavery under the European Convention on Human Rights and the Jus Cogens Prohibition of Human Trafficking' (2015) 27 *Denning Law Journal*, p 136.
180 *SM v Croatia*, op. cit.

While the type of exploitation and extent of exploitation is important in addressing the issue of THB, as Stoyanova says, "human trafficking is not a form of exploitation" itself.[181] Rather it focuses on activities preparing for or anticipating exploitation.[182] This includes "the recruitment, transportation, transfer, harbouring or receipt of persons".[183] The *mens rea* for these offences can vary from intentional to reckless,[184] with penalties being higher for those intentionally engaging in THB, however the level of proof in court might be more difficult to achieve. The UK with its possibility of life imprisonment has adopted the *mens rea* of "intention" or "knows or ought to have known".[185] Equally some engaged in THB might be "physically distanced from the potential or actual exploitation",[186] leading to further evidentiary issues for the requisite *mens rea*. Adults (those over the age of 18) can consent to certain levels of exploitation, however not when "treats or use of force or other forms of coercion, of abduction, of fraud, of deception, of the abuse of power or of a position of vulnerability or the giving or receiving of payments of benefits to achieve the consent of a person having control over another person" are involved.[187] Van Kempen and Lestrade point out that the question then arises as to how these terms are to be interpreted in domestic criminal law, in particular the terms "abuse of power or position of vulnerability".[188] The dividing line then between THB and other domestic crimes such as fraud, deception, abduction, pimping and procurement needs to be addressed.[189]

It is possible to breach Article 4 ECHR in cases which do not involve THB. There will also be instances of THB which do not breach Article 4 ECHR. The question of whether legal and practice provisions drafted at national level to combat either one or other of these crime areas is sufficiently precisely drafted to meet the requirements of national criminal laws, or sufficiently broadly drafted to cover both crime areas. There will be issues not only of overlapping legal frameworks, but also gaps in legal frameworks. This is an issue which is taken up by the UK in its response to its pre-Brexit legal requirement to implement EU Directive 2011/36/EU[190] in enacting legislation, in E&W the Modern Slavery Act 2015, a twin track approach to both THB and "slavery, servitude, forced and compulsory labour", thereby aiming to ensure that no form of serous abuse of fellow humans falls through the legislative cracks.

181 Stoyanova (2017), op. cit., p 42.
182 Ibid.
183 THB Protocol, Article 3(a.).
184 Stoyanova (2017), op. cit., p 46.
185 Modern Slavery Act 2015, section 1.1a and section 2.4, Human Trafficking and Exploitation (Scotland) Act 2015, section 1 and section 4.1 (knew or ought to have known), Human Trafficking and Exploitation (Criminal Justice and Support for Victims) Act (Northern Ireland) 2015, section 4.1 (intention).
186 Stoyanova (2017), op. cit., p 43.
187 THB Protocol, Article 3(a.).
188 Van Kempen and Lestrade, op. cit., p 227.
189 Stoyanova (2017), op. cit., p 41.
190 Directive 2011/36/EU, op. cit.

Modern Slavery

Further terminology arises in the context of THB, that of "modern slavery" (MS). Drew argues that "modern forms of slavery have been identified to reflect new forms of exploitation but also progress in standards".[191] However, as discussed above, the term "exploitation" has yet to be defined. While *Rantsev* used the term "modern slavery" to denote THB,[192] this phrase more often arises in non-legal contexts. However, it is also the terminology used by the UK in its legislation, primarily implemented for the E&W jurisdiction, but also with provisions of relevance to the devolved jurisdictions of Scotland and Northern Ireland (NI). There are similar provisions enacted by their respective regional legislatures for both Scotland and NI. The UK Modern Slavery Act 2015 has been enacted with a view to meeting the UK's requirements under the EU Directive 2011/36/EU, which it joined late, but pre-Brexit. It has also involved some deep thinking on behalf of the UK legislature, and the sub-national NI and Scottish legislatures, on the issue, all three of which have "gold plated" the EU directive provisions, adding a further dimension to the issue in a European context. A full examination of the UK's response to Directive 2011/36/EU, to include those of the UK sub-national legislatures, will be made in Chapter 7.

Prostitution

The issue of prostitution needs to be taken into consideration when examining the transnational crime of THB. A key word in the protocol is that of a "child", which was defined as being "any person under eighteen years of age".[193] The most problematic aspect of THB is "prostitution" and "sexual exploitation", particularly where children (persons under the age of 18) are involved. Much has been written about prostitution, expressing conflicting views on whether prostitution is itself a right for predominantly women to exercise, or whether all prostitution is in fact forced prostitution, due to a lack of other viable economic or cultural options. This is a complex debate which will not be entered into here. There is no consensus in Europe on how to address the issue of prostitution,[194] with some very varying, not only practices, but also laws, operating within the EU. A relevant international treaty in force, which "consolidated a number of [previous] instruments",[195] is the 1949 UN Convention on the Suppression of the Traffic in Persons and the Exploitation of the Prostitution of Others (often known, now confusingly, as the Trafficking Convention), which states in its preamble that

191 Drew, op. cit., p 487.
192 *Rantsev v Cyprus and Russia*, op. cit., p 60, paragraph 280.
193 Palermo Protocol, Article 3.d.
194 Editor, 'Prostitution: Prostitute Required to Make Social Security Contributions – Forced Prostitution –Art. 3 & 4(2), Case Comment' (2008) 1 *European Human Rights Review*, p 136, commenting on Case *Tremblay v France*, Application no. 37194/02, ECtHR, of 11 September 2007.
195 Drew, op. cit., p 483.

"prostitution is incompatible with human rights and human dignity".[196] It has, at the time of writing, 25 signatories and 82 partners, which is not as broad a take up as the THB Protocol, with its currently 117 signatories and 181 parties. This divergence in national practices when it comes to prostitution and sexual exploitation results in these issues being national issues, requiring national responses, as "the prostitution debate always moves into the context of a particular society at national level".[197] This was reflected in the ECHR case of *Tremblay v France*,[198] when the question of whether "prostitution is always forced" was not addressed. However, the issue of forced prostitution was declared to be "incompatible with the rights and dignity of the human person".[199] There is therefore, much greater clarity internationally when the prostitution or sexual exploitation is forced (or at least forced as understood by the law enforcement community), or where it involves children (persons under the age of 18).[200] The issue of forced prostitution arose again in the Grand Chamber ruling of *SM v Croatia*,[201] where THB was considered to be a "separate issue" to forced prostitution, leading to questions as to whether forced prostitution is to be seen as a separate offence under Article 4 ECHR or part of the forced labour definition.[202]

Conclusion

In the absence of the international criminal law formally recognising THB as an international crime – and *ius cogens* under Article 53 of the Vienna Convention, or even a clearer understanding of the emerging *ius cogens* under Article 64, we are left with the need to negotiate the interlegality of different THB and related texts, coming from a variety of regulatory actors. These vary from the UN Palermo Convention and its THB protocol to a variety of UN Conventions, ILO conventions and at a European regional level, the CoE THB convention, and relevant rulings of the ECtHR. In addition, for EU member states, the EU, benefiting from the principle of supremacy in its relations with its own member states, is also an important regulatory actor. While analysing the relevant texts and case law, we need to be aware of the distinction of interpreting a legal text through the lens of human rights law as opposed to criminal law, with criminal law requiring full respect of the principle of legality, which will be examined in Chapter 4.

In negotiating this interlegality, we are left with the debate whether the criminal definition of THB is greater than the sum of its parts; slavery, servitude, forced labour and compulsory labour, and problems with the definition of exploitation. In addition, there is the issue of how exactly these provisions have been enacted

196 Editor, 'Prostitution', op. cit., p 136.
197 Stoyanova (2017), op. cit., p 60.
198 *Tremblay v France*, Application no. 37194/02, ECtHR, 11 September 2007.
199 Editor, 'Prostitution', op. cit., p 136.
200 Vinkovic, op. cit., p 98.
201 *SM v Croatia*, op. cit.
202 K. Hughes, 'Human Trafficking, SM v Croatia and the Conceptual Evolution of Article 4 ECHR' (2022) 85 *Modern Law Review* 4.

into domestic law, and whether the domestic implementation has added further complexity to the need to develop transnational criminal law. Problems with the international definitions have been replicated in domestic criminal law, with Stoyanova pointing out that national legislation will have to resolve these "definitional ambiguities",[203] as national criminal law needs to be sufficiently clear and precise in order to enable effective investigation and prosecutions.[204]

An approach to the interpretation of legal text, and an understanding of the crime of THB should take, this book argues, a human security approach. This approach should prioritise the security of individuals, wherever they come from whatever their nationality, and whatever their immigration status in that state. This would therefore be broader than the traditional human rights approach, which prioritises those who can get a legal system to work to their benefit, whether that be through their legal status in that jurisdiction, or through access to the necessary legal teams. The interpretation of legal texts also needs to be done in a way in which practitioners, whether they be law enforcement officials, investigators (where these are different to law enforcement, as is the case in some legal jurisdictions), or prosecutors can operationalise the legal frameworks in a way that allows them to effectively interact with their counterparts in another legal jurisdiction along the THB supply chain. The priority should be, at all stages of the interpretation, development, and operation of the transnational legal framework for THB is to effectively combat this crime and provide the freedom from fear for potential victims required by the Canadian approach to human security.

Bibliography

Allain, J. and Hickey, R., 'Property and the Definition of Slavery' (2012) 61 *International and Comparative Law Quarterly* 4, 915–938.

Case Comment, 'Rantsev v Cyprus and Russia (App. No.25965/04): Trafficking in Human Beings – Sexual Exploitation – "Artiste" Visa Regime in Cyprus' (2010) 3 *European Human Rights Law Review*, 325–330.

Cameron, I., 'European Court of Human Rights January 2005 – March 2006' (2007) 13 *European Public Law* 1, 3–31.

Dörr O. and Schmalenback, K., *Vienna Convention on the Law of Treaties A Commentary*, Springer, 2018.

Drew, S., 'Human Trafficking: A Modern Form of Slavery?' (2002) 4 *European Human Rights Law Review*, 481–492.

Editor, 'Prostitution: Prostitute Required to Make Social Security Contributions – Forced Prostitution – Art. 3 & 4(2), Case Comment' (2008) 1 *European Human Rights Review*, 135–137.

European Court of Human Rights, Guide to Article 4 – Prohibition of Slavery and Forced Labour, Council of Europe, updated on 31 December 2018.

Gallagher, A., *The International Law of Human Trafficking*, Cambridge University Press, 2010.

203 Stoyanova (2017), op. cit., p 73.
204 Ibid., p 345.

Glasius M. and Kaldor, M., *A Human Security Doctrine for Europe: Project, Principles, Practicalities*, Routledge, 2006.

Hathaway, J., 'The Human Rights Quagmire of Human Trafficking' (2008) 49 *Virginia Journal of International Law* 1, 1–59.

Haverkamp, R., Herlin-Karnell, E., and Lernestedt, C., *What is Wrong with Human Trafficking? Critical Perspectives on the Law*, Hart Publishing, 2018.

Hughes, K., 'Human Trafficking, SM v Croatia and the Conceptual Evolution of Article 4 ECHR' (2022) 85 *Modern Law Review* 4, 1044–1061.

ILO, Human Trafficking and Forced Labour Exploitation – Guidelines for Legislation and Law Enforcement Special Action Programme to Combat Forced Labour, ILO, 2005.

Kirchner, S. and Frese, V. M., 'Slavery under the European Convention on Human Rights and the Jus Cogens Prohibition of Human Trafficking' (2015) 27 *Denning Law Journal*, 130–145.

Kubáklová, V., 'The Twenty Years' Catharsis: E. H. Carr and IR', in Kubáklová, V., Onuf, N. and Kowert, P., *International Relations in a Constructed World*, Routledge, 1998, 41–73.

Lagerwall, A., 'Article 64 Emergence of a New Peremptory Norm of General International Law ("Jus Cogens")', in O. Corten and P. Klein, *The Vienna Convention on the Law of Treaties: A Commentary*, Oxford University Press, 2011, Volume II, 1455–1480.

Mantouvalou, V., 'Servitude and Forced Labour in the 21st Century: The Human Rights of Domestic Workers' (2006) 35 *Industrial Law Journal* 4, 395–414.

McGeehan, N. L., 'Misunderstood and Neglected: The Marginalisation of Slavery in International Law' (2011) 16 *The International Journal of Human Rights* 3, 436–460.

Stoyanova, V., *Human Trafficking and Slavery Reconsidered: Conceptual Limits and States' Positive Obligations in European Law*, Cambridge University Press, 2017.

Stoyanova, V., 'Article 4 of the ECHR and the Obligation of Criminalising Slavery, Servitude, Forced Labour and Human Trafficking' (2014) 3 *Cambridge Journal of International and Comparative Law* 2, 407–443.

Stoyanova, V., 'Dancing on the Borders of Article 4: Human Trafficking and the European Court of Human Rights in the Rantsev Case' (2012) 30 *Netherlands Institute of Human Rights* 2, 163–194.

Villiger, M. E., *Commentary on the 1969 Vienna Convention on the Law of Treaties*, Martinus Nijhoff Publishers, 2009.

Vinkovic, M., 'The "Unbroken Marriage" – Trafficking and Child Labour in Europe' (2010) 13 *Journal of Money Laundering Control* 2, 87–102.

Legislation

Council Framework Decision 2002/584/JHA on the European Arrest Warrant, OJ L 190/1.

CoE Convention on Action against Trafficking in Human Beings, Warsaw, 16 May 2005, CETS No. 197.

CoE Convention on the Protection of Children against Sexual Exploitation and Sexual Abuse 2007, CETS No. 201.

CoE Convention against Trafficking in Human Organs 2015, CETS No. 216.

Directive 2011/36/EU of the European Parliament and of the Council of 5 April 2011 on preventing and combating trafficking in human beings and protecting its victims, and replacing Council Framework Decision 2002/629/JHA, OJ L 101/1.

Human Trafficking and Exploitation (Criminal Justice and Support for Victims) Act (Northern Ireland) 2015.

Human Trafficking and Exploitation (Scotland) Act 2015.

ILO Forced Labour Convention, 1930 (No. 29), UNTS, 39(612).

Modern Slavery Act 2015.

Protocol of 1995 to the Labour Inspection Convention, 1947, P081.

UK EU Trade and Cooperation Agreement, OJ L 149/10.

Cases

Case C-69/89 *Nakajima v Council* [1991] ECR I-2069.

Case 149/96, *Portugal v Council* [1999] ECR I-8395.

Case 70/87 *Fediol v Commission* [1989] ECR 1219.

Chowdury and Others v Greece, Application no. 21884/15, ECtHR, 30 March 2017.

CN and V v France, Application no. 67724/09, ECtHR, 11 October 2012.

Prosecutor v Kunarac, Vukovic and Kovac, Appeals Chamber, International Tribunal for the Former Yugoslavia, Case No. IT-96–23 & TI-96–23/1-A, 12 June 2002.

Prosecutor v Sesay, Lallon and Gbao (Trial Chamber – Special Court for Sierra Leone) SCSL-04–15-T, 2 March 2009.

Rantsev v Cyprus and Russia, Application no. 25965/04, ECtHR, 7 January 2010.

Seguin v France, Application no. 42400/98, 43722/98, 50331/99, ECtHR, 16 April 2002, 7 January 2003, and 8 July 2003.

Siliadin v France, Application no. 73316/01, ECtHR, 26 October 2005.

SM v Croatia, Application no. 60561/14, ECtHR, 25 June 2020.

Tremblay v France, Application no. 37194/02, ECtHR, 11 September 2007.

United States v Matta-Ballesteros, US Court of Appeal for the 9th Circuit, 71 F3d 754, 764 n 5 (1995).

United States v Oswald Pohl and Others, judgment of 3 November 1947, US Military Tribunal Nuremberg, available online at http://werle.rewi.hu-berlin.de/POHL-Case.pdf.

Van Droogenbroeck v Belgium, Application no. 7906/77, Commission's report, 9 July 1980, Series B no. 44.

Van der Mussele v Belgium, Application no. 8919/80, ECtHR, 23 November 1983.

W, X Y and Z v United Kingdom, Applications nos. 2435–8/67. Commission ruling, 19 July 1968 (unnumbered paragraphs).

3 Transnational Crime

THB as International Human Rights to THB as Transnational Crime

Milivojevic and Ćopić point out that it was the "21st century abolitionist movement", in its calls for the abolition of slavery, which "firmly" located the global framework for combatting THB "within a law and order framework".[1] An analysis of the provisions of the Palermo Convention, which should be read in conjunction with its THB Protocol in the context of the need to build transnational legal frameworks will be made in Chapter 4. Many would argue that the THB Protocol has been weak on the issues of prevention of the crime and victim assistance, with a need to rely on a wider range of international treaties, to include other UN treaties. In addition, states could be found to be in breach of their international human rights obligations if they fail to protect victims "who are subjected to abuses by private parties".[2] Much has been written about THB as an issue for international human rights law, as discussed earlier in Chapter 2. However, as pointed out by Stoyanova, "[h]uman rights law and criminal law have different objects of regulation",[3] as normally it is not states, to which international human rights law is addressed, that traffics victims, rather it is individuals in or passing through those states.[4]

A positive obligation, based on Article 1 ECHR is placed on states to criminalise abuse at the domestic level,[5] failure of which will lead to the state being in breach of human rights law. This positive obligation on states to implement the relevant laws will be further analysed in Chapter 4. In addition to the positive obligation on states to criminalise abuse,[6] the ECtHR rulings in

1 S. Milivojevic and S. Ćopić, 'Victims of Sex Trafficking, Gender, Myths and Consequences', in S. G. Shoham, P. Knepper, M. Kett, *International Handbook of Victimology*, CR Press, p 283.
2 V. Stoyanova, 'Article 4 of the ECHR and the Obligation of Criminalising Slavery, Servitude, Forced Labour and Human Trafficking' (2014) 3 *Cambridge Journal of International and Comparative Law* 2, p 416.
3 Ibid., p 418.
4 Ibid., p 416.
5 Ibid., p 412.
6 Ibid., p 413, relying on *X v The Netherlands* (Application no. 726631/17), judgment 27 July 2021, and *MC v Bulgaria* (application 39272/98), judgment 4th December 2003).

DOI: 10.4324/9781003429791-3

Siliadin[7] and *CN and V v France*[8] are interpreted to say that a state can fail in its duty under human rights law if it not only does not criminalise slavery, servitude or forced labour (the subject matter covered by the ECHR, as discussed in Chapter 2) but also if there is "ambiguity of the crimes at national level" or if there is a "restrictive interpretation" of those domestic provisions in the national courts.[9] In addition, Obokata points out that international human rights law "often places an obligation on states to protect not only its nationals, but also foreigners", with the obligation being to "prosecute and punish criminals who victimise foreign nationals in their territories and jurisdictions".[10] This will be examined further in Chapter 4.

It is important, however, to remember that international human rights law on the one hand, and national or transnational criminal law on the other take "two contradictory interpretative approaches".[11] Transnational criminal law focuses on "sovereignty, effective law enforcement and the objectification of individuals as criminals".[12] The transnational suppression conventions rely on "domestic protection of human rights and secondarily on general international human rights law", and make "little express protection of human rights" themselves.[13] Boister has argued that Transnational Criminal law needs to be integrated with "the general human rights framework, thus instilling the basic constitutional values of international law".[14]

As has been seen with the approach of the ECtHR in *Rantsev v Cyprus and Russia*,[15] in interpreting Article 4 ECHR as including THB, human rights law "celebrates" expansive interpretation of norms, while criminal law, which needs to be based on the principle of legal certainty in domestic legal systems forbids "such expansions".[16] Any flexibility in the interpretation of either international or transnational criminal law "poses a danger to individual human rights if it is implemented".[17] For Gallant, the essence of legality, or legal certainty is that "a person should reasonably be able to tell what laws will apply to her or him, and the rest of society should be able to determine if such laws are being arbitrarily applied to her or him".[18] The "rights of the accused" also "ban expansive interpretations", while

7 *Siliadin v France,* Application no. 73316/01, ECtHR, 26 October 2005.
8 *CN and V v France,* Application no. 67724/09, ECtHR, 11 October 2012.
9 Stoyanova, op. cit., p 424.
10 T. Obokata, *Transnational Organised Crime in International Law*, Hart Publishing, 2010, p 53.
11 Stoyanova, op. cit., p 420.
12 N. Boister, 'Transnational Criminal Law?' (2003) 14 *European Journal of International Law* 5. p 979.
13 Ibid.
14 Ibid.
15 *Rantsev v Cyprus and Russia*, Application no. 25965/04), ECtHR, 7 January 2010, paragraph 282.
16 Stoyanova, op. cit., p 420.
17 K. Gallant, *The Principle of Legality in International and Comparative Criminal Law*, Cambridge University Press, 2009, p 408.
18 Ibid., p 407/408.

"human rights law … celebrates liberal interpretation of concepts" for the purposed of holding states to account.[19] While there are clear links between the two types of law, their dynamic and operation differ quite substantially.[20]

Stoyanova points out that an accused of a criminal offence could legitimately claim "*nullum crimen sine lege*" if liberal interpretations of criminal laws were to be pleaded against him in court and be thereby acquitted.[21] In particular "human rights interpretative techniques can conflict with the principles underlying" both national and transnational legal systems[22] as operated by both law enforcement practitioners and prosecutors. An analysis of the principle of legality will be made in Chapter 4. At the same time, it is not sufficient for states merely copy and paste from, *inter alia*, the Palermo Convention, or its THB protocol, provisions on organised crime or THB for use in their internal legal systems.[23] Definitions, procedures and processes must be developed to meet the requirements of legal certainty, effectiveness, and usability within that jurisdiction. However, in absorbing the transnational legal concepts into domestic law, to include their translation into national languages and into national legal and practice frameworks, differences will emerge from one jurisdiction to the next. These differences will have to be negotiated by policy makers and practitioners who operate in the transnational law enforcement and justice arenas, to enable countries to be able to effectively interact with each. Onuf's approach to constructivism,[24] focusing on the role of individuals within structures that are being developed, and the need to develop mutual meaning making between counterparts across jurisdictions, to develop and operate new structures, will be required to effectively operationalise transnational legal and law enforcement frameworks. In addition, the relevant international treaties tend "to be a legal response to a specific threat, developed in relative isolation from conventions dealing with other threats".[25] There will be a need negotiate the interlegality between these different treaties, with this author advocating an approach which priorities human security.

Transnational Crime

National crimes with transnational effect will remain national crimes until, through "international political will" they are "transformed into transnational crimes" through suppression conventions.[26] "Criminality that crosses borders" is therefore a much "wider field of enquiry".[27] The development of transnational criminal law, and its operation in practice has a "dynamic multilevel

19 Stoyanova, op. cit., p 407.
20 Ibid., p 417.
21 Ibid., p 423.
22 Ibid., p 422.
23 Ibid.
24 N. Onuf, *World of Our Making*, University of South Carolina Press, 1989.
25 Boister (2003) op. cit., p 958/9.
26 Ibid., p 973.
27 Ibid.

character".[28] This involves a "transnational construction and flow of legal norms", the implications of which "depend on national contexts".[29] As agents of the state, whether these be lawyers, law enforcement staff, investigators or prosecutors, interact with their counterparts along specific THB chains, that process of interaction further develops structures which might only be sketchily set out in a transnational law enforcement treaty, whether bilateral or multilateral. Country A's interaction with country B might therefore develop different THB structures and operating procedures to, say similar interactions between that same country A and country C, if countries B and C have substantially different legal and operational frameworks, which might also reflect the different types of societies that they represent.

Crimes as defined in the suppression treaties are not stand-alone crimes as the "suppression conventions are ... not designed to be self-executing".[30] Normally a domestic legislative act is required to be able to operate the provisions in the suppression conventions. The normative authority for the relevant crimes derives from the law of the "state that applies them, not from international law".[31] While there is horizontal pressure from other states to operate transnational criminal law, there is "not a uniform reproduction [of the transnational criminal law provisions] in each state".[32] The role of transnational criminal law and its implementing provisions is on making the system work "through joint action rather than rule uniformity".[33] The lack of uniformity brings with it its own constructivism challenges.

Many would point out, that while the THB Protocol requires signatory states to legislate for the transnational crime, that THB can also arise, and often does arise, in a purely domestic context. The moral, and the legal obligation under human rights law, depending on how regional or universal human rights treaties are interpreted, or for relevant countries, Islamic law, as discussed in Chapter 1, is on states to prohibit all forms of THB which may occur within or across its jurisdictional boundaries. The question of whether the definition of THB as set out in the THB Protocol is broad enough to cover all possible forms of exploitation, to include THB related crimes, arises, and will be addressed in the context of the UK of its modern slavery (MS) approach in Chapter 7.

While international crimes of concern to "international society as a whole",[34] transnational crimes are only of concern to a particular jurisdiction when there is "a direct injury threatened or caused" for that state to become involved in the

28 M. R. Machado, 'Similar in Their Differences; Transnational Legal Processes Addressing Money Laundering in Brazil and Argentina', in G. Shaffer, *Transnational Legal Ordering and State Change*, Cambridge University Press, 2013, p 86/87.
29 Ibid. p 87.
30 N. Boister, *An Introduction to Transnational Criminal Law*, Oxford University Press, 2012, p 13.
31 Ibid., p 14
32 Ibid., p 22.
33 Ibid., p 23.
34 Boister (2003) op. cit., p 963.

investigation and prosecution of that crime.[35] There needs to be some sort of link between the crime and the jurisdiction investigating and prosecuting. These connections are set out, for pursuing organised crime, in Article 3(2) of the Palermo Convention, to which the THB Protocol, for better or worse, is attached. Issues arise as to whether THB predominantly occurs in the context of "organised" crime, as defined in the Palermo Convention, or whether it is more likely to be classified as "serious" or "entrepreneurial" crime. The Palermo Convention does define "serious" crime,[36] but only in the context of activities undertaken by an "organised" crime group. Crime is often classified as "serious and organised" in domestic legislation, with the two terms, "serious" and "organised" being separate legal concepts. Law enforcement practice point to the "fluidity and diversity characterising the operation of criminal organisations"[37] which some law enforcement personnel refer to as entrepreneurial organisations, with criminal organisations, outside specific geographic or cultural contexts areas such as Southern Italy or perhaps Russia, operating "increasingly on a network basis and without clear cut structures",[38] which puts the term "organised crime" in a problematic position. Another convention negotiated around the same time by the EU member states, the Europol Convention, 1995, for its part "did not contain any specific definition of organised crime" focusing instead on particular criminal offences.[39] McRedmond argues that organised crime should be seen as "lying on a continuum where some forms of serious crime are more organized than others", however she argues that "the cloud of organized crime is a distraction from the job of prosecuting the crime of human trafficking".[40] These serious crimes which are not "organised" also be addressed by transnational justice and law enforcement measures.

Despite their flaws, the point of the "suppression conventions" like the Palermo Convention and its protocols is to suppress "harmful behaviour by non-state actors", which Boister argues "can already … be said to establish a system of" transnational criminal law.[41] The intention is to "minimise or eliminate the potential havens from which certain crimes can be committed and to which criminals can flee to escape prosecution and punishment". They standardise "co-operation among governments" which otherwise "have few other law enforcement concerns in common". In addition, "they create an expectation of co-operation that governments challenge at the cost of some international

35 Ibid., p 964.
36 UN Convention against Transnational Organized Crime, 2000, UNTS 2225, p 209, Article 2.b
37 V. Mitsilegas, 'Defining Organised Crime in the European Union: The Limits of European Criminal Law in the Area of "Freedom, Security and Justice"' (2001) 26 *European Law Review* 6, p 568.
38 Ibid., p 568.
39 Ibid., p 566.
40 P. McRedmond, 'Defining Organized Crime in the Context of Human Trafficking', in G. Wylie and P. McRedmond, *Human Trafficking in Europe*, Springer, 2010, p 195.
41 Boister (2003) op. cit., p 955.

embarrassment".[42] The Palermo Convention obliges "parties to afford each other cooperation" in extradition and mutual legal assistance measures.[43] It may not be necessary to create "interstate offences" to meet transnational threats, however "one of the central purposes of suppression conventions" is to create domestic legal frameworks "in order to make international cooperation in the suppression of the particular form of conduct effective".[44] The norms and networks developed under the suppression conventions may be used to expand into cognate areas of transnational crimes, should the relevant state signatories so decide. As stated by Boister, one of the "key functions" of the Palermo Convention is to "serve in a residual role as the basis for international cooperation regarding 'serious crime'". The Palermo Convention defines serious crime "very broadly as one which carries a maximum period of deprivation of liberty of at least four years or more in the particular party's national law".[45]

For a territorial connection to be established for transnational organised crime, as set out in the Palermo Convention, there needs to be a crime committed in a. either one or more states, b. the crime occurs in one state, but there is a substantial territorial connection with another state, either in the planning, perpetration, subsequent behaviour, or effects of that crime. It can also result when an organised crime group operates in several different jurisdictions.[46] There may or may not be an actual physical crossing of a border. In this era of globalisation, there are many ways in which criminal behaviour in one state can affect or have an impact in another state. It is clear, and is evidenced whenever comprehensive audits are undertaken, that "Transnational criminal groups and criminals live and operate in a borderless world".[47] For its part, THB has been classified as "one of the fasted growing crimes worldwide" with the UNODC saying that it has "reached 'epidemic proportions'".[48] It is very difficult to put exact figures on THB offenders, however, the more that law enforcement looks for it, the more they find, with those law enforcement officials (at Europol), who are actively engaged in this area speaking of only "going after the low hanging fruit" due to the volume of the crime *vis-a-vis* the resources allocated – by governments (in the EU) focused on the issue – to tackle it.[49]

As Boister states,[50] if there is to be no Transnational Criminal Law then we must rely on "purely national offences" which involve a "vertical – state to

42 Ibid.
43 Boister (2012) op. cit., p 83.
44 Boister (2003) op. cit., p 967.
45 Boister (2012) op. cit., p 85.
46 C. Rijken, *Trafficking in Persons Prosecution from a European Perspective*, TMC Asser Press, 2003, p 47.
47 B. Zagaris, 'International Enforcement Law Trends for 2010 and Beyond: Can the Cops Keep Up with the Criminals?' (2011) 34 *Suffolk Transnational Law Review*, 1, p 4.
48 N. Tavakoli, 'A Crime that Offends the Conscience of Humanity: A Proposal to Reclassify Trafficking in Women as an International Crime' (2009) 9 *International Criminal Law Review*, p 79.
49 Europol presentation at the IALS, London, 3 October 2017.
50 Boister (2003) op. cit., p 973.

individual" relationship. These will remain purely national concerns unless "they exhibit a strong transnational dimension" which require individual jurisdictions, and other connected jurisdictions to act transnationally to properly regulate their own internal jurisdictions. "International political will" then "transform[s] these domestic crimes into transnational crimes".[51] Thankfully, given the analysis above of the limitations of the Palermo Convention, he states that this field of enquiry "includes all such criminality irrespective of whether it has been suppressed in a convention or not".[52]

Jessup, the originator of the term "transnational law" used it to "describe 'all law which regulates action or events that transcend national frontiers'".[53] This term thereby avoided the need to prove that "international society acting as a community [was] generating international law".[54] Boister has opted for a definition of Transnational Criminal Law that is "the indirect suppression by international law through domestic penal law of criminal activities that have actual or potential trans-boundary effects".[55] It is without doubt that Transnational Criminal Law, even when legislated for in "suppression conventions" is incomplete, and "relies on domestic law to flesh out" the details.[56] It assumes that domestic legal systems have "fully developed penal systems" something which in reality, is not always the case.[57] Transnational criminal law, however, is to be distinguished from the extra-territorial (and therefore unilateral) effect of domestic laws on what are otherwise purely national crimes.[58] Sovereignty is closely connected with domestic criminal law. Interstate cooperation arises when the need to properly operate the domestic criminal system requires transnational cooperation.[59] Even at the time of the League of Nations not only were states to be subject to international law, but also "the populations *within* the sovereign states themselves became the objects of international discourses and regulation".[60] The League of Nations was concerned with "the life of individuals as well as of nations".[61]

The "jurisdictional barriers between states will continue to be eroded by transnational criminality", which will result in increased "political pressure for the convergence of the substantive criminal laws of states".[62] This can be developed either bi-laterally or multi-laterally, between states faced with particular criminal threats, such as along a THB global supply chain, or at a global level, needing

51 Ibid.
52 Ibid., p 974.
53 Ibid.
54 Ibid., p 975.
55 Ibid., p 955.
56 Ibid., p 958.
57 Ibid.
58 Ibid., p 965.
59 Ibid., p 956.
60 S. Legg, '"The Life of Individuals as Well as of Nations": International Law and the League of Nations' Anti-trafficking Governmentalities' (2012) 25 *Leiden Journal of International Law*, 3, p 648.
61 Ibid. p 649.
62 Boister (2003) op. cit., p 976.

much greater traction of concepts and procedures among states, resulting in less complete or obviously flawed agreements such as the Palermo Convention or its THB Protocol. Gaps in these global regimes can also be addressed by states acting at a more specialised multi-lateral or bi-lateral basis.

Key stakeholders, whether at the policy, law enforcement or prosecution level, need to "become better at networking and cooperating" to keep up with "transnational criminals" who in addition to operating within their respective jurisdictions, also "operate in a borderless world".[63] It will not be sufficient for states to just operate within regional integration associations such as the well-developed, and still developing provisions within the EU. It will be also necessary for them to also operate along the THB chain of jurisdictions, through countries of origin, transit, and destination, wherever those chains lead. In the absence of the recognition of THB as an international crime it will be impossible to compel unwilling or uninterested jurisdictions to engage in these developments. However, those states which are signatories to the THB Protocol have at least expressed an interest in combatting this crime, and it should be easier to convince those states that the "serious" and "entrepreneurial" versions of THB also need to be tackled, along with the "organised" versions of this crime. If the interest is there, then the practice may follow, even if substantial capacity building partnerships must be entered into between more experienced, and possibly better resourced countries at one end of an often-used THB chain, with interested but less resourced or experienced jurisdictions at other points of the chain. Gallagher reports that there is now a dedicated UN funding mechanism to assist developing countries with economic and technical assistance in this area.[64]

Challenges will necessarily arise in developing transnational law enforcement and prosecution provisions along a THB chain. Differences in the design of a state, its criminal law, rules of evidence, understanding and use of fundamental/human and due process rights, and the design and operational style of their law enforcement bodies will need further and detailed examination. In addition, the differences in the definitions used to enact domestic THB law, as discussed in Chapter 2, will also pose problems. These are all challenges that have been encountered within the EU in the development of its area of freedom, security and justice (AFSJ), and in the EU's relationship in this area with the USA, which has led to some very high-profile culture clashes, leading to detailed case law and subsequent treaties, attempting to resolve issues which arise on a regular basis. Problems will arise, but the evidence exists that given the necessary political impetus, these problems can be surmounted. Some of the solutions developed by the EU in the AFSJ will be examined in Chapter 6 in the context of building a transnational legal framework to combat THB.

In designing human security focused transnational law enforcement networks, several issues need to be addressed, which add to the complexity of the challenge,

63 Zagaris, op. cit., p 10.
64 A. Gallagher, *The International Law of Human Trafficking*, Cambridge University Press, 2010, p 76.

but when addressed, should lead to more viable long-term solutions. The development of these networks or geographical regional groupings need to "be more transparent and open to greater public participation" than has been the case for the development of the existing organised crime or drug trafficking networks, of which there are many.[65] In this way they will "ensure greater legitimacy" and support from the public.[66] They "must be produced by an authentic political process" in all relevant jurisdictions "in order to justify the use of state and interstate authority against individuals".[67] There is also a need, as stated by Zagaris, for jurisdictions to "develop international enforcement regimes that are balanced and maintain fundamental international human rights".[68] To this may be added, from the EU's experience in developing the AFSJ, fundamental (as understood under the EU legal framework) and due process rights, such as the right to a lawyer, the right to transnational and interpretation, consular support, etc. The EU's approach to transnational justice issues within the AFSJ provides potential tools for building a transnational legal framework.

Gallagher argues that "the core obligation of the Convention is that of criminalization",[69] however beyond criminalisation the Palermo Convention provides for a range of instruments to be used by states in combating both organised crimes generally, and THB as understood in the THB protocol. These closely reflect those being used and developed further within the EU's AFSJ, from which much may be learnt by other Palermo Convention and THB protocol signatory states. National responses to the Palermo Convention had not been unified, as "there still are discrepancies" in national implementing legislation, and some states have not made any move to modify pre-existing legislation on the topic of organised crime.[70] Boister states that "experience suggests that provision of national legislative frameworks and conclusion of bilateral agreements are necessary to enable these arrangements".[71] Further work clearly needs to be done to fully operationalise both the Palermo Convention and its THB Protocol, despite their flaws. This will have to be led by interested state parties, as there is no "enforcement mechanism to secure compliance by states".[72] In addition, a number of state parties have argued that they are unable "to implement the Convention due to a lack of capacity and infrastructure".[73] Boister notes that the British Commonwealth Secretariat, through its Legal and Constitutional Affairs Division "has developed considerable expertise in the provision of technical support to common law states

65 Boister (2003) op. cit., p 958.
66 Ibid.
67 Ibid., p 957.
68 Zagaris, op. cit., p 10.
69 Gallagher, op. cit., p 75.
70 Obokata, op. cit., p 36.
71 N. Boister, 'The Cooperation Provisions of the UN Convention against Transnational Organised Crime: a "Toolbox" Rarely Used?' (2016) 16 *International Criminal Law Review*, p 50.
72 Obokata, op. cit., p 209.
73 Ibid.

in the implementation of suppression conventions".[74] No doubt there are similar examples in other parts of the world.

In these further developments, it is argued that a human security approach should be taken, in both the deliberations of the policy makers and the law enforcement and justice practitioners who will necessarily be required to implement these further treaties, and other provisions, to include the drafting of law enforcement practice manuals, which are usually security classified. States may be reluctant to engage with some or all other states on this level based on national security. However, the EU member states, in developing the AFSJ, were able to disentangle the concerns for national security from the need to combat cross border criminality in a collaborative way, for all be it not perfect, but effective mechanisms to be put in place and operate throughout the EU. It could also be asked what concept of security is being used by the EU in the AFSJ, with national security and internal security being matters reserved to individual member states.[75] Arguably human security should be used in the context of THB.

State Security versus Human Security

The basic premise of human security thinking is the "equal value of all human lives" rather than, in its original area of enquiry, "in the context of war" of prioritising the interests of one side over another, the approach taken in the now prevalent securitisation and homeland security debate.[76] When THB is seen as being closely connected to illegal migrant flows, and the immigration control discourse, THB provisions and human security interests can often end up taking a back seat to illegal or irregular migration provisions. It may be difficult to fully reconcile these two concerns, however, even in immigration control regimes asylum and *non-refoulement* provisions are clearly provided for. Immigration law properly applied will not put an illegal migrant in a dangerous position.

As referred to in Chapter 1, the key difference in approach between human security and the traditional concept of state security, is the priority given to human rights. Traditional state security would prioritise some individuals over others, thereby leaving some individuals without protection.[77] Rijken points out that refusal by jurisdictions to interact with other jurisdictions to combat transnational crime in the context of THB using sovereignty as an excuse actually weaken that state's sovereignty, leaving it vulnerable to exploitation by transnational crime and human traffickers.[78] By engaging with other jurisdictions to combat transnational criminality, states may have actually strengthen their own sovereignty, and increased the security of its residents

74 Boister (2012), op. cit., p 258.

75 Treaty on the Functioning of the European Union, OJ L 326/47, Articles 72 and 73.

76 M. Glasius and M. Kaldor, 'A Human Security Vision for Europe and Beyond' in M. Glasius and M. Kaldor, *A Human Security Doctrine for Europe: Project, Principles, Practicalities*, Routledge, 2006, p 17.

77 The Barcelona Report of the Study Group on Europe's Security Capabilities, A Human Security Doctrine for Europe, Barcelona, 15 September 2004, p 14.

78 Rijken, op. cit., p 244.

and citizens. In addition, "many steps in closer cooperation with and the granting of competence to authorities [such as law enforcement and prosecution officials] on a non-national level require the explicit consent of the state".[79]

In the context of globalisation, individuals at risk in one part of the globe have an impact on others, so putting of individuals at risk at one's own state's border, even if they are deemed to be irregular migrants, and not welcome in the state, puts those legitimately within the state at risk. It is impossible to fully secure any state's border, and once in the state, those vulnerable to being trafficked, and those doing the trafficking, will have an adverse impact on that state. As stated by the Human Security Commission, there is an "interdependence and interlinkages among the world's people".[80] An underclass available for exploitation in any state is leaving criminal gangs the opportunity to raise funds which can then be deployed into other areas of serious or organised crime, such as drugs or weapons crime, or being used to fund terrorist activities. Funds will also be available to criminals for bribery and corruption. As stated in Chapter 1, the European Security Strategy 2003[81] has identified as a key issue "organised crime, which includes cross-border trafficking in women, illegal migrants and children, with the effect that state authority and state institutions run the risk of being undermined".[82] As pointed out by Dandurand and Chin, it is unclear why organised crime is "increasingly defined as a national security problem and not as a fundamental human security issue.[83] They point out that a human security approach brings much greater focus on the victims.[84] Vulnerable and marginalised groups are "too easily and too often labelled as part of the problem and left to fend for themselves against these powerful and dangerous enemies", transnational serious and organised crime groups and terrorist organisations.[85]

The human rights approach also prioritises some individuals over others, leaving many outside its protection. Only some can effectively claim human rights in courts. In addition, as pointed out by Boister,[86] "there is little express protection of human rights within the suppression conventions". The CoE, for its part, has prioritised a human rights approach to THB, with the EU directive,[87] for its part,

79 Ibid., p 245.

80 Commission on Human Security, Human Security Now, The Commission, New York, 2003, p 130.

81 European Security Strategy, Brussels, 12 December 2003, fifth threat, p 4.

82 M. den Boer, 'Governing Transnational Law Enforcement in the EU: Accountability after Fusing Internal and External Security', in M. den Boer & J. de Wilde, *The Viability of Human Security*, Amsterdam University Press, 2008, p 73.

83 Y. Dandurand and V. Chin, 'Human Security Objectives and the Fight against Transnational Organized Crime and Terrorism' in S. Okubo and L. Shelly, *Human Security, Transnational crime and Human Trafficking; Asian and Western Perspectives*, Routledge, 2011, p 36.

84 Ibid.

85 Ibid., p 40.

86 Boister (2003) op. cit., p 959.

87 Directive 2011/36/EU of the European Parliament and of the Council of 5 April 2011 on preventing and combating trafficking in human beings and protecting its victims, and replacing Council Framework Decision 2002/629/JHA, OJ L 101/1.

saying that it takes an "integrated, holistic, and human rights approach" to combatting human trafficking.[88] This difference in approach in Europe will be examined in Chapter 6.

While human rights should be made to operate more effectively for more people, there is also a need for a human security approach to be taken by the various branches of government operating in this area. The human security approach seeks to "forge alliances that can yield much greater force together than alone".[89] Networks need therefore to be developed both within and between states, to properly address the issues which arise, at both the law enforcement and victim protection levels. All those agencies and bodies within states need to be networked with their counterparts in other relevant states. The relevance of the states will be determined by the nature of the THB and related crimes affecting their state. This may require a geographic regional approach; however, it is much more likely to be affected by THB routes, requiring connections to be developed between states of origin, transit, and destination of the THB victims. This will typically involve countries which are better resourced engaging with countries which are less so, with knowledge and know how as well as resources being shared and mutually developed.

Putting the Provisions into Practice

While some academics would state that the key point of the Palermo Convention and the THB Protocol is the criminalisation of the offence, others, such as Boister point out that the "great detail suggests that international cooperation rather than criminalisation is, in fact, [their] the main subject matter".[90] A "tool box" for transnational cooperation to combat transnational organised crime was enumerated,[91] all be it requiring further detail to be developed for full operationalisation. What is of concern, however, is their lack of further development and implementation.[92] Success cannot just be measured by whether laws have been enacted, but when they have been used, and been proven to be effective in tackling their target crime, whether that is organised (or transnational serious) crime of THB. State law enforcement and justice officials need to "try to nullify the advantages criminals derive form operating across borders" and, while recognising the different constitutional, legal, evidentiary and practice rules in different states, "reduce, circumvent, or transcend the frictions that impede" transnational law enforcement.[93] Practitioner designed transnational networks for intelligence sharing have traditionally been the response among the law enforcement community to combatting transnational crime. As pointed out by Zagaris a weakness of networks "is that they reduce transparency and impede

88 Ibid., preamble Paragraph 7.
89 Commission on Human Security, op. cit., p 130.
90 Boister (2016), op. cit., p 41.
91 Ibid., p 45.
92 Ibid., p 48.
93 Zagaris, op. cit., p 25.

accountability".[94] In addition, at a practitioner level, while a tip off may well be useful, and lead to effective crime disruption, this will not provide the full level of responses necessary to bring a complex transnational criminal case to court, and effectively combat structures or networks engaged in the criminal behaviour. In addition, there may be well founded fears about data protection rules, which are very robust in Western Europe.[95]

Properly designed structures, as opposed to *ad hoc* tip offs through practitioner networks, will also lead to the sharing of higher quality classified intelligence, better transnational intelligence analysis, and more complex, but effective transnational law enforcement responses, leading to, in the case of THB, victim recovery, asset seizure, criminal arrests, and in due course convictions. Decisions to develop transnational criminal and law enforcement and justice measures will lead to complex, multi-level negotiations, between government departments, prosecutors, and law enforcement personnel in the relevant jurisdictions, and "cannot therefore be taken lightly".[96] Developments within the EU took many years of negotiations, and some redrafts of legal provisions, before they were found to operate effectively. Boister points out that the International Association of Prosecutors and the World Summit of Prosecutors General appear to be slowly harmonising "prosecutorial practice in regard to transnational crime".[97]

Boister points out that "this field of enquiry includes ... regimes of purely procedural international cooperation established by extradition and mutual assistance treaties".[98] However this is exactly the weakness of the transnational criminal law suppression treaties, as having, either fully or partially, defined the crime, the necessary procedural rules, and practice manuals needed to fully operationalise the provisions in the suppression convention, remain absent. As stated by Gallagher, the suppression conventions would be "enhanced by the inclusion of a detailed legal framework on mutual legal assistance in investigations, prosecutions and judicial proceedings in relation to applicable offences".[99] In the absence of these provisions being addressed at a global level, then it is necessary, and possibly more practical, given the diversity of criminal law, evidence and law enforcement practice, for individual states or groups of states, to complete the necessary frameworks, either on a bilateral, regional or multilateral basis.

Law Enforcement Networks

The Palermo Convention "sets out a range of measures to be adopted by States Parties" to facilitate transnational law enforcement,[100] taking, in Article 27(1)

94 Ibid., p 23.
95 Among the signatory states of the Council of Europe Convention for the Protection of Individuals with regard to Automatic Processing of Personal Data (CETS No. 108), and subsequently enacted legislation at EU and individual state levels.
96 Zagaris, op. cit., p 24.
97 Boister (2012) op. cit., p 258.
98 Boister (2003) op. cit., p 974.
99 Gallagher, op. cit., p 76.
100 Ibid., p 75.

entitled Law enforcement cooperation, "a broad approach encompassing all forms of cooperation".[101] However many states have not "adopted the institutional architecture to enable effective cooperation".[102] While the Palermo Convention can be used directly, for those states which have managed to develop regular and effective transnational law enforcement activity based on the convention "experience suggests that the provision of national legislative frameworks and [the] conclusion of bilateral agreements are necessary to enable these arrangements".[103] In addition asset recovery seems to be the most often used of the provisions, while extradition seems to be rare.[104] This may be because transnational law enforcement networks are well developed in tackling proceeds of crime and money laundering. While this is an important tool in combating transnational organised crime (which will be discussed below), it is only one tool in the Palermo Convention armoury. Perhaps some of the other measures appeared to be more complicated, and there were few examples of their successful use for new states to build on. However, the EU has now managed to effectively operationalise the balance of the Palermo Convention toolbox for its own use, within the AFSJ, and the experience gained, *inter alia*, can be used for the further development of effective transnational criminal law to combat, among other relevant crimes, trafficking in human beings. In addition, training is now provided from several sources, to include the UN.[105]

Inter-governmental Organisations

The development of transnational criminal law structures and frameworks to combat THB can be facilitated by a range of inter-governmental organisations (IGOs) and agencies. For example, the Organisation for Security and Cooperation in Europe (OSCE), the Financial Action Task Force (FAFT), the Egmont Group, the CoE, Interpol, and Europol are already active in this or related areas. These IGOs are more active than in the past, and "have spread far beyond regulators to legislators, judges and enforcement officials".[106] They often supplement their traditional role of "collecting and disseminating information on global or regional best practice to actively offering technical assistance to poorer and less experienced members".[107] The UN itself has calculated that (in 2004) 17 international organisations, many operating under the UN mandate, have "a mandate more or less closely related to trafficking in persons".[108] As pointed by Obokata, it is

101 Boister (2016), op. cit., p 49.
102 Ibid., p 63.
103 Ibid., p 50.
104 Ibid., p 65.
105 Ibid., p 50/51.
106 Zagaris, op. cit., p 22.
107 Ibid.
108 UNODC Global Report on Trafficking in Persons 2012, p 96. These international organisations are; Office of the High Commissioner for Human Rights (OHCHR), Division for the Advancement of Women (DAW) and United Nations Development

"necessary to examine the extent to which international bodies and organisations are able to promote inter-agency co-operation".[109] As he says, often "these organisations do not have a clear picture of what other organisations are doing" leading to duplication.[110] In addition there is a lack of efficient use of resources, and conflicting messages to their participating states.

The then G8, in May 1998, issued a Communique of the Birmingham Summit, which was committed to in Moscow, in 1999, which stated that the Lyon-Roma (migration experts sub-group of practitioners), which it sponsors, would "intensify its efforts to develop, enact and facilitate national, multilateral and international principles, agreements, strategies and actions to prevent and counter the smuggling of and trafficking in human beings".[111] It would interpret both crimes as being "grave crimes which may contribute to human rights abuses".[112] In tackling the crime states must protect the status of refugees, and "respect human rights and sustain the lawful movement of persons across national borders".[113] Law enforcement measures must be strengthened, and where possible "States should adopt common standards with respect to such laws and measures".[114] In addition, states should "strive to improve communication, information sharing and cooperation for the purposes of disrupting, suppressing and eradicating such smuggling and trafficking activities and bringing to justice those persons involved in such activities".[115] In addition the communication called for states to "ensure appropriate assistance for those persons where circumstances warrant and provide for their safe return".[116]

The Global Action Plan attached to the Birmingham G8 Communique provided that domestic laws should be strengthened to combat both THB and smuggling, and common standards should be adopted to "enhance practical measures for cooperation in investigations, prosecutions and the targeting of

Fund for Women (UNIFEM) – both now part of UN Women, Department of Peacekeeping Operations (DPKO), United Nations Interregional Crime and Justice Research Institute (UNICRI), Office of the United Nations High Commissioner for Refugees (UNHCR), United Nations Population Fund (UNFPA), Joint United Nations Programme on HIV/AIDS (UNAIDS), United Nations Development Programme (UNDP), United Nations Children's Fund (UNICEF), United Nations Office on Drugs and Crime (UNODC), International Organization for Migration (IOM), World Health Organization (WHO), International Labour Organization (ILO), United Nations Educational, Scientific and Cultural Organization (UNESCO), International Civil Aviation Organization (ICAO) and ICPO-Interpol.

109 Obokata, op. cit., p 220.

110 Ibid.

111 Guiding Principles and Plan of Action to combat the Smuggling of and Trafficking in Human Beings Annex 2 (G 8 THB paper), The Communique of the Birmingham Summit (May 1998) committed the G8 States to: Moscow, October 20, 1999, p 1.

112 Ibid.

113 Ibid.

114 Ibid., p 2.

115 Ibid.

116 Ibid.

smuggling and trafficking associations".[117] Mutual legal assistance arrangements were to be negotiated,[118] along with asset confiscation agreements, with the intention of including "the confiscation of assets upon conviction for the crime of smuggling of and trafficking in human beings".[119] Central authorities or contact points in each of the G8 states were to be established to "facilitate the exchange of information" and the analysis of that information on smugglers and traffickers, to include their movements and methodologies.[120] The use of commercial carriers by smugglers and traffickers was to be suppressed and reduced,[121] and the return of the smuggled or trafficked persons was to be facilitated and "after appropriate legal action", also the return of the smugglers and the traffickers.[122] G8 countries were to engage in collecting and exchanging information "regarding fraudulent, lost and stolen documents used, and authentic travel or identity documents misused",[123] and there was to be consideration of the "provision of programs of technical and training assistance to other countries".[124] In addition awareness raising and education programmes were to be undertaken.[125] The UN has referred to this programme as the four Ps of the Global Plan of Action; "Prevention, Protection and assistance, Prosecution and Partnerships".[126]

Civil Society Non-governmental Organisations

Combating THB also involves civil society and non-governmental organisations. Some have been set up by law enforcement professionals, such as the International Association of Chiefs of Police and the International Association of Prosecutors.[127] There appears, yet to be no dedicated transnational THB police network. Many groups are already operating in anti-money laundering, which, in the context of THB, is the Banker's Alliance against Human Trafficking.[128] Another (interdisciplinary) organisation is Finance Against Trafficking,[129] designed for companies to avoid "reputational risk and prosecution" in handling dirty money.[130]

117 Ibid.
118 Ibid., p 3.
119 Ibid.
120 Ibid.
121 Ibid.
122 Ibid.
123 Ibid.
124 Ibid.
125 Ibid., p 4.
126 UNODC Global Report on Trafficking in Persons 2012, p 94.
127 Zagaris, op. cit., p 14.
128 OSCE, *Leveraging Anti-Money Laundering Regimes to Combat Trafficking in Human Beings*, OSCE, 2014, p 25.
129 Ibid.
130 Ibid., p 25.

Money Laundering and Proceeds of Crime

Given the problems with victim testimony for THB crimes, an issue which will be discussed further in Chapter 4, AML and financial investigative techniques, in the view of the OSCE, "could provide crucial evidence at trial, thus reducing the need to rely on complex and expensive witness protection measures".[131] AML "tools, procedures and expertise" are "significant and large untapped potential" in combatting THB "in most jurisdictions".[132] While THB as a crime shows many distinctive characteristics, its allied financial crimes "are identical to those used for other types of crime".[133] The OSCE points out that the Egmont Group of Financial Intelligence Units, based in Canada, are key players in improving "co-operation related to proceeds of THB".[134] In Europe CARIN, "an informal network for asset tracing and recovery", based at Europol, is a key player in this area. It has counterparts in other parts of the world.[135]

The OSCE points out that there is a need for "increased cooperation and information exchange" between AML and anti-THB law enforcement, between them and the relevant NGOs,[136] and between countries of origin, transit and destination of THB victims.[137] In contrast to drug trafficking, THB proceeds of crime are "often small and low-profile" requiring the regulated financial sector to adopt different techniques for its identification.[138] For example, funnel accounts have been found to be used frequently in the US by THB criminals.[139] As stated by the OSCE, "by fully leveraging the private sector's access to the financial transactions of criminal, countries can often be more effective in identifying suspicious financial activity".[140] If this issue is effectively addressed, it may be possible for the regulated sector to identify patterns, which would lead AML Suspicious Activity Reports (SARs) to start an anti-trafficking investigation, rather than AML investigations being tagged on at the end of a pre-existing THB case. Key to developments in this area will be the issue of resourcing, as the OSCE has reported on "a shortage of trained financial investigators working on THB cases".[141] The OSCE has reported on different methodologies being preferred by human traffickers operating in different parts of the globe. For example, in Europe, traffickers "tend to focus on cash intensive businesses" while in the US "there is a greater use of casinos, wire transfers" etc.[142] As well as deflating criminals ability to further operate, and reduce the

131 Ibid., p 16.
132 Ibid., p 15.
133 Ibid., p 9.
134 Ibid., p 21.
135 Ibid., p 22.
136 Ibid., p 16.
137 Ibid., p 9.
138 Ibid., p 18.
139 See www.acams.org/aml-resources/human-trafficking.
140 OSCE, op. cit., p 9.
141 Ibid., p 17.
142 Ibid., p 14.

incentive to do so, given the limited resources in many countries, and the lack of state compensation funds, the proceeds of AML or proceeds of crime recovery against THB "remains one of the only viable ways of providing financial compensation to victims of trafficking".[143]

Conclusion

The THB Protocol is optional. As stated by Tavakoli, some key states have yet failed to ratify it despite being "identified as a country from which a large number of trafficked women originate",[144] although this is now a reducing number of countries. Once ratified, however, the THB Protocol and its associated Palermo Convention, with which it should be read, "suffers from the fact that the treaty provisions for enforcement are weak and hardly ever used".[145] This is despite the fact that THB is now estimated to be "the fasted growing form of organized crime and ranks as the third largest source of illicit profit after narcotics and arms trafficking".[146] While it is always possible that THB may be reclassified as an international crime,[147] as discussed in Chapter 2, there is a need for most states to negotiate and implement agreements at a bilateral or multilateral level to effectively operationalise the provisions of the THB Protocol. These negotiations would be best done along specific THB supply chains, which are increasingly being identified by law enforcement working in this area. Bi- or multi-lateral treaties signed by governments, building on the provisions of the Palermo Convention and its THB Protocol, can provide the legal framework within which practitioners, lawyers, law enforcement, investigators (for those jurisdictions where these are different to law enforcement), and prosecutors, can work to operationalise the legal framework in order to effectively combat the particular THB supply chain that has been identified, taking a human security approach.

The effective operationalisation of the provisions on the THB Protocol will require many levels of engagement of practitioners along the identified THB supply chain, with a lot of detailed work required to build effective investigations/law enforcement frameworks, leading to effective prosecutions of the criminals and the securing of the safety of the victims or potential victims. Different designs of states, and the allocation of the roles of prosecution, investigation and law enforcement can differ considerably from one state to the next, issues which have been addressed for the benefit of EU member states in the developing of their AFSJ. While this AFSJ has its own flaws, and needs further development, it can still act as a model which can be developed by others to address transnational THB.

143 Ibid., p 18.
144 Tavakoli, op. cit., p 96.
145 Boister (2003) op. cit., p 960.
146 OSCE, op. cit., p 12.
147 Boister (2003) op. cit., p 972.

Bibliography

Boister, N., *An Introduction to Transnational Criminal Law*, Oxford University Press, 2012.

Boister, N., 'The Cooperation Provisions of the UN Convention against Transnational Organised Crime: a "Toolbox" Rarely Used?' (2016) 16 *International Criminal Law Review*, 39–70.

Boister, N., 'Transnational Criminal Law?' (2003) 14 *European Journal of International Law* 5, 953–976.

Commission on Human Security, *Human Security Now*, The Commission, New York, 2003.

Dandurand Y., and Chin, V., 'Human Security Objectives and the Fight against Transnational Organized Crime and Terrorism' in Okubo, S., and Shelly, L., *Human Security, Transnational crime and Human Trafficking: Asian and Western Perspectives*, Routledge, 2011, 36–55.

den Boer, M., 'Governing Transnational Law Enforcement in the EU: Accountability after Fusing Internal and External Security', in den Boer, M. and de Wilde, J. (eds), *The Viability of Human Security*, Amsterdam University Press, 2008, 71–96.

European Security Strategy, Brussels, 12 December 2003, 15895/03.

Gallagher, A., *The International Law of Human Trafficking*, Cambridge University Press, 2010.

Gallant, K., *The Principle of Legality in International and Comparative Criminal Law*, Cambridge University Press, 2009.

Glasius M., and Kaldor, M., 'A Human Security Vision for Europe and Beyond', in Glasius M., and Kaldor, M., *A Human Security Doctrine for Europe: Project, Principles, Practicalities*, Routledge, 2006, 3–19.

Guiding Principles and Plan of Action to Combat the Smuggling of and Trafficking in Human Beings Annex 2 (G 8 THB paper), The Communique of the Birmingham Summit (May 1998) committed the G8 States to: Moscow, October 20, 1999.

Legg, S., '"The Life of Individuals as Well as of Nations": International Law and the League of Nations' Anti-trafficking Governmentalities' (2012) 25 *Leiden Journal of International Law* 3, 647–664.

Machado, M. R., 'Similar in their Differences; Transnational Legal Processes Addressing Money Laundering in Brazil and Argentina', in Shaffer, G., *Transnational Legal Ordering and State Change*, Cambridge University Press, 2013, 50–88.

McRedmond, P., 'Defining Organized Crime in the Context of Human Trafficking', in Wylie, G., and McRedmond, P., *Human Trafficking in Europe*, Springer, 2010, 181–197.

Milivojevic, S., and Ćopić, S., 'Victims of Sex Trafficking, Gender, Myths and Consequences', in Shoham, S. G., Knepper, P., Kett, M., *International Handbook of Victimology*, CR Press, 283–302.

Mitsilegas, V., 'Defining Organised Crime in the European Union: The Limits of European Criminal Law in the Area of "Freedom, Security and Justice"' (2001) 26 *European Law Review* 6, 565–581.

Obokata, T. *Transnational Organised Crime in International Law*, Hart Publishing, 2010.

Onuf, N., *World of Our Making*, University of South Carolina Press, 1989.

OSCE, *Leveraging Anti-Money Laundering Regimes to Combat Trafficking in Human Beings*, OSCE, 2014.

Rijken, C., *Trafficking in Persons Prosecution from a European Perspective*, TMC Asser Press, 2003.

Stoyanova, V., 'Article 4 of the ECHR and the Obligation of Criminalising Slavery, Servitude, Forced Labour and Human Trafficking' (2014) 3 *Cambridge Journal of International and Comparative Law* 2, 407–443.
Tavakoli, N., 'A Crime that Offends the Conscience of Humanity: A Proposal to Reclassify Trafficking in Women as an International Crime' (2009) 9 *International Criminal Law Review*, 77–98.
The Barcelona Report of the Study Group on Europe's Security Capabilities, A Human Security Doctrine for Europe, Barcelona, 15 September 2004.
Zagaris, B., 'International Enforcement Law Trends for 2010 and Beyond: Can the Cops Keep Up with the Criminals?' (2011) 34 *Suffolk Transnational Law Review*, 1.
UNODC, *Global Report on Trafficking in Persons 2012*, UNODC, New York, 2012.

Legislation

Council of Europe Convention for the Protection of Individuals with regard to Automatic Processing of Personal Data, CETS No. 108.
Directive 2011/36/EU of the European Parliament and of the Council of 5 April 2011 on Preventing and Combating Trafficking in Human Beings and Protecting its Victims, and Replacing Council Framework Decision 2002/629/JHA, OJ L 101/1.
Treaty on the Functioning of the European Union, OJ L 326/47.
UN Convention against Transnational Organized Crime 2000, *UNTS 2225*, p 209.

Cases

CN and V v France, Application no. 67724/09, ECtHR, 11 October 2012.
Rantsev v Cyprus and Russia, Application no. 25965/04, ECtHR, 7 January 2010.
Siliadin v France, Application no. 73316/01, ECtHR, 26 October 2005.

4 Building a Transnational Legal Framework

Introduction

While some of the law enforcement provisions, covered in Chapter 3, are more advanced in their development, particularly in combatting the proceeds of crime and AML offences, under the early leadership of FATF, further work needs to be done both in THB law enforcement and in the related rights and justice side of the evolving legal framework. As with the development of the EU's AFSJ, law enforcement often starts putting the building blocks of cross border law enforcement in place before the related prosecutor or rights frameworks. However, an effective framework requires all such aspects to be fully developed and operating well to be able to effectively combat cross border criminality, and in the case THB, effectively protecting the vulnerable that are exploited or trafficked for the purpose of exploitation. A human security approach to transnational law enforcement development requires the focus to be maintained on the victim of THB.

Transnational prosecution and rights frameworks are not common at a global level. One of the more advanced regional groupings in the world in this context is the EU, with a currently evolving and developing legal framework, which could prove instructive in how future transnational law enforcement, justice and rights frameworks could be developed. The Palermo Convention[1] and its THB Protocol[2] provides a framework, but not all the necessary detail, for cross border operations to combat THB. It is up to individual jurisdictions, and groups of jurisdictions working together, probably along particular THB supply chains, where there is repeat and continual offending, to develop effective law enforcement, justice, and rights frameworks to assist in combating this crime and protecting the vulnerable. Solutions for one group of countries may not be solutions for another group. However, the provisions that the EU has developed (for a group of then 28 countries, to include the UK pre-Brexit) will inform how those EU countries operate with non-EU (or, as they are known in EU jargon, 'third countries') in the future. The UK, now such

1 UN Convention against Transnational Organized Crime 2000 (Palermo), UNTS 2225, p 209.

2 UN Protocol to Prevent, Suppress and Punish Trafficking in Persons, Especially Women and Children, supplementing the United Nations Convention against Transnational Organized Crime 2000, UNTS, 2237, p 319.

DOI: 10.4324/9781003429791-4

a third country, has replicated most of such provisions in the UK-EU Trade and Cooperation Agreement (TCA), relying at times on similar CoE provisions.[3] How the EU addresses for itself and its members THB, as informed by its, and its member states' CoE obligations, will be the focus of Chapter 6.

Effective legal frameworks to combat THB along relevant transnational supply chains are going to require some more legal and practice innovation beyond what is already in place. As stated by Shaffer building transnational legal frameworks are often "initiated, negotiated and implemented" by a mixture of different types of people, addressing the issue from a variety of perspectives which is "neither uniform in its legal views or united in a policy agenda".[4] These players would include "agents, practitioners and institutions of law" to include "government lawyers, legal departments of international organizations, judges, private lawyers, corporate legal officers, legal academics, and lawyers for nongovernmental organizations".[5]

Constructivism, as a theoretical approach discussed in Chapter 1, helps understand the mutual meaning making which needs to be engaged in by these players when developing new structures to facilitate the development of new transnational legal frameworks, with the process of interaction between all the relevant players leading to the development of new ways of working. As stated by Shaffer, "transnational networks engage national policymakers within particular normative frames",[6] and the argument of this book is that the normative frame to be adopted when combatting THB should be that of human security. If at the beginning of the design of the process the concept of human security is expressly placed to the fore, there will be an increased chance of the resulting transnational legal framework delivering the aspired for human security. This will require a shift in emphasis from the traditional law enforcement focus of pursuing the criminal, or the equally prevalent transnational driver of state security, both of which would be highly inappropriate when addressing transnational THB.

Mutual meaning making through a constructivist approach to developing new transnational law enforcement networks then informs and leads to the development of "institutional path dependencies",[7] as initially innovative practitioners find process and procedures that work in a particular context, with those new approaches being adopted as the relevant standard by their home institution and used in training future practitioners. As stated by Shaffer, these newly adopted "transnational legal processes are thus not homogeneous across countries, because they can

3 Second Additional Protocol (2001) to the Council of Europe Convention on Mutual Assistance in Criminal Matters 1959, CETS 182.

4 G. Shaffer, 'Conclusion: The Study of Transnational Legal Ordering', in G. Shaffer, *Transnational Legal Ordering and State Change*, Cambridge University Press, 2013, p 214.

5 Ibid.

6 G. Shaffer, 'The Dimensions and Determinants of State Change', in G. Shaffer, *Transnational Legal Ordering and State Change*, Cambridge University Press, 2013, p 32.

7 Ibid., p 33.

affect different dimensions of the state within different countries",[8] with differing solutions being found for different inter-jurisdictional relationships. Where effective solutions to regularly occurring problems are found, these can lead to "legal and institutional change"[9] both in the transnational context, but also in the domestic context, as "new conceptions of meaning are conveyed that may be gradually accepted as normal and authoritative" as "elite perspectives" are changed as new solutions to frequent problems are found.[10]

Principle of Legality

Key in the development of effective, legitimate, and human security focused transnational law enforcement networks to combat, *inter alia*, THB, is the principle of legality, which derives "from the general principles of international law".[11] The principle of legality crystallised in the wake of WWII, when the full extent of the activities of both Hitler and Stalin became widely known. The principle of legality is now found in most legal jurisdictions, regardless of the nature of the legal system, or the source claimed to be its origin. The principle of legality has been refined and developed in individual jurisdictions, however, at its most basic, and in its most globally recognised format it comprises two maxims: *nullum crimen sine lege* and *nulla poena sine lege*. The first, *nullum crimen sine lege* ("no crime without law") is "commonly said that the principle is designed to keep out *ex post facto* laws".[12] The allied principle of *nulla peona sine lege* provides that there shall not be a punishment if that punishment is not provided for by the law.[13] Shahabuddeen points out that both principles were considered in 1935 in the international law case of *Consistency of Certain Danzig Legislative decrees with the Constitution of the Free City*,[14] with Garibaldi pointing out that the "idea that limitations on individual rights should be imposed by law precedes, by far, the debates that shaped the Universal Declaration" on Human Rights.[15] The principle of legality is currently underpinned by the international human rights framework, in particular, the Universal Declaration of Human Rights, the International Covenant on Civil and Political Rights and the International Covenant on Economic, Social

8 Ibid.
9 Shaffer, 'Conclusion', op. cit., p 214.
10 Shaffer, 'Dimensions', op. cit., p 32.
11 B. Zagaris, 'International Enforcement Law Trends for 2010 and Beyond: Can the Cops Keep up with the Criminals?' (2011) 34 *Suffolk Transnational Law Review*, 1, p 12.
12 M. Shahabuddeen, 'Does the Principle of Legality Stand in the Way of Progressive Development of Law?' (2004), 2 *Journal of International Criminal Justice* 4, p 1008.
13 Ibid.
14 *Consistency of Certain Danzig Legislative Decrees with the Constitution of the Free City*, Permanent Court of International Justice, Advisory Opinion No. 27, 1935 P.C.I.J. Series A/B, No 65 (Dec. 4), at 51 and 52.
15 O. M. Garibaldi, 'General Limitations on Human Rights: The Principle of Legality' (1976) 17 *Harvard International Law Journal* 3, p 510.

and Cultural Rights.[16] At the level of international law, the principle of legality applies whether international law arises out of conventions, customs or general principles.[17] This principle requires that an offence involving a transnational crime "should be dealt with in any state that has jurisdiction using the same general principles, procedures and penalties" as for domestic crimes.[18] This, as pointed out by Boister, "is not commonly the case".[19]

Barker states that "criminal law begins" when "effective limits" are put on "arbitrary power to judge and punish" through the principle of legality.[20] This principle has featured more recently in the International Criminal Court for the former Yugoslavia, in *Kunarac*[21] and in the European Court of Human Rights in *Puhk v Estonia*,[22] relying on Article 7 ECHR,[23] and in *Veeber v Estonia* (No. 2).[24] States cannot exercise their right to punish, or *ius puniendi*, "beyond what they are allowed to by criminal norms".[25] Olásolo points out that "prohibited acts and penalties must be pre-established by norms that can be considered 'laws'", which "can only be issued by a legislative power".[26] He goes on to say that the *ius puniendi* of a State, or the international community, or in the context of this paper, a number of states working together in a transnational criminal context, "the principle of legal certainty" is an "essential component of the fundamental rights of any person".[27] It must therefore be at the heart of the design of any transnational criminal framework, to include those designed to combat transnational THB. It has been long recognised that domestic "criminal law reflects a strong idea of national identity and values".[28] The resulting differences in national criminal laws needs to be addressed when designing transnational criminal laws, as "individuals must be able to foresee the criminalisation of their behaviour", and they must "at least be able to identify the risk of criminalisation".[29] As stated by Peristeridou, "foreseeability has both a national and a

16 Ibid., p 503.
17 Zagaris, op. cit., p 11.
18 N. Boister, 'Transnational Criminal Law?' (2003), 14 *European Journal of International Law* 5, p 958.
19 Ibid.
20 B. M. Barker, 'Police Discretion and the Principle of Legality' (1966) 8 *Criminal Law Quarterly*, p 400.
21 *Prosecutor v Kunarac, Vukovic and Kovac*, Appeals Chamber, International Tribunal for the Former Yugoslavia, Case No. IT-96–23 and TI-96–23/1-A, 12 June 2002, para 372.
22 *Puhk v Estonia*, Application no 55103/00, ECtHR, 10 February 2004, paragraph 24.
23 Shahabuddeen, op. cit., p 1008.
24 *Veeber v Estonia* (No. 2) Application no. 45771/99, ECtHR, 21 January 2003, paragraph 31.
25 H. Olásolo, 'A Note on the Evolution of the Principle of Legality in International Criminal Law' (2007) 18 *Criminal Law Forum*, p 302.
26 Ibid.
27 Ibid., p 301.
28 C. Peristeridou, *The Principle of Legality in European Criminal Law*, Intersentia, 2015, p 301.
29 Ibid., p 290.

transnational connotation".[30] As with national criminal legal systems, transnational ones "should function in a predictable manner",[31] to include maintaining the "prohibition of retroactive application of criminal law".[32] Transnational legal systems, therefore, need to be designed, and be publicised in advance of their requirement to be used. Peristeridou argues that "even a minimum harmonisation of criminal offences contributes to legal certainty and foreseeability regarding criminal law offences in different states".[33] It is arguable that the existence of the suppression treaties, to include the Palermo Convention and its THB Protocol go some way towards such a transnational harmonisation. However, individual jurisdictions need to take whatever measures that are necessary to comply with their own understanding of the principle of legality in coming to whatever arrangements that they need to come to with other jurisdictions in developing their transnational law enforcement and justice frameworks. While they do these, two issues arise, "namely the reliability to the law but also the acceptability of its interpretation".[34]

Within the current EU, the principle of legality appears to derive from two quite distinct sources, the civil law system, with its express and highly developed principle of legality framework "with a given structure",[35] and the less clear common law system. However, there appears to be a "strong convergence among legal systems" due to the overarching influence of the ECHR.[36] Arguably "the ECJ has developed the legality principle in a common law manner".[37] As pointed out by Peristeridou[38] the general principle has been "developed through ECJ judgments throughout the 1980s",[39] most recently in the *Intertakno* case,[40] and previously in the context of criminal law in *Criminal Proceedings against X*.[41] It has been codified in Article 49 of the Charter of Fundamental Rights, Principle of legality and proportionality of criminal offences and penalties, and Article 7 ECHR, No punishment without law. Peristeridou argues that the EU needs to further develop its approach in this area, as a "European legality principle seems not only necessary but, most importantly, desirable".[42]

30 Ibid., p 294.
31 Ibid., p 59.
32 Ibid., p 60.
33 Ibid., p 254.
34 Ibid., p 294/5.
35 Ibid., p 78.
36 Ibid., p 24.
37 Ibid., p 177.
38 Ibid., p 179.
39 Ibid., p 21.
40 C-308/06 *The Queen, on the Application of the International Association of Independent Tanker Owners (Intertanko) and Others v Secretary of State for Transport*, OJ C 183, 19/07/2008, p 2, paragraph 69–70.
41 Joined Cases C-74/95 and C-129/95 *Criminal Proceedings against X*, OJ C 54, 22/02/1997, p 4, paragraph 25.
42 Peristeridou, op. cit., p 12.

Peristeridou distinguishes between the principle of legality (above) and the procedural principle of legality, which she says, "governs the prosecution of criminal offences and the discretion of the prosecutor".[43] Both of these issues are relevant in developing an effective transnational criminal law framework. The linked concepts such as "the principle of guilt, the presumption of innocence" etc. all need to be elaborated in such a framework.[44] To these requirements Boister has added "fair labelling, individuality of guilt, the prohibition on retroactive application, and right to fair trial".[45] Within the EU's AFSJ "a very complicated matrix" covering constitutional principles and policies, together with a variety of procedural provisions have all been used to contribute to the developing principle of legality at an EU level.[46] Where shared legal understandings or traditions do not already exist among states, extra effort will be needed to address these issues in a transnational setting before effective transnational law enforcement and justice provisions to combat THB can be fully developed. In addition, the public needs to be informed for effective "presumption of knowing the law" in a transnational context, or "within a plurality of legal orders",[47] particularly in the context of the Palermo Convention and its THB Protocol.

Obligations on States to Implement Relevant Laws

The THB Protocol, at Article 1, provides that it "supplements" the Palermo Convention and it is to be "interpreted together with the Convention". In addition, the provisions of the Convention are to apply "mutatis mutandis, to this Protocol, unless otherwise provided herein", with offences to be established pursuant to Article 5 of the THB Protocol, which requires the criminalisation of the offence of THB, "shall be regarded as offences established in accordance with the [Palermo] Convention". These provisions are echoed in Article 37 of the Palermo Convention, which states that that convention "may be supplemented by one or more protocols", and that, "Any protocol to this Convention shall be interpreted together with this Convention, taking into account the purpose of that protocol". Therefore, for the parties to the THB Protocol, Article 34 of the Palermo Convention obliges them to "take the necessary measures, including legislative and administrative measures", in accordance with their domestic laws, "to ensure the implementation of its obligations" under the protocol, as well as their further obligations under the Convention itself. Article 34 Palermo Convention goes on to say that the offences specified in the convention, "shall be established in the domestic law … independently of the transnational nature or the involvement of an organized criminal group". It is also open to state parties to "adopt more strict or severe measures than those provided for by

43 Ibid., p 15.
44 Ibid., p 58.
45 N. Boister, *An Introduction to Transnational Criminal Law*, Oxford University Press, 2012, p 21.
46 Peristeridou, op. cit., p 290.
47 Ibid., p 254.

this Convention".[48] As stated by Obokata, this includes the requirement to "prohibit so-called inchoate offences such as attempt and conspiracy to commit organised crime, including THB and joint criminal enterprise, as well as secondary participation (e.g. aiding and abetting)".[49] In addition to the obligation to effectively legislate for the crime of THB, the Palermo Convention also requires that the twin crimes of money laundering[50] and seizure of the proceeds and instrumentalities of crime[51] be criminalised in signatory member states, as discussed in Chapter 3.

There are also lengthy provisions in the Palermo Convention on extradition. As is typical with transnational law, the details of how the extradition is to operate, subject to the express provisions of Article 16 Palermo Convention, "shall be subject to the conditions provided for by the domestic law of the requested State party or by applicable extradition treaties".[52] For those states which, under their domestic laws, do not require a further extradition treaty, then there is an obligation to extradite pursuant to the provisions of the Palermo Convention itself, pursuant to Article 16.6 for those who do require a treaty framework, then the states "may consider this Convention the legal basis for extradition in respect of any offence to which this [Article 16.4] applies". When operating an extradition process, the accused needs to "be guaranteed fair treatment at all stages of the proceedings, including enjoyment of all rights and guarantees provided by the domestic law of the State Party in the territory of which that person is present".[53] The detail of how this is to happen would need to be pre-arranged between jurisdictions, and preferably covered by a bi-lateral or multi-lateral convention in line with the principles of both legality and procedural legality discussed above. Any divergence in defining THB in domestic jurisdictions, as discussed in Chapter 2, would also have to be dealt with at this point, in order to ensure that transnational law enforcement of THB meets the needs of relevant double criminality tests.

Mutual legal assistance also needs to be given transnationally during their investigations, prosecutions, and judicial proceedings.[54] Investigations can be directed by either law enforcement officials or investigating magistrates in different jurisdictions, depending on the constitutional and criminal structure of a particular state. It is unclear whether this distinction was in the minds of the authors of the Palermo Convention. These have all however, now been developed by the EU, and are being regularly used in the AFSJ. There is an express obligation in the convention to provide law enforcement cooperation,[55] which includes the "rapid exchange of information" across the jurisdictions. A list of what is considered

48 Palermo Convention, op. cit., Article 34.
49 T. Obokata, 'Human Trafficking', in N. Boister and R. J. Currie, *Routledge Handbook of Transnational Criminal Law*, Routledge, 2015, p 175.
50 Palermo Convention, op. cit., Article 7.
51 Ibid., Article 12.
52 Ibid., Article 16.7.
53 Ibid., Article 16.13.
54 Ibid., Article 18.
55 Ibid., Article 27

mutual legal assistance, which is to be afforded to other states is set out in Article 18.3.[56] As stated by Obokata, "the law enforcement community must be equipped with appropriate investigative powers, in addition to regular powers to stop, search and seize, so that it can facilitate proactive intelligence-led law enforcement".[57] The emphasis here on intelligence-led law enforcement[58] is important, intelligence being something different from information, as reliance on victim testimony is particularly problematic in the context of THB. The Palermo Convention provides that it is possible for law enforcement to engage in the "collection, exchange and analysis of information",[59] something that is regularly done within the EU, and to examine the setting up of Joint Investigation Teams (JITs).[60] JITs are also regularly used for law enforcement within the EU and Australia, where further detailed laws and practice has been developed.

Training and technical assistance, to the extent necessary[61] also needs to be provided transnationally, and if they are permitted by domestic legislation, to use special investigative techniques, to include controlled delivery,[62] and "other special investigative techniques, such as electronic or other forms of surveillance and undercover operations" in a transnational context.[63] These are all tools that are used effectively across borders within the EU, however only after much training, additional agreement, to include at the level of detail, ensuring the inter-compatibility of telecommunication facilities, etc. so that different law enforcement authorities can properly communicate with each other during a transnational operation, and the development of relevant law enforcement practice manuals.

It is expected that further bilateral or multi-lateral treaties would cover, in whole or in part, the provisions in the Palermo Convention on mutual legal assistance,[64] with the EU having some very detailed and well used provisions in this area, which may prove to be useful models for other countries or regions of the world to use in designing their own provisions. In addition, further mandatory provisions in the Palermo Convention include the protection of witnesses,[65] and

56 Ibid., Article 18.3. These include a. Taking evidence or statements from persons; b. Effecting service of judicial documents; c. Executing searches and seizures, and freezing; d. Examining objects and sites; e. Providing information, evidentiary items and expert evaluations; f. Providing originals or certified copies of relevant documents and records, including government, bank, financial, corporate or business records; g. Identifying or tracing proceeds of crime, property, instrumentalities or other things for evidentiary purposes; h. Facilitating the voluntary appearance of persons in the requesting State Party; i. Any other type of assistance that is not contrary to the domestic law of the requested State Party.

57 Obokata (2015), op. cit., p 176.

58 A. James, *Examining Intelligence-led Policing, Developments in Research, Policy and Practice*, Palgrave Macmillan, 2013.

59 Palermo Convention, Article 28.

60 Ibid., Article 19.

61 Ibid., Article 29.

62 Ibid., Article 2(i).

63 Ibid., Article 20.

64 Ibid., Article 18.6.

65 Ibid., Article 24.

the giving of assistance and protection to victims.[66] There are two further obligations in the THB Protocol to "protect and assist the victims of such trafficking, with full respect for their human rights", as discussed below, and "to promote cooperation among State Parties in order to meet those objectives".[67] There is therefore an obligation to work in a transnational context, and not just to criminalise, or protect victims in a domestic jurisdiction.

In addition, it is recommended that there is an establishment of a criminal record,[68] possibilities for the transfer of sentenced persons,[69] and that the transfer of criminal proceedings from one jurisdiction to another be considered.[70] The Palermo Convention further provides that each state party will "ensure that conditions imposed in connection with decisions on release pending trial or appeal take into consideration the need to ensure the presence of the defendant at subsequent criminal proceedings".[71] The "grave nature of the offences" covered by the Palermo Convention and its protocols should be borne in mind "when considering the eventuality of early release or parole".[72] Legal procedure and legal defences remain a matter for the jurisdiction in which the offence is tried.[73]

The above complex detail needs to be negotiated by practitioners transnationally in a constructivist manner. The detail of what will be required to be agreed between jurisdictions cannot be covered in an international treaty, although the parameters for those negotiations do need to be set out in a treaty, and review mechanisms put in place to ensure a balanced development of the required objectives. As pointed out by Zagaris, this requires a three-stage process, the "regularization of relations among law enforcement officials of different states; accommodation among systems that retain their essential differences; and homogenization of systems towards a common norm".[74] The exact order in which these develop will depend on the previous levels of engagement between the two or more criminal jurisdictions, and the preferred methods of operation of the relevant state parties. If there are sufficient levels of transnational criminality between the relevant states, then the levels of diplomatic, legal and practitioner investment necessary will be well worth while.

From a human rights perspective, the positive obligations on states to implement relevant laws on THB are therefore much broader than the obligation to effectively criminalise, which has been the focus of many academic writers to date. Taking a Eurocentric approach, the ECtHR case of *Rantsev v Cyprus and Russia*,[75] is pointed to by many academics as setting out the state obligation to

66 Ibid., Article 25.
67 THB Protocol, Article 2.
68 Palermo Convention, Article 22.
69 Ibid., Article 17.
70 Ibid., Article 21.
71 Ibid., Article 11.3.
72 Ibid., Article 11.4.
73 Ibid., Article 11.6.
74 Zagaris, op. cit., p 26.
75 *Rantsev v Cyprus and Russia*, Application no. 25965/04, ECtHR, 7 January 2010.

effectively criminalise. *Rantsev* however, underlined the state obligation to do a lot more than just criminalise THB. The judgment in *Rantsev* relied on Article 4 ECHR, which, as pointed out by the ECtHR, "makes no provisions for exceptions and no derogation … even in the event of a public emergency threatening the life of the nation".[76] The judgment reflected the need to meet the three "P"s of preventing trafficking, protecting victims, and punishing traffickers.[77] In addition to the often commented on requirement to effectively "penalise and prosecute effectively any act aimed at maintaining a person in a situation of slavery, servitude or forced or compulsory labour"[78] with the court expressly referring to both the THB Protocol and the CoE Council of Europe Convention on Action against Trafficking in Human Beings[79] (discussed further in Chapter 6), further obligations are placed on states.

The *Rantsev* ruling also held that there is an obligation "to take operational measures to protect victims, or potential victims, of trafficking", in circumstances where "[s]tate authorities were aware, or ought to have been aware, of the circumstances giving rise to a credible suspicion that an identified individual had been, or was at real and immediate risk of being trafficked or exploited".[80] This included the need to regulate "businesses often used as a cover for human trafficking" and ensuring that the states' immigration rules needing to "address relevant concerns relating to encouragement, facilitation or tolerance of trafficking", two issues which are outside the scope of this book.[81] These positive obligations, in the eyes of the ECtHR under Article 4 (Prohibition of slavery and forced labour), also relevant to Article 5 ECtHR (Right to liberty and security), included the need for effective policing, with an entire paragraph in the judgment being devoted to the "difficulties involved in policing modern societies" and the need for law enforcement to make "operational choices… in terms of priorities and resources".[82] Nevertheless, there is a "requirement to investigate" potential THB, which should "not depend on a complaint from the victim or next-of-kin". Law enforcement need to "act of their own motion" once the matter has come to their attention.[83] While the ECtHR did not make express reference to the provisions in the Palermo Convention on this point, its provisions are echoed in this reasoning. The investigation into THB needs to be "independent from those implicated in the events" and "be undertaken as a matter of urgency".[84] The ECtHR did expressly address the issue of transnational law enforcement in *Rantsev*, stating that "trafficking offences may occur in the State of origin, any State of transit and

76 Ibid., paragraph 283.
77 Ibid., paragraph 285.
78 Ibid., paragraph 284.
79 CETS 197 CoE Convention on Action against Trafficking in Human Beings, Warsaw, 16.V. 2005.
80 *Rantsev v Cyprus and Russia*, op. cit., paragraph 285.
81 Ibid., paragraph 283.
82 Ibid., paragraph 286.
83 Ibid., paragraph 287.
84 Ibid.

the State of destination", and that "relevant evidence and witnesses may be located in all States".[85] The competent authorities in ECHR contracting states are obliged not only to conduct investigations into offences occurring within their own states, but "are also subject to a duty in cross-border trafficking cases to cooperate effectively with the relevant authorities of other States concerned in the investigation of events which occurred outside their territories".[86] There is, however, no right "to have criminal proceedings instituted".[87] In *Rantsev* there was a violation of Article 4 ECHR by Russia "of its procedural obligations to investigate the alleged trafficking",[88] with Russia having an obligation to "investigate the possibility that individual agents or networks operating in Russia", or to Cyprus, were involved in THB.[89] Russia was obliged not only to investigate domestically, but also transnationally.

The ECtHR went on to say that such a duty was in keeping with the obligations of acceding states to the THB Protocol "to adopt a comprehensive international approach to trafficking in countries of origin, transit and destination".[90] European Human Rights law therefore clearly requires a full operationalisation of the provisions of the Palermo Convention and THB Protocol to protect individuals being trafficked into and out of ECHR states, regardless of which ever other countries are involved along the THB supply chains. There was no limitation in the *Rantsev* judgment to cooperation between signatory states only to the ECHR. Rather there was a direct reference to "State of origin, any State of transit and the State of destination".[91] This would apply if there were a territorial connection with one of the ECHR states, as discussed in Chapter 3.

The Victims

In developing transnational criminal law to combat THB, it is important to bear in mind the vulnerability of the victims. While the Palermo Convention contains no human rights protection, they are in the THB Protocol,[92] with specific reference being made to "full respect for [the] human rights" of the victims.[93] However, as Gallagher points out, "to the general disappointment of many commentators", there is "very little in the way of 'hard' or detailed obligations".[94] This would be

85 Ibid., paragraph 288.
86 Ibid.
87 Case comment, '*Rantsev v Cyprus and Russia* (App. No.25965/04): Trafficking in Human Beings – Sexual Exploitation – "Artiste" Visa Regime in Cyprus' (2010) 3 *European Human Rights Law Review*, p 326.
88 Ibid., p 328.
89 Ibid.
90 *Rantsev v Cyprus and Russia*, op. cit., paragraph 288.
91 Ibid.
92 N. Boister, 'The Cooperation Provisions of the UN Convention against Transnational Organised Crime: a "Toolbox" Rarely Used?' (2016), 16 *International Criminal Law Review* 1, p 64.
93 THB Protocol, Article 2.c.
94 A. Gallagher, *The International Law of Human Trafficking*, Cambridge University Press, 2010, p 81–82.

in contrast now to the provisions on victim support and protection in many domestic jurisdictions, and would be a key issue in developing transnational law enforcement and justice frameworks with those jurisdictions. These provisions may well have to be expressly written into bilateral and multi-lateral THB treaties developing transnational relationships.

Obokata is of the view that the victim protection provisions in the THB Protocol "clearly illustrates recognition by the international community that trafficking is also a human rights issue".[95] In Europe the *Rantsev* case confirmed "for the first time a positive obligation on state authorities to protect victims or potential victims" of THB under Article 4 ECHR, "from real and immediate risks which are known to the authorities".[96] This obligation to take operational measures is subject to the caveat that it "does not impose an impossible or disproportionate burden on the authorities".[97] It should be noted at this point that law enforcement often finds that effective policing to combat THB requires "intense and costly resourcing" to obtain the necessary actionable intelligence.[98]

Often victims will have been living chaotic lives before having come under the control of their exploiters. Issues of whether the victims over the age of 18 consented to the exploitation, or the inability to prove that they had not consented to the level of exploitation encountered, will often present problems for presenting victim testimony in court. Victims may have originally been capable of effectively presenting evidence in court, but the level of exploitation and trauma that they have now undergone at the hands of their exploiters have rendered them highly vulnerable, and giving evidence at trial is only adding to the mental instability that they are now suffering. Other victims will have come from marginalised communities, or "the most vulnerable sectors of society", "those who are marginalized due to socio-economic factors and those who face racial, ethnic or gender discrimination".[99] They may well be "reluctant to co-operate with law enforcement due to a lack of trust, serious threats to their personal security and intimidation by traffickers" as well as, where relevant, "their irregular migration status".[100] As stated by Walsh, victims may present with "anxiety, panic attacks, memory loss, depression, substance abuse and eating disorders, or a combination of these", making the role of the first responder very difficult.[101]

For these reasons, among others, relying on victims to testify in court is fraught with danger, with many reporting that most victims or suspected victims "encountered by police fled before initial interviews could be conducted or shortly

95 T. Obokata, *Trafficking of Human Beings from a Human Rights Perspective; Towards a Holistic Approach*, Martinus Nijhoff Publishers, 2006, p 34.
96 Case comment, '*Rantsev v Cyprus and Russia*', op. cit., p 330.
97 Ibid.
98 K. Lebov, 'Human Trafficking in Scotland' (2010) 7 *European Journal of Criminology* 1, p 85.
99 OSCE, *Leveraging Anti-Money Laundering Regimes to Combat Trafficking in Human Beings*, OSCE, 2014, p 13.
100 Ibid., p 15.
101 M. Walsh, 'Human Trafficking' (2009) 1 *Judicial Studies Institute Journal*, p 113.

afterwards".[102] The identity and privacy of the victims needs to be ensured by each state,[103] and each state needs to provide support to victims of THB in the course of "relevant court and administrative proceedings", to include having the victims "views and concerns" presented and considered "at appropriate stages of criminal proceedings against offenders, in a manner not prejudicial to the rights of the defence".[104] Obokata argues that victims should also have the right to "participate in the investigation and judicial process against the traffickers" as this allows the victims voice to be heard, which has "a therapeutic value", in assisting in "handling their anger and trauma in a constructive way". This would then lead in many cases to a "restoration of their sense of control, dignity, and self-worth".[105]

Victim rehabilitations provisions, as required to be considered under the THB Protocol, at Article 6.3, may not be present, or be insufficient to effectively bring the victim to the stage where they are confident in giving evidence in court. There may be a problem with "weak victim and witness protection systems" which exist in many countries.[106] The THB Protocol asks states to "consider implementing measures to provide for the physical, psychological and social recovery of victims" either directly by the state, or in cooperation with NGOs, to include the provision of appropriate housing, "counselling and information, in particular as regards their legal rights, in a language that the victims of trafficking … can understand, medical, psychological and material assistance" and "employment, education and training opportunities".[107] The particular needs of the individual, to include their "age and gender and special needs" should be taken into account, "in particular the special needs of children, including appropriate housing, education and care".[108] Physical safety of the victim also needs to be provided "while they are within" the state's territory,[109] and also required is the possibility of "obtaining compensation for damage suffered".[110] However, as Obokata points out, the issue of compensation must be handled with care, as its key point is to affirm the dignity of the victim. However, if the process for applying for compensation is too difficult or is seen as "buying silence" or as "blood money" then this process may be counterproductive.[111]

In addition, victims, while given protection themselves, may be vulnerable to other members of their families in their country of origin becoming victims, in retaliation, of the human traffickers. Transnational law enforcement and justice frameworks designed to combat THB should not, therefore, be designed to rely

102 Lebov, op. cit., p 88.
103 THB Protocol, Article 6.1
104 Ibid., Article 6.2.
105 Obokata, (2006), op. cit., p 158.
106 OSCE, op. cit., p 16.
107 THB Protocol, Article 6.3.
108 Ibid., Article 6.4.
109 Ibid., Article 6.5.
110 Ibid., Article 6.6.
111 Obokata, (2006), op. cit., p 161.

on victim testimony in court. Other methods of developing intelligence and evidence for trial should instead be focused on, such as covert surveillance etc. This is known as intelligence led policing.[112]

The THB Protocol goes on to provide that states should also "consider adopting legislative or other appropriate measures" to allow THB victims to "remain in its territory, temporarily or permanently, in appropriate cases", giving "appropriate consideration to humanitarian and compassionate factors".[113] Complex issues arise at state borders, an issue taken up by Stoyanova in her book.[114] In addition, states should "facilitate and accept" the repatriation of THB victims "without undue or unreasonable delay", to their state of nationality or permanent of residence "with due regard for the safety of that person".[115] This repatriation should "preferably be voluntary".[116] However, there should continue to be compliance with "rights, obligations and responsibilities of States and individuals under international law", etc. in particular in the context of the protection of refugees, and the "principle of non-refoulement".[117] Not covered at the level of the THB Protocol, but covered in the ECHR for its member states, is the obligation, under Article 6 ECHR, is the "right to a fair trial" and a "duty to enable access to justice".[118] This would include "the establishment of legal aid systems" and the "possibility to retain legal counsel – including victims of human trafficking".[119]

Breath of Criminality in the THB Protocol

A wide breath of activity is required to be criminalised under the THB Protocol. As discussed in Chapter 2, under Article 3 exploitation within THB "shall include, at a minimum, the exploitation of the prostitution of others or other forms of sexual exploitation, forced labour or services, slavery or practices similar to slavery, servitude or the removal of organs". The term "as a minimum" indicates that this is not a closed list, but rather that THB could arise in circumstances not anticipated by the drafters of this protocol. Many of the circumstances which were anticipated by the THB Protocol are covered by further detailed international law provisions. As also discussed in Chapter 2, what is not covered by the THB Protocol is prostitution not connected with the Article 3.a provision of "threat or use of force or other forms of coercion, of abduction, of fraud, of deception, of the abuse of power or of a position of vulnerability or of the giving or receiving of

112 J. H. Ratcliffe, *Intelligence-Led Policing*, 2nd edition, Routledge, 2016.
113 THB Protocol, Article 7.
114 V. Stoyanova, *Human Trafficking and Slavery Reconsidered: Conceptual Limits and States' Positive Obligations in European Law*, Cambridge University Press, 2017.
115 THB Protocol, Article 8.
116 Ibid., Article 8.2.
117 Ibid., Article 14.1.
118 S. Kirchner and V. M. Frese, 'Slavery under the European Convention on Human Rights and the Jus Cogens Prohibition of Human Trafficking' (2015) 27 *Denning Law Journal*, p 137.
119 Ibid., p 137.

payments or benefits to achieve the consent of a person having control over another person, for the purpose of exploitation". The academic and policy debates on what constitutes voluntary prostitution are lengthy and detailed.

A child, for the purposes of the THB Protocol, means "any person under eighteen years of age",[120] regardless of the national law on either majority or sexual maturity. The protection of children also covers the issue of illegal adoption with a view to exploitation.[121] It is unclear whether illegal adoption, or as described by Gallagher, "abusive, illegal, unethical, or otherwise undesirable adoption practices"[122] is included in the definition of THB. However, any practice, to include "stealing, buying and selling of children"[123] leading to "practices similar to slavery" to include delivery of a child by a parent or guardian into bonded labour or a forced marriage is included.[124] A further examination of the vulnerability and rights of the child victim will be made in Chapter 5. The issue of "stealing, buying and selling of children" as a stand-alone offence and its connection with trafficking "have not been explored in any great depth" by transnational legislators, despite the attempts of many academics to address the issue.[125] This is clearly an issue which needs to be revisited by legislators.

A further distinct issue in the context of THB is the removal of organs. This is expressly provided for in the THB Protocol, in its THB definition at Article 3.a, having been inserted late into the drafting process.[126] Since the coming into force of the protocol greater clarity has been brought to the seriousness of this issue. A distinction has been made in subsequent years between trafficking in organs, cells and tissues, and trafficking in persons for purposes of organ removal.[127] A human security approach would require that both issues be addressed, even if the trafficking in organs, cells and tissues do not map onto the THB Protocol definition of THB.

Conclusion

As can be seen from the above, THB is a "highly complex" area of law.[128] In addition to the hard law provisions enumerated above, a number of "soft law" provisions are also relevant. These include, as pointed out by Gallagher, the internal UN documents which were drafted with no state input, the UN Principles and Guidelines on Human Rights and Human Trafficking, and the UN Children's fund's Guidelines for the Protection of Child Victims of Trafficking.[129] In

120 THB Protocol, Article 3.d.
121 Gallagher, op. cit., p 41.
122 Ibid., p 40.
123 Ibid., p 41.
124 Ibid., p 40.
125 Ibid.
126 Ibid., p 39.
127 Ibid., p 39.
128 Obokata, (2006), op. cit. p 38.
129 Gallagher, op. cit., p 140.

addition several other documents, resolutions and intergovernmental action plans emanating from UN bodies are also relevant.[130]

With a positive legal obligation to enact and operate transnational law enforcement and justice frameworks to combat THB, while complying with the principle of legality, most legal jurisdictions' treaty-based networks still need to be developed between states, both from a law enforcement and victim protection perspective. Obokata has called for a framework that "unifies … responses at the national, regional and international level" so as to "promote effective global action against trafficking".[131] Boister points out that states are reluctant to sign transnational organised crime bilateral treaties with "non-parties of the ICCPR [International Covenant on Civil and Political Rights] because of wariness of harsh penalty regimes".[132] This issue needs to be expressly addressed by states in their negotiations with other countries, under their obligations under both the Palermo Convention, and for contracting parties, the ECHR, as highlighted in *Rantsev*, regardless of which other third country they need to work with in order to combat THB. Traditional reluctance to deal with a country with a poor human rights record needs to be reconciled with European human rights requirements to proceed against human traffickers and protect their victims in a transnational context. A human security approach to THB requires that victims of THB, regardless of where they come from, be protected. Drafters will have to put a lot of thought into the relevant treaty provisions, law enforcement practice manuals and internal prosecution and victim practice provisions to effectively address these issues in a transnational context.

At the level of practice however, law enforcement agencies have been "concentrating more on arrest and deportation of illegal migrants", a significant number of whom would be classified as victims in a THB context.[133] This has allowed the organisers of THB to remain free to recruit more victims and to arrange for more irregular crossing of borders. A high level of resourcing is required to combat THB, together with considerable effort to effectively tackle the underlying organised crime, both domestically and transnationally.[134] Consent to being "trafficked" or more accurately to be smuggled, or exploited, remains a complex legal issue in many jurisdictions, to include, as discussed in Chapter 2, at the ECtHR.[135] However, once coercion, deception, abuse of authority etc. is established, this should nullify the issue of consent.[136]

Operationalising national and transnational law to combat THB is required but will be highly problematic. Making a national or transnational legal system work to the benefit of a victim is always problematic as THB victims "are in the weakest

130 Ibid., p 140/141.
131 Obokata, (2006), op. cit., p 38.
132 Boister, (2016), op. cit., p 64.
133 Obokata, (2006), op. cit., p 80.
134 Ibid.
135 *Chowdury and Others v Greece*, Application no. 21884/15, ECtHR, 30 March 2017.
136 Gallagher, op. cit., p 28.

position and least able to speak out and demand their rights".[137] As pointed out by the OSCE, even in countries which maintain "strong legal standards on the protection of victims' rights" effective implementation of THB laws remain "elusive".[138]

Bibliography

Barker, B. M., 'Police Discretion and the Principle of Legality' (1966) 8 *Criminal Law Quarterly*, 400–407.

Boister, N., 'The Cooperation Provisions of the UN Convention against Transnational Organised Crime: a "Toolbox" Rarely Used?' (2016) 16 *International Criminal Law Review* 1, 39–70.

Boister, N., 'Transnational Criminal Law?' (2003) 14 *European Journal of International law* 5, 953–976.

Boister, N., *An Introduction to Transnational Criminal Law*, Oxford University Press, 2012.

Case comment, 'Rantsev v Cyprus and Russia (App. No.25965/04): Trafficking in Human Beings – Sexual Exploitation – "Artiste" Visa Regime in Cyprus' (2010) 3 *European Human Rights Law Review*, 325–330.

Gallagher, A., *The International Law of Human Trafficking*, Cambridge University Press, 2010.

Garibaldi, O. M., 'General Limitations on Human Rights: The Principle of Legality' (1976) 17 *Harvard International Law Journal* 3, 503–558.

James, A., *Examining Intelligence-Led Policing, Developments in Research, Policy and Practice*, Palgrave Macmillan, 2013.

Kirchner, S. and Frese, V. M., 'Slavery under the European Convention on Human Rights and the Jus Cogens Prohibition of Human Trafficking' (2015) 27 *Denning Law Journal*, 130–145.

Lebov, K., 'Human Trafficking in Scotland' (2010) 7 *European Journal of Criminology* 1, 77–93.

Obokata, T., 'Human Trafficking', in Boister N., and Currie, R. J., *Routledge Handbook of Transnational Criminal Law*, Routledge, 2015.

Obokata, T., *Trafficking of Human Beings from a Human Rights Perspective; Towards a Holistic Approach*, Martinus Nijhoff Publishers, 2006.

Olásolo, H., 'A Note on the Evolution of the Principle of Legality in International Criminal Law' (2007) 18 *Criminal Law Forum*.

OSCE, *Leveraging Anti-Money Laundering Regimes to Combat Trafficking in Human Beings*, OSCE, 2014.

Peristeridou, C., *The Principle of Legality in European Criminal Law*, Intersentia, 2015.

Ratcliffe, J. H., *Intelligence-Led Policing*, 2nd edition, Routledge, 2016.

Shaffer, G., *Transnational Legal Ordering and State Change*, Cambridge University Press, 2013.

Shahabuddeen, M., 'Does the Principle of Legality Stand in the Way of Progressive Development of Law?' (2004), 2 *Journal of International Criminal Justice* 4, 1007–1017.

137 Kirchner and Frese, op. cit., p 134.
138 OSCE, op. cit., p 17.

Stoyanova, V., *Human Trafficking and Slavery Reconsidered: Conceptual Limits and States' Positive Obligations in European Law*, Cambridge University Press, 2017.
Walsh, M., 'Human Trafficking' (2009) 1 *Judicial Studies Institute Journal*, 104–129.
Zagaris, B., 'International Enforcement Law Trends for 2010 and Beyond: Can the Cops Keep up with the Criminals?' (2011) 34 *Suffolk Transnational Law Review*, 1.

Legislation

CoE Convention on Action against Trafficking in Human Beings, Warsaw, 16 May 2005, CETS 197.
Second Additional Protocol (2001) to the Council of Europe Convention on Mutual Assistance in Criminal Matters 1959, CETS 182.
UN Convention against Transnational Organized Crime 2000, UNTS 2225, p 209.
UN Protocol to Prevent, Suppress and Punish Trafficking in Persons, Especially Women and Children, supplementing the United Nations Convention against Transnational Organized Crime 2000, UNTS, 2237, p 319.

Cases

C-308/06, *The Queen, on the application of the International Association of Independent Tanker Owners (Intertanko) and others v Secretary of State for Transport*, OJ C 183, 19 July 2008, p 2.
Chowdury and Others v Greece, Application no. 21884/15, ECtHR, judgment 30 March 2017.
Consistency of Certain Danzig Legislative decrees with the Constitution of the Free City, Permanent Court of International Justice, Advisory Opinion No. 27, 1935 P.C.I.J. Series A/B, No 65 (4 December).
Joined Cases C-74/95 and C-129/95, *Criminal proceedings against X*, OJ C 54, 22 February 1997, p 4.
Prosecutor v Kunarac, Vukovic and Kovac, Appeals Chamber, International Tribunal for the Former Yugoslavia, Case No. IT-96-23 and TI-96-23/1-A, 12 June 2002.
Puhk v Estonia, Application no. 55103/00, ECtHR, 10 February 2004.
Rantsev v Cyprus and Russia, Application no. 25965/04, ECtHR, 7 January 2010.
Veeber v Estonia (No. 2) Application no. 45771/99, ECtHR, 21 January 2003.

5 Children

Introduction

When building the transnational law enforcement framework to combat THB, it is important to provide special consideration to the rights and vulnerabilities of children.[1] Gallagher points out that "the matter of child trafficking did not especially occupy delegations during the negotiations" of the THB Protocol.[2] There are clearly gaps in dealing with children which latter legal provisions either have or should address. Taking a human security approach to tackling THB, these further risks affecting children will also be addressed in this chapter. The THB protocol calls for full respect to be given to human rights while protecting and assisting victims of THB,[3] and to promote cooperation among states in meeting those objectives.[4] There are a wide variety of international legal documents which enumerate such rights of children, to include the UN Convention on the Rights of the Child 1989 (CRC),[5] and its two Optional Protocols.[6] Also relevant are the International Labour Organization (ILO) conventions, however, even the ILO Convention on the Worst Forms of Child Labour 1999 (No 182) (WFCL) does not expressly call for the criminalisation of behaviour leading to the worst forms of child labour, leaving it to ILO Recommendation 190 – Worst Forms of Child Labour Recommendation, 1999 to expressly speak about criminalisation. A substantial amount of interlegality, as discussed in Chapter 2, is required to effectively negotiate this area of law, with the assistance of the Vienna Convention on the Law of Treaties 1969. Nevertheless, the THB Protocol does expressly speak of criminalisation and offences. It is also very clear that a child is to be defined for

1 THB protocol, Article 2(a).
2 A. Gallagher, *The International Law of Human Trafficking*, Cambridge University Press, 2010, p 84.
3 THB protocol, Article 2(b).
4 Ibid, Article 2(c).
5 UN Convention on the Rights of the Child, General Assembly Resolution 44/25, 20 November 1989.
6 Optional Protocol to the Convention on the Rights of the Child on the involvement of children in armed conflict, 2000, UNTS 2217, p 27531, and the Optional Protocol to the Convention on the Rights of the Child on the sale of children, child prostitution and child pornography, 2000, UNTS 2171, p 227.

DOI: 10.4324/9781003429791-5

THB as someone under the age of 18,[7] something which is not that clear in many of the relevant ILO or UN conventions. The beginning of a child's life is also an emerging issue in THB.

Child trafficking, using the state's current definition of THB (discussed further in Chapter 7), is seen as a substantial issue in the UK. The CoE THB monitoring body, GRETA (discussed further in Chapter 6), reported that UK nationals were the most common country of origin for children in its National Referral Mechanism (NRM) in 2019, at 52%, "followed by Vietnam (9%), Eritrea (6%), Albania (6%) and Sudan (5%)".[8] Ninety-five per cent of child referrals were in England, with "174 children identified in Wales, 156 in Scotland and 16 in Northern Ireland".[9] The high level of UK children in the NRM is attributed to exploitation for the purposes of forced criminality, in particular county line crime.[10]

The THB Protocol, at Article 3 speaks about "the abuse of power or of a position of vulnerability". While this phrase will have different meanings in different contexts, it will have a particular meaning in the context of child THB victims. Article 3 of the protocol speaks about exploitation, which "at a minimum [means] the exploitation of the prostitution of others or other forms of sexual exploitation, forced labour or services, slavery, or practices similar to slavery, servitude, or the removal of organs". While the means[11] of THB is relevant in the context of adult victims (as discussed in Chapter 2), this is not required when a child is being trafficked,[12] providing additional protection to children. The THB Protocol goes on to say that "Each State Party shall take into account, in applying the provisions of this article, the age, gender and special needs of victims", "in particular the special needs of children, including appropriate housing, education and care".[13] The THB Protocol does call for "State Parties [to] provide or strengthen training for law enforcement, immigration and other relevant officials" to not only prevent trafficking, but to also ensure that both the traffickers are prosecuted and the rights of victims are protected.[14] This training should "take into account" not only "the human rights" but also the "child- and gender-sensitive issues" arising from the crime, and states should "encourage cooperation with non-governmental organizations, other relevant organizations and other elements of civil society" in order to properly address these issues.[15] A state's membership of global and regional human rights

7 THB protocol, Article 3(d).

8 GRETA Evaluation Report, United Kingdom Third Evaluation Round: Access to Justice and Effective Remedies for Victims of Trafficking in Human Beings, GRETA (2021)12, Council of Europe, 2021, p 12, point 15.

9 Ibid.

10 Ibid.

11 Article 3(a) of the THB protocol "means of the threat or use of force or other forms of coercion, of abduction, of fraud, of deception, of the abuse of power or of a position of vulnerability or of the giving or receiving of payments or benefits".

12 THB protocol, Article 3.c.

13 Ibid, Article 6.4.

14 Ibid, Article 10.2.2.

15 Ibid.

provisions, will affect how these rights are determined, and whether those provisions are properly and effectively interpreted and implemented in individual states. Failure to so properly interpret and implement could lead to state liability within their own jurisdictions. In addition, it could lead to a lack of cooperation with transnational law enforcement and justice provisions operating from other jurisdictions which maintain higher human rights and justice standards, which, for their part, cannot be seen to compromise these standards.

What Is a Child?

The THB Protocol clearly defines a child as someone under the age of 18 years, overriding, for the purposes of the THB offence, any contrary provisions in earlier ILO conventions on age and labour. In addition, as can be seen from the ECHR case of *Siliadin v France*,[16] as discussed in Chapter 2, work in the family or household chores can in extreme circumstances be classified servitude. The facts in *Siliadin*, involved a child in forced domestic service in France. It is worth noting that in *Siliadin* "the court emphasised the girl's age constantly throughout the whole judgment".[17] As pointed out by Cullen, there was for a long time "no specific standards on child domestic workers",[18] either at the ILO or at the CoE. The ILO has since enacted the Domestic Workers Convention 2011 (ILO No. 189), which at the time of writing has 36 ratifications, including a few European countries. This convention does call for the "effective abolition of child labour" in Article 3, although Article 4 provides those domestic workers who are under the age of 18, and above the minimum age of employment should not be deprived of compulsory education and the work should not "interfere with opportunities to participate in further education or vocational training". Further accessions and implementation of this convention would assist in avoiding legislative gaps in domestic criminal and labour laws.

Standard THB provisions within the EU and the CoE address the issue of child forced labour. The EU states that it is "inspired by" … "but does not participate formally in the respective activities of the ILO",[19] with EU member states being left to engage exclusively with the ILO. All EU member states are long standing parties to the ILO Minimum Age Convention,[20] and on the Worst Forms of

16 *Siliadin v France*, Application no. 73316/01, ECtHR, p 33, paragraph 129.
17 V. Stoyanova, 'Dancing on the Borders of Article 4: Human Trafficking and the European Court of Human Rights in the *Rantsev* Case' (2012) 30 *Netherlands Institute of Human Rights* 2, p 180.
18 H. Cullen, *The Role of International Law in the Elimination of Child Labour*, Martinus Nijhoff Publishers, 2007, p 156.
19 M. Hartwig, 'The Elimination of Child Labour and the EU', in G. Nesil, L. Nogler, and M. Pertile, *Child Labour in a Globalized World: A Legal Analysis of ILO Action*, Ashgate 2008, p 254.
20 ILO's Minimum Age Convention 1973 (C138).

Child Labour.[21] The EU THB directive itself makes express reference to the UN CRC 1989,[22] in the context of child victims of THB.

Child Prostitution, Pornography, and Child Sex Tourism

The concept "sexual exploitation", in the context of adults, caused problems at the drafting of the THB Protocol, with the decision being taken, given the lack of agreement, "that there was no need to define the term".[23] In fact "no international instrument actually defines prostitution".[24] The drafters of the THB Protocol were clear that it should "not extend to prostitution or pornography per se".[25] In the context of adult sexual exploitation, "several different definitions" in this issue have emerged since the conclusion of the THB protocol, confirming "that many of the earlier controversies ... are alive and well".[26] From an ILO perspective, Kooijmans states that neither ILO Convention No 182 (WFCL) "nor the ILO at large take a position on the question whether prostitution could potentially be a legitimate form of work".[27] However, the ILO is of the view that children are considered not capable of volunteering for such type of work.[28] There has been some debate about the level of coercion required for engagement in worst form of child labour under clauses (a) "all forms of slavery or practices similar to slavery" and (b) "prostitution and the production of pornography or pornographic performances". Kooijmans points out, the classification of child prostitution and child pornography under a different heading from the clause a. classification, "all forms of slavery or practices similar to slavery, such as the sale and trafficking of children, debt bondage and serfdom and forced or compulsory labour", "indicates that it is irrelevant [in the context of ILO Convention No 182 (WFCL)] whether or not the involvement in prostitution had the consent of the child and/or its parents or guardians".[29] This is important as in a number of cases it

21 ILO Worst Forms of Child Labour Convention 1999 (C182).
22 Directive 2011/36/EU of the European Parliament and of the Council of 5 April 2011 on Preventing and Combating Trafficking in Human Beings and Protecting its Victims, and Replacing Council Framework Decision 2002/629/JHA, OJ L 101/1, preamble, paragraph 22.
23 Gallagher, op. cit., p 38.
24 F. Humbert, *The Challenge of Child Labour in International Law*, Cambridge University Press, 2009, p 75.
25 Gallagher, op. cit., p 39.
26 Ibid.
27 J. Kooijmans, 'Prostitution, Pornography and Pornographic Performances as Worst Forms of Child Labour: A comment on Article 3(b) of ILO Convention 182', in G. Nesil, L. Nogler, and M. Pertile, *Child Labour in a Globalized World: A Legal Analysis of ILO Action*, Ashgate 2008, p 131.
28 ILO, Human Trafficking and Forced Labour Exploitation – Guidelines for Legislation and Law Enforcement Special Action Programme to Combat Forced Labour, ILO, 2005, p 25.
29 Kooijmans, op. cit., p 134.

is "the parents who sell their children into sexual slavery".[30] Neither parental nor child consent is relevant under the THB Protocol.[31]

The ILO Convention No 182 (WFCL) Article 3.b prostitution etc. classification is understood to be "regardless of means of dissemination or consumption" a matter which was "left to the national law maker".[32] This has been further developed by some with reference to the UN CRC, Optional Protocol on the sale of children, child prostitution and child pornography,[33] which at the time of writing has 178 parties. It defines child prostitution as "the use of a child in sexual activities for remuneration or any other form of consideration".[34] It further defines child pornography as "any representation, by whatever means, of a child engaged in real or simulated or explicit sexual activities or any representation of the sexual parts of a child for primarily sexual purposes".[35]

The ILO itself says that child prostitution and pornography, a child being under 18, has always constituted "forced labour and a modern form of slavery".[36] This is in contrast to the rights-based UN CRC refers to "unlawful" sexual exploitation, recognising that "in some states sexual emancipation is reached at an earlier state than full majority", leaving some under 18-year-olds in a very vulnerable legal position.[37]

Sex tourism and technologically mediated child pornography are expressly referred to in the CRC optional protocol, which takes a more up to date approach to the issue of child pornography than ILO Convention No 182 (WFCL). Tackling technologically mediated child pornography, sex tourism or recruitment to prostitution poses its own problems from a transnational law enforcement perspective. As stated by Kirby and Penna "[a]s the 'wired' population expands" "offenders – both opportunistic and organised – exploit the potential of these opportunities to commit crime".[38] At the regional level the CoE has its 2007 Convention on the Protection of Children Against Sexual Exploitation and Sexual Abuse.[39] However, as pointed out by Vinkovic, "due to the cooperative nature of the" CoE this contains "nether effective victim protection mechanisms not a developed punishment system for perpetrators".[40] Reliance is made on individual contracting states effectively legislating and operationalising its provisions.

30 ILO (2005), p 26.
31 UN Protocol to Prevent, Suppress and Punish Trafficking in Persons, Especially Women and Children, supplementing the United Nations Convention against Transnational Organized Crime, 2000, UNTS, 2237, p 319, Article 3.c.
32 Humbert, op. cit., p 97.
33 CRC Optional Protocol – Sale of Children, op. cit.
34 Ibid, Article 2.b.
35 Ibid, Article 2.c.
36 ILO (2005), p 25.
37 Humbert, op. cit., p 75.
38 S. Kirby and S. Penna, 'Policing Mobile Criminality: Towards a Situational Crime Prevention Approach to Organised Crime', in R. Clarke, K. Bullock and N. Tilley, *Situational Prevention of Organised Crime*, Willan, 2010, p 198.
39 CETS 201.
40 M. Vinkovic, 'The "Unbroken Marriage" – Trafficking and Child Labour in Europe' (2010) 13 *Journal of Money Laundering Control* 2, p 93.

The above complex legal framework for defining relevant crimes against children forms the backdrop for the development of transnational law enforcement and justice provisions. ILO Convention No 182 (WFCL) calls for states, at Article 8, to "assist one another in giving effect to the provisions of this Convention through enhanced international cooperation" which must, on any rational reading of the provisions, include transnational law enforcement, as well as "including" the other measures enumerated in the article, "support for social and economic development, poverty eradication programmes and universal education". ILO Recommendation 190, paragraph 12 calls for the criminalisation of "all forms of slavery or practices similar to slavery, as well as the use, procuring or offering of a child for prostitution, the production of pornography or pornographic performances, and for illicit activities". It calls for the use of "other criminal, civil or administrative remedies such as special supervision of enterprises which have used the worst forms of child labour; and, in cases of persistent violation, consideration of temporary or permanent revoking of permits to operate".[41]

The CRC Optional Protocol while being attached to the rights focused CRC, takes an "explicitly criminal justice approach to the issue and detailing obligations accordingly",[42] which includes requiring the relevant offences to be made extraditable.[43] Transnational cooperation is also important in combatting the worst form of child labour, to include the trafficking of children for sexual exploitation.[44] ILO Convention No 182 (WFCL)'s supporting recommendation (190) recommends, at paragraph 16, "enhanced international cooperation and/ or assistance" to include "mutual legal assistance" and "technical assistance including the exchange of information". In addition, paragraph 15 of the recommendations calls for the development of extraterritorial effect of domestic criminal laws, to be able to prosecute a state's nationals when they "commit offences under its national provisions", "even when these offences are committed in another country". Kooijmans states that ILO Recommendation 190 reflects "a global consensus on its contents" which should be used as a guideline for all states "at local or international level".[45] However, more concrete developments can be reported in a Eurocentric context in technologically mediated child pornography, and detailed provisions for transnational law enforcement in the context of the sale of children, child prostitution, child pornography and child sex tourism.

The lack of a UN legal framework to combat cyber-crime has resulted in the global focus shifting to the CoE's Convention on Cyber Crime 2001.[46] This treaty, drafted by the CoE in conjunction with the USA, but without the support of Russia, operates as either the lead international treaty for its now 68 ratifications

41 D. Rishikesh, 'The Worst Forms of Child Labour: A Guide to the ILO Convention 182 and Recommendation 190', in G. Nesil, L. Nogler, and M. Pertile, ***Child Labour in a Globalized World A legal analysis of ILO Action***, Ashgate 2008, p 89.

42 Gallagher, op. cit., p 67.

43 CRC Optional Protocol – Sale of Children, op. cit., Article 5.

44 Kooijmans, op. cit., p 137.

45 Ibid.

46 CoE Convention on Cybercrime (Budapest), CETS No. 185.

(23 of which are non-CoE members), or as a formal model law for adoption in other parts of the world.[47] It has express provisions on "Offences related to Child Pornography", Article 9, which would go some way to addressing the need to combat the technologically mediated offences under ILO Convention No 182 (WFCL), Article 3.b. It should be noted that ILO Convention No 182 (WFCL) does not expressly call for the criminalisation of activities leading to the worst forms of child labour, but rather that states should take "effective measures to secure the prohibition and elimination of the worst forms of child labour as a matter of urgency".[48] It would be open to states, in acceding to the Convention on Cyber Crime, and implementing resulting national provisions, to prohibit activities leading to a broader range of worst form of child labour, such as for example, facilitating child sex tourism. They could adopt the procedures in the Convention on Cyber Crime to deal with resulting interjurisdictional issues or use them as a model for further bilateral or multilateral treaties on transnational law enforcement.

There are, at a transnational law enforcement level (apparently the same) 24/7 response networks, operating under one of two distinct practitioner frameworks. Either the 24/7 law enforcement framework[49] is operating under the G8's "Lyon-Roma High Tech-Crime Group",[50] which responds to "urgent requests for co-operation in cases involving electronic evidence",[51] or the network operates based on Article 35 of the above-mentioned Convention on Cybercrime. While the G8 network, as reported in 2007,[52] has a much wider global reach,[53] contracting states to the Convention on Cybercrime, in addition to accessing the network for alerts, also benefit from conflict of jurisdiction rules which facilitates

47 M.G. Porcedda, 'Transatlantic Approaches to Cybersecurity and Cybercrime', in P. Pawlak, *The EU–US Security and Justice Agenda in Action*, Chaillot Papers, Institute for Security Studies, European Union 2011, p 43.

48 ILO Worst Forms of Child Labour Convention, Article 1.

49 Communication from the Commission to the Council, the European Parliament, the Economic and Social Committee and the Committee of the Regions, Creating a Safer Information Society by Improving the Security of Information Infrastructures and Combating Computer-related crime, Brussels, 26.1.2001 COM (2000) 890 final, at 5.4 Practical Co-operation at International Level, p 21.

50 Communication from the Commission to the European Parliament, the Council and the Committee of the Regions, Towards a general policy on the fight against cyber-crime, Brussels, 22.5.2007, COM (2007) 267 final, *1.2.2. Traditional Crime on Electronic Networks* p 5.

51 Communication from the Commission (2001), op. cit., 5.4, Practical Co-operation at International Level, p 21.

52 The OAS document, The G8 24/7 Network of Contact Points, Protocol Statement, presented to the OAS Regional *Cyber Crime* Workshop, April 2007, and available at www.oas.org/juridico/english/cyb20_network_en.pdf.

53 In the 2007 returns Brazil, Chile, Dominican Republic, Hong Kong (China), India, Indonesia, Israel, Jamacia, Korea, Mauritius, Mexico, Morocco, Namibia, New Zealand, Nigeria, Pakistan, Singapore, Taiwan, Thailand, Tunisia, Malaysia, Peru, and the Philippines were all reported as members. No doubt more countries have joined in the intervening period.

international cooperation, with the Convention on Cybercrime "acting as a mutual legal assistance treaty in the absence of an agreement between the cooperating parties".[54] Those countries in the G8 network which are not also members of the Convention on Cybercrime, will be lacking this further elaboration of a transnational legal and law enforcement framework, and will have to fall back on any traditional bi-lateral arrangements which may or may not be in place. It is arguable that the Convention on Cybercrime 24/7 Network could be adopted to cover the online recruitment for THB, should its members, or the EU members among themselves, so agree. The EU's Global Alliance Against Child Sexual Abuse Online is an example of the potential for developments in this area.[55]

The CoE operates the Convention on the Protection of Children against Sexual Exploitation and Sexual Abuse (Lanzarote Convention),[56] while the EU enacted[57] Directive 2011/93/EU on combatting the sexual abuse and sexual exploitation of children and child pornography.[58] At the time of writing the Lanzarote Convention has 48 signatures and ratifications, being all of the member states of the CoE, with now non-CoE states Russia and Tunisia having also signed and ratified this convention. The EU directive operates against the backdrop of Article 24 of the EU Charter of Fundamental Rights 2000,[59] and the Council Decision to combat child pornography on the internet,[60] and related policy areas, such as the backdrop of the then EU Youth Strategy,[61] and the EU's Safer Internet Programme.[62]

54 Porcedda, op. cit., p 43.
55 See https://ec.europa.eu/home-affairs/what-we-do/policies/organized-crime-and-human-trafficking/global-alliance-against-child-abuse.
56 Council of Europe Convention on the Protection of Children against Sexual Exploitation and Sexual Abuse, 2007, CETS No. 201.
57 With pre-Brexit UK and Ireland opt ins, and Denmark opt out.
58 Directive 2011/93/EU of the European Parliament and of the Council of 13 December 2011 on combating the sexual abuse and sexual exploitation of children and child pornography, and replacing Council Framework Decision 2004/68/JHA, OJ L 335, 2011/12/18, p 1.
59 EUCFR Article 24.1 on the rights of the child, provides that "Children shall have the right to such protection and care as is necessary for their well-being". (OJ C 326, 26.10.2012, p 391.)
60 Council Decision 2000/375/JHA of 29 May 2000 to combat child pornography on the Internet, OJ L 138, 09/06/2000 p 1.
61 Communication from the Commission to the Council, the European Parliament, the European Economic and Social Committee and the Committee of the Regions – An EU Strategy for Youth: Investing and Empowering – A renewed open method of coordination to address youth challenges and opportunities, COM/2009/0200 final.
62 The Safer Internet programme (2009–2013) (Decision 1315/2008/EC of the European Parliament and of the council of 16 December 2008 establishing a multiannual community programme on protecting children using the Internet and other communication technologies, OJ L 348, 24.12.2008, p. 118–127) was the successor to the Safer Internet plus programme (2005–2008) (Decision no 854/2005/ EC of the European Parliament and of the council of 11 May 2005 establishing a multiannual Community Programme on promoting safer use of the Internet and new online technologies, OJ L 149, 11.6.2005, p. 1–13.)

As with the UN, EU and CoE provisions on THB,[63] both EU Directive 2011/93/EU and the Lanzarote Convention provide that a child is someone under the age of 18 years.[64] Both documents contain provisions on the substantive criminal laws on sexual abuse,[65] with the Lanzarote Convention defining offences concerning child prostitution[66] and the EU directive, child exploitation.[67] Both documents cover combating child pornography,[68] and include offences concerning the participation of a child in pornographic performances.[69] They also cover solicitation of children for sexual purposes,[70] and provisions on aiding or abetting an attempt of any CoE or EU directive offences.[71] The Lanzarote Convention for its part, has provisions on the corruption of children,[72] while Directive 2011/93/EU goes further on the issue of sexually explicit images, with child pornography to include "realistic images of a child engaged in sexually explicit conduct or realistic images of the sexual organs of a child, for primarily sexual purposes".[73]

The Lanzarote Convention provides for covert operations and the use of "units or investigative services to identify the victims of offences" through "analysing child pornography material, such as photographs and audio-visual recordings" to include those obtainable online.[74] The EU directive talks about "interception of communications, covert surveillance including electronic surveillance, monitoring of bank accounts or other financial investigations" and the use of "concealed identity" by law enforcement authorities on the internet.[75] It also provides that "effective investigative tools, such as those which are used in organised crime and other serious crimes cases" should be available to "persons, units or services" responsible for investigating crimes under the directive.[76] The EU directive also speaks about either the removal of child pornographic content from the internet, or where is this is not possible the blocking of access from EU member states jurisdictions.[77] In addition the Lanzarote Convention provides that the initiation of investigations or proceedings "shall not be dependent upon the report or accusation made by a victim", and that proceedings should continue "even if the victim has withdrawn his or her statements",[78] recognising that victims of child

63 THB Protocol, Article 3.d, CoE Convention on Action against Trafficking in Human Beings 2015, (Warsaw Convention), Article 4.d and EU THB directive, Directive 2011/36/EU, Article 2.6.
64 CETS 201 Article 3, Directive 2011/93/EU, Article 2.
65 Lanzarote Convention, Article 18, Directive 2011/93/EU, Article 3.
66 Lanzarote Convention, Article 10.
67 Directive 2011/93/EU, Article 4.
68 Lanzarote Convention, Article 11, Directive 2011/93/EU, Article 5.
69 Lanzarote Convention, Article 21, Directive 2011/93/EU, Article 4.2.
70 Lanzarote Convention, Article 23, Directive 2011/93/EU, Article 6.
71 Lanzarote Convention, Article 24, Directive 2011/93/EU, Article 7.
72 Lanzarote Convention, Article 22.
73 Directive 2011/93/EU, Article 2.iv
74 Lanzarote Convention, Article 30.
75 Directive 2011/93/EU, preamble paragraph 27.
76 Directive 2011/93/EU Article 15.3.
77 Directive 2011/93/EU, preamble, paragraph 47.
78 Lanzarote Convention, Article 32.

sexual exploitation are inherently vulnerable and highly susceptible to intimidation. This provision is replicated in the EU directive.[79] The Lanzarote Convention provides that the "confidentiality rules imposed ... on certain professionals (working with children should) not constitute an obstacle" to reporting that they have "reasonable grounds for believing that a child is the victim of sexual exploitation or sexual abuse",[80] a provision which is replicated in the EU directive.[81]

It is recognised in both the EU and CoE provisions that when conducting the criminal investigation and prosecution special measures need to be put in place to protect child victims.[82] Both CoE and EU provisions provide that prosecution for child sex abuse offences should be possible for a period of time after the victim has reached the age of majority.[83] Both legal documents call for the establishment of jurisdiction not only when the offence is committed in their territory, to include, as stated in the Lanzarote Convention, "on board a ship flying the flag of that Party" and "on board an aircraft registered under the laws of that Party" but also where the offender is one of its nationals,[84] following the active personality principle to criminal jurisdiction. The Lanzarote Convention calls for the jurisdiction to be extended to a "person who has his or her habitual residence in its territory",[85] something which is a further jurisdictional option under the EU directive.[86] The EU directive also provides for further extension of jurisdiction for offences "committed for the benefit of a legal person established in its territory".[87] Both legal documents provide the optional extension of jurisdiction for when the offence is committed against one of its national or habitual resident,[88] thereby following the passive personality principle. Both also provide that the prosecution of offences should not be subordinated to the condition that a victim needs to make a report in the place where the offence was committed, or for there to be a "denunciation from the State of the place where the offence was committed".[89]

When it comes to punishment of child sex abuse crimes, both documents have provisions on aggravating circumstances,[90] and corporate liability.[91] Both the EU and the CoE set out a list of aggravating circumstances in their legal documents,[92] the EU provisions listing being "offences against children in a particularly vulnerable position", offences committed within the family, offences committed by several persons acting together, offences committed within an organised crime

79 Directive 2011/93/EU, Article 15.1
80 Lanzarote Convention, Article 12.
81 Directive 2011/93/EU, Article 16.
82 Directive 2011/93/EU Article 20 and Lanzarote Convention, Articles 30–32.
83 Directive 2011/93/EU, Article 15.2. Lanzarote Convention, Article 33.
84 Directive 2011/93/EU, Article 17.1, Lanzarote Convention, Article 25.1.
85 Lanzarote Convention, Article 25.1.a.
86 Directive 2011/93/EU, Article 17.2.c.
87 Directive 2011/93/EU, Article 17.2.b.
88 Lanzarote Convention, Article 25.2, Directive 2011/93/EU, Article 17.2.a.
89 Lanzarote Convention, Article 25.6, Directive 2011/93/EU, Article 17.5.
90 Directive 2011/93/EU Article 9, Lanzarote Convention, Article 28.
91 Lanzarote Convention, Article 26, 27, Directive 2011/93/EU, Articles 12 and 13.
92 Lanzarote Convention Article 28 and Directive 2011/93/EU, Article 9.

framework, the offender has "deliberately or recklessly endangered the life of the child" or the "offence involved serious violence or caused serious harm to the child". In addition to provisions on victim support[93] and preventative measures,[94] both the EU directive on child sex abuse and the Lanzarote Convention contain provisions on disqualifications arising from child sex abuse convictions.[95] Victim protection provisions are set out in Article 31 of the Lanzarote Convention, while the EU would be relying on separate EU legal provisions in this area.[96]

As pointed out by Farka, the age of consent varies greatly among states.[97] Missing from the Lanzarote Convention but present in Directive 2011/93/EU are the Article 8 provisions providing for EU member states to make their own provisions on "consensual sexual activities" between "peers, who are close in age and degree of psychological and physical development or maturity, in so far as the acts did not involve any abuse". The EU directive further has provisions on measures against advertising abuse opportunities and child sex tourism,[98] with the CoE convention covering the issue of advertising the offences[99] but failing to call for the criminalisation of child sex tourism, although Article 9.2 of the Lanzarote Convention does seek the participation of the travel and tourism industries in policies to protect sexual abuse of children. The EU directive also contains measures against websites containing or disseminating child pornography.[100] There are no corresponding provision in the Lanzarote Convention.

At the CoE level, the Convention on Cybercrime[101] does require the prohibition of online child pornography, as one of its content-related offences.[102] It does not, unfortunately, cover the issue of online pornography generally, or the online facilitation of trafficking of adults. For the Convention on Cybercrime a child, in the context of online child pornography, is defined as someone under the age of 18, but individual acceding jurisdictions can opt for an under 16 age limit.[103] At the time of writing the Convention on Cybercrime is the leading global convention on cybercrime, with 68 ratifications.

The Lanzarote Convention calls on contracting parties to engage in cross border law enforcement to combat sexual exploitation and sexual abuse of

93 Directive 2011/93/EU Article 18, 19, Lanzarote Convention, Articles 10, 11, 14.
94 Directive 2011/93/EU Articles 22–24, Lanzarote Convention, Articles 6–9, 15–17.
95 Directive 2011/93/EU Article 10, Article 27.2.b Lanzarote Convention.
96 E.g. Directive 2012/29/EU of the European Parliament and of the Council of 25 October 2012 establishing minimum standards on the rights, support and protection of victims of crime, and replacing Council Framework Decision 2001/220/JHA, OJ L 315, 2012/11/14, p 57.
97 I. Farka, 'Extra-Territorial Jurisdiction: A Prosecutorial Tool to Combat Child Trafficking from Albania', in G. Wylie and P. McRedmond, *Human Trafficking in Europe: Character, Causes and Consequences*, Palgrave Macmillan, 2010, p 210.
98 Directive 2011/93/EU, Article 21.
99 Lanzarote Convention, Article 8.2.
100 Directive 2011/93/EU, Article 25.
101 CETS No. 185.
102 Budapest Convention, Article 9.
103 Ibid, Article 9.3.

children,[104] using both the provisions of that document and "relevant applicable international and regional instruments, arrangements agreed on the basis of uniform or reciprocal legislation and internal laws, to the widest extent possible". These transnational arrangements are for three purposes: "investigation and proceedings", "preventing and combatting" these crimes, and "protecting and providing assistance to victims". While there is no express reference in the EU Directive 2011/93/EU to transnational law enforcement, this is built into the EU legal and operational framework of the AFSJ. As with THB, "sexual abuse and sexual exploitation, including child abuse material and solicitation of children for sexual purposes" are listed as crimes for which both Europol[105] and Eurojust,[106] are competent to act, if it is serious crime affecting two or more EU member states.

The UN's CRC's Optional Protocol on the Sale of Children, Child Prostitution and Child Pornography 2000 requires that its Article 3.1 offences of "sexual exploitation of the child", "transfer of organs of the child for profit" and the "engagement of the child in forced labour" all "be included as extraditable offences in every extradition treaty subsequently concluded" by state parties to the Optional Protocol 2000.[107] If there is no such extradition treaty, but a state party to the Optional Protocol 2000 receives a request of extradition for the Article 3.1 offences, then "it may consider the present Protocol to be a legal basis for extradition in respect of such offences".[108] The European Arrest Warrant[109] for internal EU transnational arrests, covers "sexual exploitation of children and child pornography" as well "trafficking in human beings", as does the post Brexit UK/EU surrender provisions under the Trade and Cooperation Agreement.[110]

Illegal Adoption

A further human security trafficking related risk for children is that of the purchase of children for illegal adoption. Article 35 of the UN CRC provides that its member states "shall take all appropriate national, bilateral and multilateral

104 Lanzarote Convention, Article 38.
105 Regulation (EU) 2016/794 of the European Parliament and of the Council of 11 May 2016 on the European Union Agency for Law Enforcement Cooperation (Europol) and replacing and repealing Council Decisions 2009/371/JHA, 2009/934/JHA, 2009/935/JHA, 2009/936/JHA and 2009/968/JHA, OJ L 135/53, Article 3 Objectives and Annex I paragraph 1.
106 Regulation (EU) 2018/1727 of the European Parliament and of the Council of 14 November 2018 on the European Union Agency for Criminal Justice Cooperation (Eurojust), and replacing and repealing Council Decision 2002/187/JHA, OJ L 295/138, Article 3.1 Competence of Eurojust and Annex 1 paragraph 1.
107 CRC Optional Protocol – sale of children, op. cit., Article 5.1.
108 Ibid, Article 5.2.
109 Council Framework Decision 2002/584/JHA of 13 June 2002 on the European arrest warrant and the surrender procedures between Member States, 2002, OJ L 190/1, Article 2.1.
110 UK EU Trade and Cooperation Agreement, OJ L 149/10, Articles 599.5.

measures to prevent the abduction of, the sale of or traffic in children for any purpose or in any form". The Optional Protocol to the CRC on the sale of children, child prostitution and child pornography, covers the issue of the sale of children, separate from child prostitution and child pornography. Its Article 2.a provides that the "Sale of children means any act or transaction whereby a child is transferred by any person or group of persons to another for remuneration or any other consideration". This scenario became an issue in the English case of *R v P*, where, despite its web of legal provisions "there [did] not appear to be any specific offence of selling a baby or a child to people who appear to be intent on treating the child properly" under English law at that time.[111] The issue of correct and adequate implementation by signatory states of international legal obligations arises in many jurisdictions.

The Hague Convention on Intercountry Adoption 1993[112] is also relevant, with Smolin writing about the Hague Convention in the context of "child laundering". For Smolin, "child laundering" is "(1) obtaining children illicitly through purchase or abduction; (2) falsifying the child's paperwork to hide both the illicit conduct and the child's history and origins; and (3) processing the child through the intercountry adoption system as an 'orphan' and then adoptee".[113] He writes from a US perspective, with, in 2006, a particular concern for children being sent to the USA from Colombia, where he speaks about children being "bought or stolen"[114] and Guatemalan children, where he speaks about baby-farming,[115] and Guatemala having "created one of the most commercialized and profiteering system of intercountry adoption yet seen".[116] Neither of these two countries had ratified the Hague Convention at the time.[117] There will be other countries in similar situations. However, as Smolin points out, the Hague convention is not a "complete response to child laundering/ adoption trafficking",[118] and that "the problems with intercountry adoption and child trafficking are systematic and recurrent, not exceptional or occasional".[119]

111 D. A. Thomas, 'Sentencing: *R v P* – sale of baby' (2012) 4 *Criminal Law Review*, p 303.

112 Hague Convention on Protection of Children and Co-operation in Respect of Intercountry Adoption, 27 May 1993 (HCCH 33).

113 D. M. Smolin, 'Child Laundering as Exploitation: Applying Anti-Trafficking Norms to Intercountry Adoption under the Coming Hague Regime' (2007) 32 *Vermont Law Rev.*, pp 2–3.

114 D. M. Smolin, 'Child Laundering: How the Intercountry Adoption System Legitimizes and Incentivizes the Practices of Buying, Trafficking, Kidnaping, and Stealing Children' (2006) 52 *Wayne Law Review*, p 144.

115 Ibid, p 168.

116 Ibid.

117 D. M. Smolin, 'Abduction, Sale and Traffic in Children in the Context of Intercountry Adoption' (2010) *Information Document No 1*, Hague Conference on Private International Law, p 20.

118 Ibid, p 22.

119 D. M. Smolin, 'Intercountry Adoption as Child Trafficking' (2004) 39 *Valparaiso University Law Review* 2. p 324.

Smolin is of the view that the real dangers arise from non-implementation or "inadequate implementation of the Hague Convention"[120] and "Hague receiving nations [choosing] not to apply Hague standards to adoptions from non-Hague sending nations".[121] He view is that the Hague Convention is an incomplete anti-trafficking treaty in the context of inter-country adoption,[122] with the treaty being "designed to function within a broader context of other legal instruments, presumably including (among others) the Convention on the Rights of the Child".[123] The Hague Convention is "designed to prevent 'only indirectly'" trafficking in children as it expects that proper "observance of the Convention's rule will bring about the avoidance of such abuses".[124] It is unlikely, however, that Smolin had in mind the UN THB Protocol as one of those other legal instruments. Given the difficulty in tracing the paperwork and money in the case of illegal inter-country adoption, the question arises whether the THB Protocol, when read with the Palermo Convention has sufficient provisions to tackle this crime, and whether those provisions have been effectively deployed to combat it. There are certainly enough provisions to tackle this type of transnational organised crime, and the allied bribery and corruption that Smolin speaks about in his analysis of "child laundering". Again, reliance on the testimony of the mothers of the children would be legally problematic, as with other forms of THB victim testimony.

If intercountry adoptions are to be permitted, and not be seen as exploitative *per se*, it is necessary that receiving countries of intercountry adoptions, which must necessarily be involved in the issuing of visas for the entry of the child, and the formal registration of the child as being adopted, need to engage in due diligences to ensure that the baby supply chain is not compromised by child laundering or other abusive practices. As stated by Smolin, "receiving nations … cannot simply outsource their own responsibilities for intercountry adoption to sending nations" which may have "limited government capacities, lack of political will" or systems compromised in corruption.[125] Following the human security approach, and freedom from fear, the commodification of children needs to be combatted, the THB understanding of country of origin, transit and destination needs to be deployed, with transnational legal and law enforcement frameworks developed to tackle this form of abuse. The EU has not itself legislated on the issue of inter-country adoption. The CoE does have the European Convention on the Adoption of Children 1967,[126] which at the time of writing is in force in 16 countries.[127] The 1967 document does not address

120 Smolin (2010), op. cit., p 3.
121 Ibid, p 4.
122 Ibid, p 7.
123 Ibid, p 8.
124 Ibid, p 7.
125 Ibid, p 21.
126 ETS No.058.
127 Austria, Czech Republic, Denmark, Germany, Greece, Ireland, Italy, Latvia, Liechtenstein, Malta, North Macedonia, Poland, Portugal, Romania, Switzerland, and the United Kingdom.

the trafficking and sale of children, something which is addressed by the much later 1993 Hague Convention on Intercountry Adoption,[128] discussed above.

While the focus of this chapter has been on children, having been born to the age of 18, a new trend in THB is being reported from Viet Nam, that of foetus trafficking.[129] This is reported as involving the sale of foetuses "while still in the womb, then born abroad and given to traffickers",[130] in the cases being reported, in China. This is presumably to avoid the impact of Viet Nam laws to combat THB and to protect children. No doubt this is also happening in other countries globally, and both national and transnational legal frameworks, and law enforcement needs to be developed to combat the organised crime groups involved. Thyu *et al.* discuss the issues of embryo and foetuses trafficking, which leads to the question where exactly the boundary line between THB and trafficking in organs, tissues and cells. Presumably, different jurisdictions will draw the line between these two issues at different places, depending on their view of when exactly life starts from the point of view of their criminal laws, and which will be reflected in their laws on abortion.

Conclusion

The situation of children needs to be specifically considered when developing transnational law enforcement frameworks, however the THB Protocol is lacking full consideration of this issue. This lack of detail requires the examination of other documents, to include the UN CRC and its two optional protocols. Also required to fill the gaps are the ILO Convention on the World Forms of Child Labour 1999 (No 182) and ILO Recommendation 190 – Worst Forms of Child Labour Recommendation 1999. There are, however, weaknesses in both the UN CRC documents and the ILO Convention No 182 (WFCL) when it comes to the definition of a child, with the THB Protocol being much clearer in stating that it is anyone under the age of 18 years. Consent, whether that be from the parent or the child itself, also muddies the waters when it comes to the operation of both the CRC and its protocols and ILO Convention No 182 (WFCL) for all forms of exploitation. In addition, the ILO Convention No 182 (WFCL) does not cover all possible instances of exploitation, as family and small-scale agricultural holdings[131] and "domestic service" are not expressly provided for.[132] There is clarity under the THB Protocol that a child cannot consent to exploitation.[133]

128 Which at the time of writing has 105 contracting parties.
129 H. L. Thyu, H. T. H. Yen, and N. Q. Bao, 'Fetus Trafficking in Viet Nam – the New Criminal Method of Human Trafficking', 2021, 10 *International Journal of Criminology and Sociology*.
130 Ibid, p 1594.
131 ILO Minimum Age Convention, Article 5.3.
132 Cullen, op. cit., p 140/1.
133 THB Protocol, Article 3.c.

Not covered in ILO Convention No 182 (WFCL), however, is "adoption or child victims of organ transplants".[134] The Optional Protocol to the CRC on the sale of children, child prostitution and child pornography does refer at Article 2 to the "sale of children … for remuneration, or any other consideration". While the issue of trafficking of children for inter country adoption is addressed in the Hague Convention on Intercountry Adoption 1993, the lack of provisions to combat transnational sale of children for adoption also needs to be addressed by legislators. The Optional Protocol to the CRC on the sale of children, child prostitution and child pornography does refer, at Article 3.b, to the "transfer of organs of the child in for profit".

The Palermo Convention together with the THB Protocol, when due consideration is given to subsequent legal provisions on the rights of children, can be deployed to combat child trafficking, to include intercountry adoption. In addition, when read with the CoE Convention on Cybercrime and the use of either, depending on the jurisdiction, the G8 or the CoE 24/7 Lyon-Roma High Tech-Crime Group, further opportunities arise to combat those human security risks which arise affecting children online.

Bibliography

Cullen, H., *The Role of International Law in the Elimination of Child Labour*, Martinus Nijhoff Publishers, 2007.

Farka, I., 'Extra-Territorial Jurisdiction: A Prosecutorial Tool to Combat Child Trafficking from Albania', in Wylie, G. and McRedmond, P., *Human Trafficking in Europe, Character, Causes and Consequences*, Palgrave Macmillan, 2010, 198–215.

Gallagher, A., *The International Law of Human Trafficking*, Cambridge University Press, 2010.

GRETA Evaluation Report, United Kingdom Third Evaluation Round: Access to Justice and Effective Remedies for Victims of Trafficking in Human Beings, GRETA (2021)12, Council of Europe, 2021.

Humbert, F., *The Challenge of Child Labour in International Law*, Cambridge University Press, 2009.

Kirby, S. and Penna, S., 'Policing Mobile Criminality: Towards a Situational Crime Prevention Approach to Organised Crime', in Clarke, R., Bullock, K., and Tilley, N., *Situational Prevention of Organised Crime*, Willan, 2010, 192–211.

Nesil, G., Nogler, L. and Pertile, M., *Child Labour in a Globalized World A legal analysis of ILO Action*, Ashgate, 2008.

Porcedda, M.G., 'Transatlantic Approaches to Cybersecurity and Cybercrime', in Pawlak, P., *The EU–US Security and Justice Agenda in Action*, Chaillot Papers, Institute for Security Studies, European Union 2011/127, 41–54.

Smolin, D. M., 'Abduction, Sale and Traffic in Children in the Context of Intercountry Adoption' (2010) Information Document No 1, Hague Conference on Private International Law.

Smolin, D. M., 'Child Laundering as Exploitation: Applying Anti-Trafficking Norms to Intercountry Adoption under the Coming Hague Regime' (2007) 32 *Vermont Law Rev.*, 1–55.

134 Rishikesh, op. cit., p 85/86.

Smolin, D. M., 'Child Laundering: How the Intercountry Adoption System Legitimizes and Incentivizes the Practices of Buying, Trafficking, Kidnaping, and Stealing Children' (2006) 52 *Wayne Law Review*, 113–200.

Smolin, D. M. 'Intercountry Adoption as Child Trafficking' (2004) 39 *Valparaiso University Law Review* 2, 281–326.

Stoyanova, V., 'Dancing on the Borders of Article 4: Human Trafficking and the European Court of Human Rights in the *Rantsev* Case' (2012) 30 *Netherlands Institute of Human Rights* 2, 163–194.

Thomas, D. A., 'Sentencing: *R v P* – Sale of Baby' (2012) 4 *Criminal Law Review*, 303–304.

Thyu, H. L., Yen, H. T. H. and Bao, N. Q., 'Fetus Trafficking in Viet Nam – the New Criminal method of Human Trafficking' (2021) 10 *International Journal of Criminology and Sociology*, 1594–1603.

Vinkovic, M., 'The "Unbroken Marriage" – Trafficking and Child Labour in Europe' (2010) 13 *Journal of Money Laundering Control* 2, 87–102.

Legislation

Charter on Fundamental Rights of the European Union 2000, OJ C 326, 26 October 2012, p 391.

CoE Convention on Cybercrime 2001, CETS No. 185.

CoE European Convention on the Adoption of Children 1967, CETS No. 058.

Communication from the Commission to the Council, the European Parliament, the European Economic and Social Committee and the Committee of the Regions – An EU Strategy for Youth: Investing and Empowering – A Renewed Open Method of Coordination to Address Youth Challenges and Opportunities, COM/2009/0200 final.

Communication from the Commission to the Council, the European Parliament, the Economic and Social Committee and the Committee of the Regions, Creating a Safer Information Society by Improving the Security of Information Infrastructures and Combating Computer-Related Crime, Brussels, 26.1.2001 COM (2000) 890 final.

Communication from the Commission to the European Parliament, the Council and the Committee of the Regions, Towards a General Policy on the Fight against Cybercrime, Brussels, 22.5.2007, COM (2007) 267 final.

Council Decision 2000/375/JHA of 29 May 2000 to Combat Child Pornography on the Internet, OJ L 138, 09/06/2000, p 1.

Council of Europe Convention on the Protection of Children against Sexual Exploitation and Sexual Abuse, 2007, CETS No. 201.

Council Framework Decision 2002/584/JHA of 13 June 2002 on the European Arrest Warrant and the Surrender Procedures between Member States, 2002, OJ L 190/1.

Decision 1315/2008/EC of the European Parliament and of the Council of 16 December 2008 Establishing a Multiannual Community Programme on Protecting Children Using the Internet and Other Communication Technologies, OJ L 348, 24.12.2008, 118–127.

Decision 854/2005/ EC of the European Parliament and of the Council of 11 May 2005 Establishing a Multiannual Community Programme on Promoting Safer Use of the Internet and New Online Technologies, OJ L 149, 11.6.2005, 1–13.

Directive 2011/36/EU, of the European Parliament and of the Council of the 5 April 2011 on Preventing and Combating Trafficking in Human Beings and Protecting its Victims, and Replacing Council Framework Decision 2002/629/JHA, OJ L 101/1.

Directive 2011/93/EU of the European Parliament and of the Council of 13 December 2011 on Combating the Sexual Abuse and Sexual Exploitation of Children and Child Pornography, and Replacing Council Framework Decision 2004/68/JHA, OJ L 335, 2011/12/18, p 1.

Directive 2012/29/EU of the European Parliament and of the Council of 25 October 2012 Establishing Minimum Standards on the Rights, Support and Protection of Victims of Crime, and Replacing Council Framework Decision 2001/220/JHA, OJ L 315, 2012/11/14, p 57.

Hague Convention on Protection of Children and Co-operation in Respect of Intercountry Adoption, 27 May 1993 (HCCH 33).

ILO Minimum Age Convention 1973 (C138).

ILO Worst Forms of Child Labour Convention 1999 (C182).

ILO, Human Trafficking and Forced Labour Exploitation – Guidelines for Legislation and Law Enforcement Special Action Programme to Combat Forced Labour, ILO, 2005.

OAS document, The G8 24/7 Network of Contact Points, Protocol Statement, presented to the OAS Regional Cyber Crime Workshop, April 2007, and available at www.oas.org/juridico/english/cyb20_network_en.pdf.

Optional Protocol to the Convention on the Rights of the Child on the Sale of Children, Child Prostitution and Child Pornography 2000, UNTS 2171, p 227.

Optional Protocol to the Convention on the Rights of the Child on the Involvement of Children in Armed Conflict, 2000, UNTS 2217, p 27531.

Regulation (EU) 2018/1727 of the European Parliament and of the Council of 14 November 2018 on the European Union Agency for Criminal Justice Cooperation (Eurojust), and Replacing and Repealing Council Decision 2002/187/JHA, OJ L 295/138.

Regulation (EU) 2016/794 of the European Parliament and of the Council of 11 May 2016 on the European Union Agency for Law Enforcement Cooperation (Europol) and Replacing and Repealing Council Decisions 2009/371/JHA, 2009/934/JHA, 2009/935/JHA, 2009/936/JHA and 2009/968/JHA, OJ L 135/53.

UK–EU Trade and Cooperation Agreement, OJ L 149/10.

UN Convention on the Rights of the Child, 1577 UNTS 3(1989).

UN Protocol to Prevent, Suppress and Punish Trafficking in Persons, Especially Women and Children, supplementing the United Nations Convention against Transnational Organized Crime 2000, UNTS, 2237, p 319.

Case

Siliadin v France, Application no. 73316/01, ECtHR, 26 October 2005.

Website

https://ec.europa.eu/home-affairs/what-we-do/policies/organized-crime-and-human-trafficking/global-alliance-against-child-abuse.

6 Europe

Introduction

As discussed in Chapter 1, Krisch's "enmeshment of laws"[1] becomes relevant when examining how laws are implemented in regions or individual states. There is a need to navigate and construct understanding when dealing with the "pluralist web of legal orders"[2] as it affects and influences the EU and its member states. Taking a Eurocentric approach to the transnational crime of THB requires several different layers and regional groupings to be considered. Most significantly are the contributions of both the EU[3] and the CoE.[4] However, other organisations must also be mentioned. For example, the Organisation for Security and Cooperation in Europe (OSCE)[5] is a consensus-based organisation, with its decisions being binding politically, but not legally. All EU and CoE member states are members of the OSCE, with the OSCE being the largest of the three.[6] It runs, *inter alia*, both police reform and THB programmes, which would involve the voluntary sharing of best practice in tackling specific issues. The OSCE THB programme covers the "4Ps": prevention, prosecution, protection, and partnership.[7] This is very similar to the anti-THB programmes being operated by the EU and the CoE. Stodiek points out that "there has been considerable overlap between the agendas of" the OSCE and the EU, with EU member states in the OSCE, by 2009, contributing 70% of the budget of the OSCE and

1 N. Krisch, *Beyond Constitutionalism: The Pluralist Structure of Postnational Law*, Oxford University Press, 2010, p 160.
2 Ibid., p 165.
3 At the time of writing 27 member states, with the UK now having left the EU post Brexit. UK THB provisions will be analysed in Chapter 7.
4 At the time of writing 46 member states, having expelled Russia on 22 February 2022.
5 At the time of writing 57 participating states located in Europe, North America, and Asia.
6 The OSCE additionally has the following countries as members: Belarus, Canada, Holy See, Kazakhstan, Kyrgyzstan, Mongolia, Tajikistan, Turkmenistan, United States, and Uzbekistan. The OSCE also operates Partnership for Co-operation programs with, in the Mediterranean, Algeria, Egypt, Israel, Jordan, Morocco and Tunisia, and in Asia with Afghanistan, Australia, Japan, The Republic of Korea and Thailand.
7 See www.osce.org/combating-human-trafficking.

DOI: 10.4324/9781003429791-6

80% of its personnel.[8] The OSCE has spoken of the need to "improve human security" in its Istanbul Summit Declaration in 1999.[9] It sees the development of common security of all of its member states as involving international cooperation,[10] with openness to cooperate with NGOs in order "to empower and engage the individual [being] a long-standing tradition in the OSCE".[11] Oberleitner points out that the OSCE is more focused on practical problem solving rather than security concepts, much of the "human security" concept can be seen to pervade its operation, through its focus on "comprehensive" and "cooperative" security, which is geared "towards protecting and empowering the individual" through the development of "trans-regional networks and in cooperation with civil society actors".[12] Through these activities "security is considered a common good and a shared value".[13] In this sense THB is seen as a "human security issue" rather than a border security concern, with Farka arguing that countries of origin should criminalise "smuggling and the participation of organized criminal groups in facilitating such smuggling".[14] This would include the forgery of travel documents and identity papers. In addition, Farka calls for the state's jurisdiction to "reach across illegally crossed borders", with a state assuming extra-territorial jurisdiction to enhance efforts "to prosecute smugglers who threatened the state's border security and increase the opportunity to protect the victims (human security)".[15] This is often best done with the assistance and support of other jurisdictions along the THB chain. In addition, stateless persons need to be protected when asserting extra-territorial jurisdiction.[16]

Unlike the OSCE, both the CoE and the EU operate as law making organisations, with both prioritising the concept of legality. Article 7 ECHR (No punishment without law) and Article 49 of the EU Charter of Fundamental Rights (CFR) (Principles of legality and proportionality of criminal offences and penalties) are key provisions. The principle of legality is a key issue when contrasting the interpretative approach to the ECHR, which is seen as a living document, to be contrasted with the need for there to be no crime without law in both the EU and its member states. The EU itself encounters issues with the traditional concept of direct effect of EU directives clashing with the need for legality in criminal law. Under CJEU case law, the *Berlusconi*

8 T. Stodiek, 'OSCE's Police-Related Activities: Lessons-Learned during the Last Decade' (2009) 30 *Security and Human Rights* 3, p 204.
9 G, Oberleitner, 'The OSCE and Human Security' (2008) 19 *Security and Human Rights* 1, p 67.
10 Ibid., p 69.
11 Ibid., p 70.
12 Ibid.
13 Ibid.
14 I. Farka, 'Extra-Territorial Jurisdiction: A Prosecutorial Tool to Combat Child Trafficking from Albania', in G. Wylie and P. McRedmond, *Human Trafficking in Europe, Character, Causes and Consequences*, Springer, 2010, p 207.
15 Ibid.
16 Ibid., p 208.

judgment,[17] extending the *Kolpinghuis*[18] judgment, leads to the "predominant view that a directive cannot by itself have the effect of determining or increasing the criminal liability of those who act in breach of the directive".[19] This is despite the fact that such a ruling would compromise "EU law's primacy and effectiveness".[20] Further case law is required on this point as the CJEU *Berlusconi* judgment predated the "recognition of the Union's criminal competences".[21] Meyer, writing about EU law, states that here is a need to understand "legality as a multilevel concept that integrates multiple legal actors and layers of legal sources today".[22] The principle of legality within the EU is seen as "a shared responsibility".[23] O'Higgins states that there must be "regard to national constitutions and to international instruments" when the CJEU develops its case law.[24]

The principle of reciprocity provides the relevant legal basis for enacting obligations under international agreements into domestic law, recognising the constitutional make up of a particular state. This is not, however, the principle operating within the now supranational EU AFSJ legal system. The EU rather uses the concepts of harmonisation, predominantly in commercial law, approximation, and mutual recognition. It recognises that "meaningful transposition of foreign legal elements in the criminal justice field" requires full conformation "with the substantive and procedural criminal legal framework of the recipient state".[25] Harmonisation, "has been a core instrument" of the EU and the CoE,[26] with EU law being described as being "arguably the most extensive and ambitious harmonisation project ever attempted".[27] The process of harmonisation "recognises the existences of differences"[28] in different legal systems, however the EU is

17 Joined cases C-387/02, C-391/02 and C-403/02, Criminal Proceedings against *Silvio Berlusconi* (C-387/02), *Sergio Adelchi* (C-391/02) and *Marcello Dell'Utri and Others* (C-403/02), [2005] ECR p I-03565.
18 Case 80/86 *Kolpinghuis Nijmegen* [1987] ECR 3969.
19 F. Meyer, 'C-387/02 Berlusconi and Others. The Berlusconi Judgment: A Cornerstone of European Legality', in V. Mitsilegas, A. di Martiona and L. Mancano, *The Court of Justice and European Criminal Law: Leading Cases in a Contextual Analysis*, Hart Publishing, 2019, p 41.
20 Ibid.
21 Ibid., p 43.
22 Ibid.
23 Ibid., p 47.
24 P. O'Higgins, 'The Interaction of the ILO, the Council of Europe and European Union Labour Standards', in B. Hepple, *Social and Labour Rights in a Global Context; International and Comparative Perspectives*, Cambridge, 2002, p 62/3.
25 I. Bantekas, 'The Principle of Mutual Recognition in EU Criminal Law' (2007) 32 *European Law Review* 3, p 367.
26 M. Andenas, C. Baasch Andersen and R. Ashcroft, 'Towards a Theory of Harmonisation' in M. Andenas, C. Baasch Andersen, *Theory and Practice of Harmonisation*, Edward Elgar, 2011, p 573.
27 Ibid.
28 S. Andreadakis, 'Regulatory Competition or Harmonisation: The Dilemma, the Alternatives and the Prospect of Reflexive Harmonisation', in M. Andenas and C. B. Andersen, *Theory and Practice of Harmonisation*, Edward Elgar, 2011, p 58.

of the view that these "differences do not necessarily pose any threat to coexistence and co-operation" at an EU level.[29] Andreadakis states that "when different cultures, nationalities and traditions manage to co-exist and create a harmonised legal system, such system combines all the virtues and values of them".[30] Approximation of criminal law, as used by the EU in the AFSJ, to include Directive 2011/36/EU on THB,[31] requires "a process whereby diverse legal elements retain their individuality, but adapt forming a coherent whole in order to accommodate a particular objective".[32] The EU's process of approximation of criminal law, and its adoption of mutual recognition, are regarded as independent process,[33] sometimes, but not always, interacting with each other in practice.[34]

Mutual recognition, as adopted by the AFSJ, is another "facet of possible co-operation" between the EU member states,[35] replacing the traditional international concept of mutual legal assistance and the traditional use of extradition treaties. As pointed out by Bantekas, the concept of mutual recognition is already well established in international law for civil judgments and arbitral awards.[36] Mutual recognition has led to less political involvement, and less use of the double criminality test under the European Arrest Warrant[37] and no such use under the European Investigation Order,[38] bringing greater speed and efficiency in EU transnational investigations and prosecutions. Lavenex argues that mutual recognition was adopted instead of the EU's preferred approach of supranational harmonisation, used by the EU in commercial matters, with the intention of "safeguarding of national sovereignty".[39] She argues, however, that mutual recognition, as exercised by "governments' cross-border law enforcement activities" has "much deeper implications in terms of horizontal transfers of sovereignty" than what happens in the EU's economic sphere.[40] This approach does give rise to issues regarding fundamental rights,[41] and "significant constitutional

29 Ibid.
30 Ibid.
31 Directive 2011/36/EU of the European Parliament and of the Council of 5 April 2011 on preventing and combating trafficking in human beings and protecting its victims, and replacing Council Framework Decision 2002/629/JHA, OJ L 101/1.
32 Bantekas, op. cit., p 368.
33 T. Obokata, *Transnational Organised Crime in International Law*, Hart Publishing, 2010, p 187.
34 Bantekas, op. cit., p 366.
35 Ibid.
36 Ibid., p 355.
37 Council Framework Decision 2002/584/JHA on the European Arrest Warrant, OJ L 190, 18/07/2002, p 1, Article 2.2.
38 Directive 2014/41/EU of the European Parliament and of the Council of 3 April 2014 regarding the European Investigation Order in criminal matters, OJ L 130/1, Article 1.2.
39 S. Lavenex, 'Mutual Recognition and the Monopoly of Force: Limits of the Single Market Analogy' (2007) 14 *Journal of European Public Policy* 5, p 766.
40 Ibid., p 775.
41 Bantekas, op. cit., p 366/7.

challenges for Member States".[42] It has also led to substantial state reform of processes, procedures, and training of relevant personnel.

As can be seen from the changes discussed above, practitioners building the Police and Judicial Cooperation in Criminal Matters (PJCCM) frameworks have had to engage in constructivism. Practitioners brought with their own socialised understandings about how to conduct law enforcement operations, and through interaction with counterparts in other EU jurisdictions, negotiated shared understandings as to how transnational law enforcement within the EU was going to work. This was initially done by former drug enforcement officers, and then widened out to a wider range of law enforcement practitioners. Similar developments were made by investigating magistrates and prosecutors, supported by developing legal frameworks.

Bantekas argues that the EU is "thus moving towards a treaty-less regime in the field of criminal justice, where relevant EU legal instruments help create a hybrid, regional set of general principles of criminal law and regional customary law, in at least the definition of particular transnational offences".[43] Certainly the EU is exploiting its post-Lisbon supranational legal space in the AFSJ to further develop transnational criminal law and law enforcement. The Treaty of Lisbon allowed for these developments, with the detail being filled in using secondary supranational law, which has been informed by constructivist practitioner consensus.

The concept of state sovereignty, and its associated problems, has arisen in other areas of the THB academic debate. Rijken has argued that "the traditional concept of state sovereignty … must be abandoned" in order to properly address the transnational crime of THB.[44] She argues for a form of state sovereignty which requires one state to "cooperate with other states in the most effective way" in order to be able to effectively protect their citizens "in the long term".[45] Going some way towards the concept of human security, she prioritises a state duty to protect its citizens and residents ahead of the non-interference concept of state sovereignty, which only creates gaps in criminal law and law enforcement, which transnational organised crime can exploit, and through which crime can profit and individuals fall victim. How to develop the form of state sovereignty and national security and law enforcement policies in a way which prioritised human security, at least for the purposes of combatting THB, either within the EU and its supranational legal structures, or between states in a more traditional international or intergovernmental relationship remains a challenge for transnational criminal law.

The traditional approach of criminal law is one of territorial, or national jurisdiction, with offences being prosecuted in the jurisdiction where they occur. Extra-territorial jurisdiction is a more recent development, and one which is provided for in the Palermo Convention at Article 15. As stated by Wylie and

42 Ibid., p 365.
43 Ibid., p 384.
44 C. Rijken, *Trafficking in Persons Prosecution from a European Perspective*, TMC Asser Press, 2003, p 271.
45 Ibid.

McRedmond, extraterritoriality can be established on three different bases, "the personality principle" which can be both active and passive, "the protective principle" and the "universality principle".[46] The active personality principle operates where a state punishes the crimes of its own citizens, even when committed abroad. The passive personality principle, the "most controversial" option,[47] involves a state being able "to prosecute a foreign national for a crime committed on foreign soil solely because the victim" is one of their nationals.[48] It has been criticised as intruding "too deeply on the sovereignty of other states".[49] It usually requires a double criminality test to be met, with the offence being recognised as a crime in both relevant jurisdictions. Arguably it should not be necessary for states to adopt the passive personality principle when prosecuting the transnational THB, as so many jurisdictions have acceded to the THB Protocol. The question arises, however, as to how many of those states are prepared to prioritise and resource the investigation and prosecution of THB. While several jurisdictions have legislation adopting the passive personality principle, in practice, it is little used for crimes other than terrorism.[50] An expansion of this principle should be considered to combat THB. If states remain unwilling or unable to resource effective investigations and prosecutions within their jurisdictions, then the use of the passive personality principle in another state for the investigation and prosecution of THB offences should be used. Similarly the protective principle might be an option, which would be based on the need to extend a state's jurisdiction to "offences committed outside its territory by non-nationals, if the conduct is considered a threat to [that] state's security".[51] In contrast, the universality principle would only arise in the more extreme cases of THB and slavery, when seen as international crimes, when a state would agree "to prosecute certain crimes, irrespective of where they are committed, or by whom, because these crimes are denounced by the international community".[52] THB as an international crime is outside the scope of this book.

Transnational Crime

The CoE is of the view that with its "some 30 conventions" setting out "a common basis for co-operation in criminal matters across Europe and sometimes beyond"[53] that the issue at the CoE level is not the "lack of legal instruments, but

46 Farka, op. cit., p 206.
47 G. R. Watson, 'The Passive Personality Principle' (1993) 28 *Texas International Law Journal* 1, p 2.
48 Ibid.
49 Ibid., p 14.
50 Ibid., p 13.
51 Farka, op. cit., p 206.
52 Ibid., p 207.
53 Council of Europe, White Paper on Transnational Organised Crime, Council of Europe, December 2014, p 5.

rather their implementation in practice".[54] Specialist organisations have been put in place at the CoE to address different aspects of transnational crime, such as the anti-money laundering body, Moneyval, the drug abuse and drug trafficking group, the Pompidou group etc. Included in this list of groups is the Group of Experts on Action against Trafficking in Human Beings, GRETA.

The CoE Action Plan on Combatting Transnational Organised Crime (2016–2020) did anticipate setting up an over-arching group to combat Transnational Organised Crime.[55] CoE developments are anticipated to, in due course mirror EU provisions to combat transnational organised crime, to include the development of a European Judicial Atlas. The CoE action plan states that these goals are seen as being "too ambitious at present".[56] Particularly challenging for CoE states is the development of the concept of "mutual recognition", which has been the focus in the EU jurisdiction, having been "introduced by the UK during its presidency of the EU in 1998".[57] Within the EU mutual recognition has been promoted through the "role of specialised bodies"[58] such as Eurojust and the European Judicial Network (EJN) – Crime, complimenting the role of Europol. Many Europol-like organisations are now operating in other parts of the globe, such as the South-Eastern European Law Enforcement Centre,[59] formerly known as the SECI centre, which is supported by the South-East Europe Prosecutors Advisory Group (SEEPAG).[60] THB was seen as a priority early on for the SECI centre,[61] and was key to the development of Europol-SECI developmental and operational relationship. Europol like bodies need to be set up in conjunction with Eurojust or EJN-Crime like bodies or frameworks to become as fully effective. The CoE does intend to "start … discussions on the possibility of linking the judicial networks or strengthening the existing co-operation agreements" between European, Eurasian and Euro-Atlantic networks.[62] While the CoE notes inter-agency cooperation at different parts of the chain, that "there is a lack of inter-agency co-operation along the enforcement chain",[63] and that this issue needs to be addressed.

54 Ibid., p 7.
55 European Committee on Crime Problems (CDPC), Council of Europe Action Plan on Combating Transnational Organised Crime (2016–2020), (2016), Council of Europe, p 8.
56 Ibid., p 11.
57 Obokata, op. cit., p 186.
58 Ibid., p 189.
59 Albania, Bosnia Herzegovina, Bulgaria, Hellenic Republic, Hungary, Moldova, Montenegro, Republic of North Macedonia, Romania, Serbia, and Türkiye.
60 See www.selec.org/about-seepag/.
61 M. Močnik, 'Balancing political interests and practical interests; The SECI Centre', in S. D. Brown, *Combating International Crime: The Longer Arm of the Law*, Routledge, 2008, p 92.
62 European Committee on Crime Problems, op. cit., p 12.
63 Ibid., p 23.

The EU's Council Framework Decision 2008/841/JHA[64] had implemented "broadly in conformity"[65] the provisions of the Palermo Convention into EU law. Their basic principles do operate within each of the laws of each of the EU member states.[66] Wylie and McRedmond refer to the "blunt instrument of the UN" and the "complexity of the EU definitions" for organised crime. They point out that the CoE's approach takes "a more pragmatic approach that recognizes that organized crime is itself complex and composed of many different facts that may change over time from one organization to another".[67] Law enforcement practitioners prefer the concepts of either serious crime or entrepreneurial crimes, rather than the more static structures envisaged in the UN definition of organised crime.

The EU, for its part, both in earlier legislation[68] and in its directive on THB,[69] has disaggregated the crime of THB from the concept of organised crime, with the presence of organised crime being an aggravating factor for the purposes of punishment. The CoE has taken a similar approach.[70] As pointed out by Shelly, "much of human trafficking is committed by smaller crime networks rather than large scale organisations".[71] Movement of people for the purpose of their exploitation "necessitates a degree of flexibility and fluidity that is not always essential when trafficking inanimate commodities such as narcotics or counterfeit goods".[72] Echoing Shelly, Makareno points out that THB usually occurs "in networked operations",[73] often undertaken, as reported in the UK, "in cooperation by several, relatively small local criminal groups".[74]

64 Council Framework Decision 2008/841/JHA of 24 October 2008 on the fight against organised crime, OJ L 300, 2008/11/11, p 42.
65 Obokata, op. cit., p 184.
66 A. Di Nicola et al., European Commission Study on paving the way for future policy initiatives in the field of fight against organized crime: the effectiveness of specific criminal law measures targeting organised crime, final report, February 2015.
67 P. McRedmond, 'Defining Organized Crime in the Context of Human Trafficking', in G. Wylie and P. McRedmond, *Human Trafficking in Europe, Character, Causes and Consequences*, Springer, 2010, p 193.
68 Council Framework Decision 2002/629/JHA on combating trafficking in human beings, OJ L 203, 01/08/2002 p. 1, which replaced Joint Action 97/154/JHA of 24 February 1997 adopted by the Council on the basis of Article K.3 of the Treaty on European Union concerning action to combat trafficking in human beings and sexual exploitation of children, OJ L 63, 04/03/1997, p 2.
69 Directive 2011/36/EU, op. cit.
70 CoE Convention against Trafficking in Human Beings 2005, (Warsaw Convention), CETS No. 197, Articles 2 and 24.
71 L. Shelly, 'Human Security and Human Trafficking', in A. Jonsson, *Human Trafficking and Human Security*, Routledge Transnational Crime and Corruption, 2009, p 13.
72 T. Makareno, 'Organized Crime or Crimes Organized? Isolating and Identifying Actors in the Human Trafficking Chain', in A. Jonsson, *Human Trafficking and Human Security*, Routledge, 2009, p 29.
73 Ibid., p 30.
74 Ibid., p 38.

Trafficking in Human Beings

CoE Convention against Trafficking in Human Beings 2005 (the Warsaw Convention),[75] which came into force in 2008, now has 48 member-state ratifications, to include non-CoE members Belarus and Israel. Russia was subject to the case law of the ECtHR under the ECHR, until its expulsion in 2022, with one of the most prominent of ECtHR cases being *Rantsev v Cyprus and Russia*.[76] Unlike both the CoE THB Convention and the THB Protocol, the EU directive on THB[77] needs to be read in the context of a separate legal system, relying as it does on supporting legal provisions and agencies in order to become fully operational. Within the EU legal system, the provisions of the EU Charter of Fundamental Rights (CFR) 2000 also operate, Article 5 of which, in addition to prohibiting slavery and forced labour, provides that THB "is prohibited".

The THB directive was enacted after the CoE THB Convention, and informed by the CoE's approach, is the third attempt of the EU to legislate in this area. The THB directive makes express references to both the Palermo Protocol and the CoE THB Convention,[78] calling for full use to be made of these international law provisions. It also expressly builds on the provisions of the ILO Convention no 29 on forced and compulsory labour, particularly in the context of forced begging.[79] It is to interact with further EU internal legal provisions, and the CoE THB Convention on Laundering, Search, Seizure and Confiscation of the Proceeds from Crime, Strasbourg, 1990.[80] Reference is also expressly made to the UN CRC 1989,[81] in the context of child victims of trafficking. Children are defined as anyone under the age of 18 in all three documents,[82] with, both the CoE and EU providing that, people of "indeterminate age" are to be presumed to be children.[83]

The CoE THB Convention, unlike the THB Protocol, has a built-in compliance monitoring mechanism, GRETA,[84] to ensure that the CoE provisions are properly implemented and operated in acceding member states. The GRETA mechanism is expressly referred to in the THB directive,[85] to which the EU has added for its own purposes, a system of national rapporteurs, or equivalent, who will "carry out assessments of trends" in this area, and to measure the "results of

75 CETS No. 197.
76 Judgment in *Rantsev v Cyprus and Russia*, Application no. 25965/04, ECtHR, 7th January 2010.
77 Directive 2011/36/EU, op. cit.
78 Ibid., preamble, paragraphs 9 and 13.
79 Ibid., paragraph 11.
80 CETS 141.
81 Directive 2011/36/EU, preamble, paragraph 22.
82 THB Protocol, Article 3.d, CoE THB Convention, Article 4.d and Directive 2011/36/EU, Article 2.6.
83 CoE THB Convention, Article 10.3, Directive 2011/36/EU, Article 13.2.
84 CoE THB Convention, Article 36 to 38.
85 Directive 2011/36/EU, preamble, paragraph 9.

anti-trafficking actions", to include gathering statistics.[86] These national rapporteurs will be coordinated by and report to the EU's anti-trafficking coordinator (ATC), who will, in her turn, be tasked with reporting every two years on progress to the Commission.[87] The CoE THB Convention reads as an evolution and further development of the provisions of the THB protocol, stating that its provisions should "not affect rights and obligations derived" from the THB Protocol.[88] The CoE THB Convention covers THB for the purposes of organ removal, with further CoE conventions covering the issue of organ trafficking[89] and child protection against sexual exploitation.[90] Unfortunately, the THB directive still does not encompass the allied crime areas of child sex tourism or online paedophilia activity. In contrast with the THB Protocol, the context of the CoE THB Convention is on the rights agenda[91] and gender equality.[92] The THB directive, for its part, says that it takes an "integrated, holistic, and human rights approach" to combatting THB.[93] Many legal academic commentators would argue that this is an important change in focus.

A particular issue for the CoE THB Convention is on the non-discrimination principle, to include non-discrimination on the basis of "sex, race, colour, language, religion, political or other opinion, national or social origin, association with a minority, property, birth or other status".[94] Direct reference is made to the need to take a "gender mainstreaming and a child-sensitive approach".[95] The issue of gender equality is reinforced later in the convention.[96] As stated by the CoE explanatory report on the convention, gender equality means an equal visibility, empowerment and participation of both sexes in all spheres of public and private life",[97] being an issue which is "integral to human rights".[98] The concept of gender mainstreaming is connected, *inter alia*, to UN Security Council Resolution 1325 (2000) on women, peace and security. This was the first time that the Security Council "formally recognized that women may be something other than victims of armed conflict who need protection".[99] There is some doubt, however, as to the efficacy of the "gender mainstreaming" initiatives taken at the

86 Ibid., Article 19.
87 Ibid., Article 20.
88 CoE THB Convention, Article 39.
89 Council of Europe Convention against Trafficking in Human Organs, 2015, CETS No. 216.
90 Council of Europe Convention on the Protection of Children against Sexual Exploitation and Sexual Abuse 2007, CETS No. 201.
91 CoE THB Convention, Article 5.3.
92 Ibid., Article 1.1.
93 Directive 2011/36/EU, preamble, paragraph 7.
94 CoE THB Convention, Article 3.
95 Ibid., Article 5.3.
96 Ibid., Article 17.
97 Explanatory Report on the Council of Europe Convention on Action against Trafficking in Human Beings, Warsaw, 16.V.2005, paragraph 54.
98 Ibid., paragraph 55.
99 D. Otto, 'The Exile of Inclusion: Reflections on Gender Issues in International Law over the Last Decade' (2009) 10 *Melbourne Journal of International Law* 1, p 6.

UN.[100] Certainly gender equality needs to be revisited in order to ensure that all people are protected from all forms of THB, noting that an increasing number of men are being found to be victims. All victims of THB need to be visible, and protection provided for an effective human security approach to be taken. For its part, there is a requirement in the THB directive for EU member states to take "a gender perspective and a child-rights approach" in taking measures to prevent THB or discourage or reduce demand for the services of victims.

A problem arises with the THB directive stating that THB is a "gender specific phenomenon", with men and women being trafficked for "different purposes".[101] It is arguable that this approach is too rigid. While it may be possible in practice to say certain types of victims fall predominantly into genders, it is not possible to say that THB, as it presents itself in practice, is in fact an exclusively gender specific phenomenon, with all types of victims being found by law enforcement officers, in all THB categories. A gendered approach cannot be allowed to lead to gender blindness and failure to protect some victims, just because they are unexpected. Under EU law gender is also one of the issues which is to be taken into account when assessing the vulnerability of victims, with the others being "pregnancy, state of health and disability".[102] There is also express reference in the EU law to "sexual exploitation, sexual abuse, rape", and "slavery-like practices" in the preamble of the directive, in the context of the need to avoid "secondary victimisation and further trauma during the criminal proceedings".[103]

The EU THB strategy speaks about the need to "enhance actions to improve victims' support and referral in the cross-border context, towards the objective of setting up a European referral cooperation mechanism".[104] Arguably this is an initiative that the post Brexit UK should become involved in, as it is now no longer involved in the European Return and Reintegration Network.[105] It is also an initiative that the UK should strive to replicate in its own transnational frameworks for THB and modern slavery.

Unlike the THB Protocol, both the CoE THB Convention and the THB directive require the criminalisation of offences committed, not just in its territory but also by one of its nationals or a stateless person who has a habitual residence in their territory, or for offences against one of its nationals, thereby adopting both

100 *Inter alia* ibid., and H. Charlesworth, and M. Wood, '"Mainstreaming Gender" in International Peace and Security: The Case of East Timor' (2001) 26 *Yale Journal of International Law*.
101 Directive 2011/36/EU, preamble, paragraph 3.
102 Ibid., paragraph 12.
103 Ibid., paragraph 20.
104 Communication from the Commission to the European Parliament, the Council, the European Economic and Social Committee and the Committee of the Regions on the EU Strategy on Combatting Trafficking in Human Beings 2021–2025, Brussels, 14.4.2021, COM (2021) 171 final, p 14.
105 Independent Anti-Slavery Commissioner Annual Report 2021–2022 Presented to Parliament pursuant to Section 42(10)(b) of the Modern Slavery Act 2015, April 2022, Crown Copyright 2022, p 20, point 1.4.10.

the active and passive personality principles to criminal jurisdiction.[106] For prosecution of offences committed in another territory, the THB directive provides that the other country's "prosecution can be initiated only following a report made by the victim in the place where the offence was committed, or a denunciation from the State of the place where the offence was committed".[107] The CoE additionally provides that offences committed on board a ship flying the flag of that country, on board an aircraft registered to that country are to be similarly criminalised.[108] As with organised crime, both the THB directive and the CoE THB Convention require the criminalisation of offences committed for the benefit of a legal person established in its territory.[109] The CoE THB Convention also provides that its contracting states should "consider adopting" laws establishing criminal offences for those knowingly using the services of THB victims,[110] a provisions which is echoed in the THB directive.[111]

Both the CoE and EU documents provide the need for contracting parties to examine making provision on the non-punishment of victims involved in unlawful activities.[112] This point has been a major issue for THB victim protection lobby groups. As will be discussed in Chapter 7, while consideration is given to this point in the UK, no blanket ban on the prosecution and punishment of victims has been imposed in the three main jurisdictions of the UK.

When it comes to investigation and prosecution, the THB Protocol calls for the training of both law enforcement and prosecution,[113] something which is missing from the CoE THB Convention. As well as training to prevent THB, the required training under the THB Protocol is to "consider human rights and child- and gender- sensitive issues".[114] The EU directive, for its part, puts emphasis on the training of THB law enforcement units, to include front-line police officers,[115] which is much broader than specialist THB units. The THB directive requires that member states ensure that THB law enforcement units have "effective investigation tools", to include "those which are used in organised crime or other serious crime cases".[116] This would include the whole range of tools legislated for by the EU for cross border law enforcement operations, to include wiretaps,[117] controlled deliveries,[118] cross border covert surveillance,[119] joint investigation teams

106 CoE THB Convention, Article 31, Directive 2011/36/EU, Article 10.
107 Directive 2011/36/EU, Article 10.3.b.
108 CoE THB Convention, Article 31.1.
109 CoE THB Convention, Article 23.2, Directive 2011/36/EU, Article 10.2.b.
110 CoE THB Convention, Article 19.
111 Directive 2011/36/EU, Article 18.4.
112 CoE THB Convention, Article 26, Directive 2011/36/EU, Article 8.
113 THB Protocol, Article 10.2.
114 Ibid.
115 Directive 2011/36/EU, Article 18.3.
116 Ibid., Article 9.4.
117 Directive 2014/41/EU, op. cit., Articles 30–31.
118 EU Convention on Mutual Assistance in Criminal Matters 2000, Article 12.
119 Schengen Convention 1990, Article 40.

(JITs),[120] or the use of undercover officers in a cross border investigation,[121] etc. Similar law enforcement provisions are provided for in the CoE Second Additional Protocol to the European Convention on Mutual Assistance in Criminal Matters 2001 (ECMACM),[122] which was written around the same time as the EU Convention on Mutual Assistance in Criminal Matters 2000, a with a substantial overlap of country membership. The Second Additional Protocol underpins many of the post Brexit UK-EU Trade and Cooperation Agreement provisions. The CoE Convention on Mutual Assistance in Criminal Matters,[123] and its two protocols,[124] are overseen by the Committee of Experts on the Operation of European Conventions on Co-operation in Criminal Maters (PC-OC).[125]

Within the EU both Europol[126] and Eurojust[127] (the agency for investigating and prosecuting magistrates) have been active for some time in combatting THB, with Europol reporting that THB is one of its priority crime areas under the 2018–2021 EU Policy Cycle. Eurojust, in its THB report in 2021, has called on its early involvement in EU transnational operations to combat THB, with "support from Europol should go hand in hand with the involvement of Eurojust".[128] Eurojust goes on to recommend that all parties to a THB JIT "discuss the possibility of seconding specialised officers to interview potential victims of trafficking and take into consideration the particularities of child victims of THB".[129] In investigations where JITs have not been set up, Eurojust speaks about the use of European Investigation Orders (EIOs),[130] using Directive 2014/41/EU.[131]

The CoE THB Convention does have extensive protection provisions which are missing from the THB Protocol with the EU Agency for Fundamental Rights pointing out that "it is clear that the CoE THB Convention applies also to victims who entered or are present illegally in [an EU] Member State".[132] The EU's THB strategy speaks about needing to be aware about the possibility of victims being re-trafficked after engaging with a state's immigration system,[133] with the

120 EU Convention on Mutual Assistance in Criminal Matters 2000, Article 13.
121 Directive 2014/41/EU, op. cit., Article 29.
122 CETS 182, which at the time of writing has 43 ratifications, including Russia, Chile, and Israel. Greece and Iceland have signed, but not ratified this protocol, Articles 17–22.
123 ETS. 30, 1959.
124 ETS. 99, 1978, and ETS. 182, 2001.
125 See www.coe.int/en/web/transnational-criminal-justice-pcoc/home.
126 See www.europol.europa.eu/.
127 See www.eurojust.europa.eu/.
128 Eurojust Report on Trafficking on Human Beings Best practice and issues in judicial cooperation, Eurojust, 2021, p 2.
129 Ibid., p 27.
130 Ibid.
131 Directive 2014/41/EU, op. cit.
132 FRA, Child Trafficking in the European Union Challenges, perspectives and good practices, European Union Agency for Fundamental Rights, 2009.
133 Communication from the Commission, (2021), op. cit., p 15.

need to ensure that the rights of children in migration systems have "specific safeguards ...put in place to ensure that their rights are respected".[134]

The CoE provisions include the need for investigations and prosecutions not to be reliant on victim testimony,[135] and the need for witness and victim protection measures.[136] There are also specific measures called for in the CoE THB Convention for endangered or missing persons.[137] The THB directive, for its part, provides that EU member states should "ensure that investigation into or prosecution of offences ... is not dependent on reporting or accusation by a victim" and that the criminal proceedings can continue "even if the victim has withdrawn his or her statement".[138] Reliance is therefore being made on intelligence led policing.[139] Secondary victimisation during the investigation or prosecution process also needs to be avoided under the THB directive.[140] These provisions would run in parallel with EU provisions on minimum standards on the rights, support and protection of victims of crime.[141]

While much has been written about the CoE's THB Convention's contribution to developing a rights based and victim centred approach, and the need to move from earlier purely law enforcement approaches, the CoE THB Convention also provide that one of its purposes is to "promote international cooperation on action against" THB.[142] However, the convention does not set up the necessary transnational legal frameworks for combatting THB, unlike those set up under the Palermo Convention, and the THB Protocol. Reliance would therefore have to be made by CoE member states on the Second Additional Protocol to the ECMACM.

Both the THB protocol and the CoE THB Convention have provisions on the control of borders,[143] the security and control of documents[144] and the legitimacy and validity of documents.[145] The CoE THB Convention additionally requires the criminalisation of acts relating to travel or identity documents.[146] These are not replicated in the THB directive, reliance being made on other detailed measures within the AFSJ legal framework. Gaps in the EU approach are reflected in the EU THB strategy for 2021–2025 which speaks about "challenges created by the

134 Ibid.
135 CoE THB Convention, Article 27.1.
136 Ibid., Article 28.
137 Ibid., Article 33.
138 Directive 2011/36/EU, Article 9.1.
139 J. H. Ratcliffe, *Intelligence-Led Policing*, 2nd ed, Routledge, 2016.
140 Directive 2011/36/EU, Article 12.4.
141 Directive 2012/29/EU of the European Parliament and of the Council of 25 October 2012 establishing minimum standards on the rights, support, and protection of victims of crime, and replacing Council Framework Decision 2001/220/JHA, OJ L 315, 14/11/2012, p 57.
142 CoE THB Convention, Article 1.1.c.
143 THB Protocol, Article 11, and CoE THB Convention, Article 7.
144 THB Protocol, Article 12, and CoE THB Convention, Article 8.
145 THB Protocol, Article 13, and CoE THB Convention, Article 9.
146 CoE THB Convention, Article 20.

digital age for law enforcement and judicial bodies in the fight against trafficking" "related to the modern law enforcement response to technological developments"[147] and the need for "dialogue with relevant internet and technology companies to reduce the use of online platforms for the recruitment and exploitation of victims".[148]

The EU's European Labour Authority (ELA),[149] which started operating from 1 August 2021,[150] has been tasked to cooperate with Europol and Eurojust in order to coordinate "promote synergies and avoid any duplication of activities" with them.[151] The ELA is also to promote cooperation with third countries and international organisations.[152] This should strengthen the EU's response to forced labour trafficking, which was reported in 2021 as accounting for 15% of all THB victims found in the EU, "with an increasing number of victims remaining undetected",[153] (in comparison to much higher forced labour numbers being reported by the UK). In addition, the EU is still reporting that most of the victims in the EU are women and girls trafficked for sexual exploitation,[154] while in the UK, there is an increased focus on forced labour, and a broadened understanding of THB, to include county line crime. Further, EU member states appear to have much work to do on labour exploitation, the less severe situation than that of THB, with Stoyanova reporting that the EU Fundamental Rights Agency is finding very "fragmented and piecemeal"[155] criminal laws across the EU.

Conclusion

Europe has several key players when it comes to developing a response to THB, with both the EU and the CoE providing extensive legal frameworks, not only in specialised CoE THB Convention and the EU directive,[156] but also in supporting provisions, as discussed above. The principle of legality is however a key issue for both the CoE and the EU both domestically and in developing transnational legal frameworks. The EU sees "legality as a multilevel concept that integrates multiple legal actors and layers of legal sources today",[157] with the principle of legality

147 Communication from the Commission, (2021), op. cit., p 11.
148 Ibid.
149 See www.ela.europa.eu/en.
150 Regulation (EU) 2019/1149 of the European Parliament and of the Council of 20 June 2019 establishing a European Labour Authority, amending Regulations (EC) No 883/2004, (EU) No 492/2011, and (EU) 2016/589 and repealing Decision (EU) 2016/344, OJ L 186, 2019/07/11, p 21.
151 Ibid., preamble para. 42, and Article 14.
152 Regulation (EU) 2019/1149, Article 42.
153 Communication from the Commission, (2021), op. cit., p 7.
154 Ibid., p 1.
155 V. Stoyanova, *Human Trafficking and Slavery Reconsidered: Conceptual Limits and States' Positive Obligations in European Law*, Cambridge University Press, 2017, p 349.
156 Directive 2011/36/EU, op. cit.
157 Meyer, op. cit., p 43.

within the EU being "a shared responsibility".[158] This process requires regard to be had to "national constitutions and to international instruments" when the CJEU develops its case law.[159] Academics argue that the "the traditional concept of state sovereignty" … "must be abandoned" to properly address transnational THB.[160] The need for states to effectively cooperate with each other to protect their own citizens, citizens from other states and stateless persons, prioritising human security over national security, requires the development of transnational law enforcement frameworks. This is the approach taken in the EU, with the development of the concept of shared national sovereignty. A broader approach to establishing jurisdiction in THB cases should also be considered in order to fully develop a human security approach to THB.

National differences can be overcome, and should not "necessarily pose any threat to coexistence and co-operation" at an EU level.[161] Andreadakis states, "when different cultures, nationalities and traditions manage to co-exist and create a harmonised legal system, such system combines all the virtues and values of them".[162] Advancing the development of transnational law enforcement, both the active and passive personality principle have been adopted by both the CoE THB Convention and the THB directive in the criminalisation of THB offences.[163]

The THB protocol frames transnational THB in the context of organised crime. The EU, in its THB directive,[164] and in its earlier THB legislation,[165] has disaggregated the crime of THB from the concept of organised crime, with the presence of organised crime being an aggravating factor for the purposes of punishment. The CoE has taken a similar approach.[166] As pointed out by Shelly, "much of human trafficking is committed by smaller crime networks rather than large scale organisations".[167] Movement of people for the purpose of their exploitation "necessitates a degree of flexibility and fluidity that is not always essential when trafficking inanimate commodities such as narcotics or counterfeit goods".[168] Both the EU and the CoE also legislate for national THB. There has also been an important change of focus in the CoE and EU provisions, with the context of the CoE THB Convention being on the rights agenda[169] and gender equality.[170] The THB directive takes an "integrated, holistic, and human rights approach".[171] A problem does arise, however with the THB directive stating that

158 Ibid., p 47.
159 O'Higgins, op. cit., p 62/3.
160 Rijken, op. cit., p 271.
161 Andreadakis, op. cit., p 68.
162 Ibid.
163 CoE THB Convention, Article 31, Directive 2011/36/EU, Article 10.
164 Directive 2011/36/EU, op. cit.
165 Council Framework Decision 2002/629/JHA, op. cit.
166 CoE THB Convention Articles 2 and 24.
167 Shelly, op. cit., p 13.
168 Makareno, op. cit., p 29.
169 CoE THB Convention, Article 5.3.
170 Ibid., Article 1.1.
171 Directive 2011/36/EU, preamble, paragraph 7.

THB is a "gender specific phenomenon", with men and women being trafficked for "different purposes".[172] This could be too rigid an approach, leading to gender blindness, as all types of victims are being found by law enforcement officers, in all THB categories.

A long-standing gap in the EU legal framework in the context of THB and related exploitation, the EU's European Labour Authority (ELA),[173] only started operating from the 1st of August 2021.[174] It has yet to become fully involved in the forced labour aspect of THB. In due course it should assist in strengthening the EU's response to this issue, with THB for forced labour being substantially less reported in the EU in comparison to in the UK, where a lot of work has been undertaken on this type of THB.

The problems with legal definitions at both international and domestic level discussed in Chapter 2 will be an issue for transnational law enforcement, which will have to negotiate the interlegality of not just THB legal frameworks, but also related legislation using Onuf-style constructivism.[175] Any gaps in enacting THB provisions in domestic law, or enacting legislation dealing with "slavery, servitude, forced or compulsory labour", as has been done in the UK jurisdictions, discussed further in Chapter 7, will pose problems. When investigating the THB offence, both the CoE[176] and the EU[177] emphasise the need for law enforcement and prosecution not to be reliant on victims' testimony, as by the very nature of the crime, victims are already highly vulnerable. As alternative methods of evidence gathering need to be used, this will often require the adoption of intelligence led policing techniques,[178] using the variety of methods provided for in the EU legal space by, inter alia, EU Convention on Mutual Assistance in Criminal Matters 2000, and the Second Additional Protocol,[179] for CoE states, as discussed above.

In addition, the issue of secondary victimisation of victims during the investigation or prosecution process has been addressed in the EU directive.[180] In this context, the EU has now identified the need for "dialogue with relevant internet and technology companies to reduce the use of online platforms for the recruitment and exploitation of victims".[181] The EU is also seeking to "enhance actions to improve victims' support and referral in the cross-border context, towards the objective of setting up a European referral cooperation mechanism",[182] which might be worth examining formally, with a treaty base, by other countries in the context of high volume THB global supply chains.

172 Ibid., paragraph 3.
173 See www.ela.europa.eu/en.
174 Regulation 2019/1149, op. cit.
175 N. Onuf, *World of Our Making*, University of South Carolina Press, 1989.
176 CoE THB Convention, Article 27.1.
177 Directive 2011/36/EU, Article 9.1.
178 Ratcliffe, op. cit.
179 CoE Second Additional Protocol to the European Convention on Mutual Assistance in Criminal Matters 2001, CETS No. 182.
180 Directive 2011/36/EU, Article 12.4.
181 Communication from the Commission, (2021), op. cit., p 11.
182 Ibid., p 14.

As discussed in Chapter 5, there continue to be some notable child-related gaps in the THB directive. It still does not cover the crime areas of child sex tourism or online paedophilia activity. Further EU and CoE documents need to be examined to find relevant provisions, which arguably should have been covered, at least additionally, in the THB legislation. The CoE operates the Convention on the Protection of Children against Sexual Exploitation and Sexual Abuse (Lanzarote Convention),[183] while the EU operates Directive 2011/93/EU on combatting the sexual abuse and sexual exploitation of children and child pornography.[184] The CoE Convention on Cyber Crime 2001,[185] and the EU's Council Decision to combat child pornography on the internet[186] are also required to complete this picture.

The approach of the CoE and the EU can be contrasted with the approach of the UK, discussed in Chapter 7, where all three of the main jurisdictions (England & Wales, Scotland and Northern Ireland) have not only legislated for THB, but also for "slavery, servitude, forced and compulsory labour", with a view to catching all forms of exploitation, and not just that exploitation which is covered by the definition of THB. This approach is known as "modern slavery" in the England & Wales jurisdiction.

Bibliography

Andenas, M. and Andersen, C. B., *Theory and Practice of Harmonisation*, Edward Elgar, 2011.

Bantekas, I., 'The Principle of Mutual Recognition in EU Criminal Law' (2007) 32 *European Law Review* 3, 365–385.

Communication from the Commission to the European Parliament, the Council, the European Economic and Social Committee and the Committee of the Regions on the EU Strategy on Combatting Trafficking in Human Beings 2021–2025, Brussels, 14.4.2021, COM (2021) 171 final.

Council of Europe, *White Paper on Transnational Organised Crime*, Council of Europe, December 2014.

European Committee on Crime Problems (CDPC), *Council of Europe Action Plan on Combating Transnational Organised Crime (2016–2020)*, (2016), Council of Europe, CDPC (2015) 17 Fin.

Di Nicola, A., *et al.*, *Study on Paving the Way for Future Policy Initiatives in the Field of Fight against Organized Crime: The Effectiveness of Specific Criminal Law Measures Targeting Organised Crime*, Publications Office of the European Union, 2015.

Eurojust, *Report on Trafficking on Human Beings Best Practice and Issues in Judicial Cooperation*, Eurojust, 2021.

183 CoE Protection of Children convention, op. cit.

184 Directive 2011/93/EU of the European Parliament and of the Council of 13 December 2011 on combating the sexual abuse and sexual exploitation of children and child pornography, and replacing Council Framework Decision 2004/68/JHA, OJ L 335, 2011/12/18, p 1.

185 CoE Convention on Cybercrime 2001 (Budapest), CETS No. 185.

186 Council Decision 2000/375/JHA of 29 May 2000 to combat child pornography on the Internet, OJ L 138, 09/06/2000 p 1.

FRA, *Child Trafficking in the European Union Challenges, Perspectives and Good Practices*, European Union Agency for Fundamental Rights, 2009.

Farka, I., 'Extra-Territorial Jurisdiction: A Prosecutorial Tool to Combat Child Trafficking from Albania', in Wylie, G. and McRedmond, P., *Human Trafficking in Europe, Character, Causes and Consequences*, Springer, 2010, 198–215.

Independent Anti-Slavery Commissioner Annual Report 2021–2022 Presented to Parliament pursuant to Section 42(10)(b) of the Modern Slavery Act 2015, April 2022, Crown Copyright 2022.

Krisch, N., *Beyond Constitutionalism: The Pluralist Structure of Postnational Law*, Oxford University Press, 2010.

Lavenex, S., 'Mutual Recognition and the Monopoly of Force: Limits of the Single Market Analogy' (2007) 14 *Journal of European Public Policy* 5, 762–779.

Makareno, T., 'Organized Crime or Crimes Organized? Isolating and Identifying Actors in the Human Trafficking Chain', in Jonsson, A., *Human Trafficking and Human Security*, Routledge, 2009, 26–47.

McRedmond, P., 'Defining Organized Crime in the Context of Human Trafficking', in Wylie, G. and McRedmond, P., *Human Trafficking in Europe: Character, Causes and Consequences*, Springer, 2010, 181–197.

Meyer, F., 'C-387/02 Berlusconi and Others. The Berlusconi Judgment: A Corner stone of European Legality', in Mitsilegas, V., di Martiona A., and Mancano, L., *The Court of Justice and European Criminal Law: Leading Cases in a Contextual Analysis*, Hart Publishing, 2019, 37–54.

Močnik, M., 'Balancing Political Interests and Practical Interests: The SECI Centre', in Brown, S. D., *Combating International Crime: The Longer Arm of the Law*, Routledge, 2008, 88–95.

Oberleitner, G., 'The OSCE and Human Security' (2008) 19 *Security and Human Rights* 1, 64–72.

Obokata, T., *Transnational Organised Crime in International Law*, Hart Publishing, 2010.

O'Higgins, P., 'The Interaction of the ILO, the Council of Europe and European Union Labour Standards', in Hepple, B., *Social and Labour Rights in a Global Context: International and Comparative Perspectives*, Cambridge University Press, 2002, 55–72.

Otto, D., 'The Exile of Inclusion: Reflections on Gender Issues in International Law over the Last Decade' (2009) 10 *Melbourne Journal of International Law* 1.

Charlesworth, H., and Wood, M., '"Mainstreaming Gender" in International Peace and Security: The Case of East Timor' (2001) 26 *Yale Journal of International Law*, 313–317.

Onuf, N., *World of Our Making*, University of South Carolina Press, 1989.

Ratcliffe, J. H., *Intelligence-Led Policing*, 2nd edition, Routledge, 2016.

Rijken, C., *Trafficking in Persons Prosecution from a European Perspective*, TMC Asser Press, 2003.

Shelly, L., 'Human Security and Human Trafficking', in Jonsson, A., *Human Trafficking and Human Security*, Routledge Transnational Crime and Corruption, 2009, 10–25.

Stodiek, T., 'OSCE's Police-Related Activities: Lessons Learned during the Last Decade' (2009) 30 *Security and Human Rights* 3, 201–206.

Stoyanova, V., *Human Trafficking and Slavery Reconsidered: Conceptual Limits and States' Positive Obligations in European Law*, Cambridge University Press, 2017.

Watson, G. R., 'The Passive Personality Principle' (1993) 28 *Texas International Law Journal* 1, 1–46.

Legislation

CoE Additional Protocol to the European Convention on Mutual Assistance in Criminal Matters, 1978, CETS. 99.
CoE Convention on Mutual Assistance in Criminal Matters 1959, CETS No. 30.
CoE Second Additional Protocol to the European Convention on Mutual Assistance in Criminal matters 2001, CETS No.182.
Council Framework Decision 2008/841/JHA of 24 October 2008 on the fight against organised crime, OJ L 300, 2008/11/11, p 42.
CoE Convention against Trafficking in Human Organs, 2015, CETS No. 216.
CoE Convention against Trafficking in Human Beings 2005, CETS No. 197.
CoE Convention on the Protection of Children against Sexual Exploitation and Sexual Abuse, 2007, CETS No. 201.
CoE Convention on Cybercrime 2001, CETS No. 185.
Council Decision 2000/375/JHA of 29 May 2000 to combat child pornography on the Internet, OJ L 138, 09/06/2000 p 1.
Council Framework Decision 2002/629/JHA on combating trafficking in human beings, OJ L 203, 01/08/2002 p 1, which replaced Joint Action 97/154/JHA of 24 February 1997 adopted by the Council on the basis of Article K.3 of the Treaty on European Union concerning action to combat trafficking in human beings and sexual exploitation of children, OJ L 63.
Council Framework Decision 2002/584/JHA on the European Arrest Warrant, OJ L 190, 18 July 2002, p 1.
Directive 2014/41/EU of the European Parliament and of the Council of 3 April 2014 regarding the European Investigation Order in criminal matters, OJ L 130/1.
Directive 2011/93/EU of the European Parliament and of the Council of 13 December 2011 on combating the sexual abuse and sexual exploitation of children and child pornography, and replacing Council Framework Decision 2004/68/JHA, OJ L 335, 2011/12/18, p 1.
Directive 2011/36/EU of the European Parliament and of the Council of 5 April 2011 on preventing and combating trafficking in human beings and protecting its victims, and replacing Council Framework Decision 2002/629/JHA, OJ L 101/1.
Directive 2012/29/EU of the European Parliament and of the Council of 25 October 2012 establishing minimum standards on the rights, support, and protection of victims of crime, and replacing Council Framework Decision 2001/220/JHA, OJ L 315, 14/11/2012, p 57.
EU Convention on Mutual Assistance in Criminal Matters 2000.
Regulation (EU) 2019/1149 of the European Parliament and of the Council of 20 June 2019 establishing a European Labour Authority, amending Regulations (EC) No 883/2004, (EU) No 492/2011, and (EU) 2016/589 and repealing Decision (EU) 2016/344, OJ L 186, 2019/07/11, p 21.
Schengen Convention 1990.

Cases

Case 80/86 *Kolpinghuis Nijmegen* [1987] ECR 3969.
Joined cases C-387/02, C-391/02 and C-403/02, *Criminal proceedings against Silvio Berlusconi* (C-387/02), *Sergio Adelchi* (C-391/02) *and Marcello Dell'Utri and Others* (C-403/02), [2005] ECR p I-03565.
Rantsev v Cyprus and Russia, Application no. 25965/04, ECtHR, 7 January 2010.

Websites

www.coe.int/en/web/transnational-criminal-justice-pcoc/home
www.ela.europa.eu/en
www.eurojust.europa.eu/
www.europol.europa.eu/
www.osce.org/combating-human-traffickingwww.selec.org/about-seepag/

7 The UK

Introduction

While the UK has now left the EU, it has implemented, and gold-plated, the EU THB directive,[1] with the three UK jurisdictions of England & Wales (E&W), Scotland, and Northern Ireland (NI) going further in their definition and punishments of the relevant crimes than was required. The UK continues to disaggregate THB from organised crime, in line with the approach of Directive 2011/36/EU. Given its distinctive approach, and its regular reporting of much higher than the EU average numbers of male and forced labour victims, the UK's approach to THB and related exploitation merits examination. In Scotland, the most recent laws on THB are to be found in the Human Trafficking and Exploitation (Scotland) Act 2015, in NI, in the Human Trafficking and Exploitation (Criminal Justice and Support for Victims) Act (Northern Ireland) 2015,[2] and in E&W, by the Modern Slavery Act 2015.[3] The Modern Slavery Act 2015 also contains several provisions which apply to all three of the UK jurisdictions. In addition, section 60(6) of the Modern Slavery Act 2015 provides that its provisions can be extended "to any of the Channel Islands or to the Isle of Man". THB, or as it is known in E&W, modern slavery (MS), is legislated for in similar, but slightly different ways, by the three different jurisdictions. Two distinct offences are provided for in all three acts, that of THB and of "slavery, servitude, forced and compulsory labour", with the *mens rea* being "intention" or "knows or ought to have known".[4] Stoyanova is of the view that the locating of the THB offence after the crimes of "slavery, servitude, forced and compulsory labour" in UK legislation "is a positive development in the European

1 Directive 2011/36/EU of the European Parliament and of the Council of 5 April 2011 on preventing and combating trafficking in human beings and protecting its victims, and replacing Council Framework Decision 2002/629/JHA, OJ L 101/1.
2 As amended by the Justice (Sexual Offences and Trafficking Victims) Act (Northern Ireland) 2022.
3 As amended by the Nationality and Borders Act 2022.
4 Modern Slavery Act 2015, section 1.1a and section 2.4, Human Trafficking and Exploitation (Scotland) Act 2015, section 1 and section 4.1 (knew or ought to have known), Human Trafficking and Exploitation (Criminal Justice and Support for Victims) Act (Northern Ireland) 2015, section 4.1 (intention).

DOI: 10.4324/9781003429791-7

Table 7.1. Legal provisions in various UK legislation

England and Wales	*Scotland*	*Northern Ireland*
Modern Slavery Act 2015	Human Trafficking and Exploitation (Scotland) Act 2015	Human Trafficking and Exploitation (Criminal Justice and Support for Victims) Act (Northern Ireland) 2015
s.1 Slavery, Servitude, Forced and Compulsory Labour	s.4 Slavery, Servitude, Forced and Compulsory Labour	s.1 Slavery, Servitude, Forced and Compulsory Labour
s.2 Human Trafficking	s.1 Human Trafficking	s.2 Human Trafficking

context"[5] given the relevant gravity of the offences. However, both offences in all three UK jurisdictions could give rise to life imprisonment, up considerably from the EU directive requirement of 5, or in aggravated circumstances, 10 years. Where the exact definition of THB is not met by the facts of the case, the second crime of "slavery, servitude, forced and compulsory labour", terms which have extensive international legal interpretation, may well apply.

Modern Slavery Act 2015 provides, at section 1, that the terms "slavery" "servitude" "forced labour" or "compulsory labour" should be "construed in accordance with Article 4" ECHR,[6] with similar provisions being provided in the Scottish act[7] and the NI act.[8] Reliance is therefore made in UK criminal law to definitions developed in ECtHR. Practice directions, such as the Lord Advocates (chief prosecutors) directions on prosecution in Scotland, or codes, such as the Victim's Code for Scotland also must be examined to complete the legal practice picture in any jurisdiction.

UK nationals, by 2019, represented "by far the highest proportion of potential victims identified at almost a quarter of all those recorded",[9] as a result of an increasing "number of children identified as being involved in county lines".[10] The CoE's GRETA's 2021 UK report states that while "prior to 1 October 2019, the most common form of exploitation in the UK for both adults and children was recorded as labour exploitation",[11] due to a change in methods of recording on

5 V. Stoyanova, *Human Trafficking and Slavery Reconsidered: Conceptual Limits and States' Positive Obligations in European Law*, Cambridge University Press, 2017, p 351.
6 CoE Convention for the Protection of Human Rights and Fundamental Freedoms, 1950, CETS No. 5.
7 Human Trafficking and Exploitation (Scotland) Act 2015, section 4.
8 Human Trafficking and Exploitation (Criminal Justice and Support for Victims) Act (Northern Ireland) 2015, section 1.
9 Independent Review of the Modern Slavery Act 2015, Final Report Presented to Parliament by the Secretary of State for the Home Department by Command of Her Majesty, May 2019, CP 100, p 8.
10 Ibid., p 8.
11 GRETA Evaluation Report United Kingdom third evaluation round Access to justice and effective remedies for victims of trafficking in human beings, GRETA (2021)12, Council of Europe, 2021, p 12, point 16.

that date, exploitation for the purposes of forced criminality was separately recorded, accounting for a large number of recorded children, particularly those from the UK, with "labour exploitation [continuing] to be the most common exploitation type for adult victims".[12] At a transnational level, trafficking of nationals from Albania, Vietnam, Nigeria, and Romania into the UK, from year to year, remains substantial.

A distinction is made in all three UK jurisdictions, for all purposes, between victims who are over the age of 18 and those who are under that age.[13] In the case of doubt, individuals are to be presumed to be under the age of 18 until the contrary is proven.[14] The approach of the courts to local authorities disputing age was addressed for E&W in the joint case of *R (on the application of A) v London Borough of Croydon, R (M) v London Borough of Lambeth.*[15] The Independent Review for the Home Office of the Modern Slavery Act 2015 expressed some concern as to how the relevant provision under the Modern Slavery Act operated on this point, and it recommended a review of the E&W legislation, and the issuance of further guidance on this point.[16] The word "travel" has also caused some concern, in policy and academic circles. However, the Crown Prosecution Service (CPS) (which covers E&W and NI) reported to the Independent Review that "it takes a broad interpretation of what is meant by 'travel', including movement over a very small space", and this approach has continued to be accepted by the courts.[17]

Exploitation for the purposes of the THB offence (or both offences in E&W) is defined in the three pieces of legislation.[18] The law in this area is supplemented by a variety of trafficking and exploitation strategies, and the operation of the National Referral Mechanism (NRM). The Independent Review expressed concerns that the Modern Slavery Act definitions did not extent to "orphanage trafficking and county lines offences".[19] County lines offences involve the supply of drugs, and possibly weapons, up and down the country, often being carried by vulnerable children, with or without duress, for adult criminals under whose control they operate. However, the CPS was happy that the definitions were broad enough to cover new forms of exploitation being encountered in practice.[20]

12 Ibid.
13 Modern Slavery Act, section 51, Human Trafficking and Exploitation (Scotland) Act 2015, section 12, and Human Trafficking and Exploitation (Criminal Justice and Support for Victims) Act (Northern Ireland) 2015, section 18.2.
14 Modern Slavery Act 2015, section 51, Human Trafficking and Exploitation (Scotland) Act 2015, section 12, and Human Trafficking and Exploitation (Criminal Justice and Support for Victims) Act (Northern Ireland), 2015, section 25(3).
15 [2009] EWHC 939 (Admin); [2009] 5 WLUK 178; [2010] 1 F.L.R. 193; [2009] Fam. Law 659; (2009) 153(20) S.J.L.B. 40.
16 Independent Review, op. cit., pages 54 and 58.
17 Ibid., p 63/4.
18 Modern Slavery Act 2015, section 3, Human Trafficking and Exploitation (Scotland) Act 2015, section 3, Human Trafficking and Exploitation (Criminal Justice and Support for Victims) Act (Northern Ireland) 2015, section 3.
19 Independent Review, op. cit., p 61.
20 Ibid.

The National Crime Agency (NCA), (the UK wide serious crime law enforcement body), is reporting for 2021 that "coerced criminality" is now the most common reported form of exploitation in the UK.[21] In addition, as discussed in Chapter 2, law enforcement have encountered problems with exploitation on the boundary line "between poor employment conditions and forced or compulsory labour".[22] Rather than extending the definition, the Independent Review recommended that the Government "should produce policy guidance to assist in the interpretation of the Act".[23] In addition issues on the border line between forced and compulsory labour and poor employment practices are to be addressed by the Gangmasters and Labour Abuse Authority (GLAA), and other traditional "civil enforcement routes, including by employment tribunals".[24] What is now known as the GLAA was originally set up in the UK in 2004, to address several serious instances which had arisen in the use of unskilled work gangs. The supplier of such labour work gangs now needs to be licensed.[25] Compliance officers act on behalf of the agency across the UK, often operating in conjunction with the local police force,[26] conducting inspections,[27] using search warrants,[28] with obstruction of their officers being a criminal offence.[29]

All three UK jurisdictions have introduced prevention orders,[30] which are usually used post-conviction, and in two, risk orders,[31] which operate prior or instead of convictions.[32] In E&W there is also the possibility of slavery and trafficking reparation orders.[33] Prevention orders are issued by a court either on sentencing, instead of, or in addition to other punishment. They can also be made on application, where an individual has been convicted of a slavery or THB offence, or he has been found not guilty of such an offence by reason of disability or by reason of insanity. The application for the prevention order can be made by a chief police officer, an immigration officer, the Director of the NCA, or the Director of the GLAA. The prevention order can prevent certain behaviour, anywhere in the UK, and can prohibit foreign travel, to include requiring surrender of a passport.

21 NCA, National Strategic Assessment of Serious and Organised Crime 2021, Crown Copyright, 2021.
22 Independent Review, op. cit., p 62.
23 Ibid.
24 Ibid.
25 Gangmasters (Licencing) Act 2004, as amended, section 6.1.
26 Ibid., section 22A.
27 Ibid., section 16.
28 Ibid., section 17.
29 Ibid., section 18.
30 Modern Slavery Act 2015, sections 14 to 22, Human Trafficking and Exploitation (Scotland) Act 2015, sections 17 to 25, and schedule 3 of the Human Trafficking and Exploitation (Criminal Justice and Support for Victims) Act (Northern Ireland) 2015.
31 Modern Slavery Act 2015, sections 23 to 29, Human Trafficking and Exploitation (Scotland) Act 2015, sections 26 to 31.
32 Independent Anti-Slavery Commissioner Annual Report 2021–2022 Presented to Parliament pursuant to Section 42(10)(b) of the Modern Slavery Act 2015, (2022), Crown Copyright, p 29, point 2.3.7.
33 Modern Slavery Act 2015, section 9.

In addition, risk orders are also available in E&W and in Scotland, in anticipation of an individual committing a THB or MS offence.

The UK Government has designed its 2014 Modern Slavery Strategy[34] around four pillars, Pursue, Prevent, Protect and Prepare.[35] The first pillar, "Pursue" covers "prosecuting and disrupting individuals and groups responsible for modern slavery". The second pillar, "Prevent", covers "preventing people from engaging in modern slavery". Both pillars are to lead to a reduction of the threat and involve law enforcement and criminal law. The third pillar, "Protect" addresses the need for the "strengthening safeguards against modern slavery by protecting vulnerable people from exploitation and increasing awareness and resilience against this crime". The fourth pillar, "Prepare" addresses "reducing the harm caused by modern slavery through improved victim identification and enhanced support and protection". The third and fourth pillars are meant to lead to a reduction in vulnerability. All four pillars are seen as being equally important in addressing what is seen not just as a transnational crime, but also a national crime of the utmost importance. The focus of this chapter will be on the "Pursue" pillar.

The National Referral Mechanism

Legislation provides a statutory duty to report victims of THB and "slavery, servitude, forced and compulsory labour". There appear to be different statutory obligations to report suspected victims of THB and related offences in the three jurisdictions,[36] however, these all operate in the same way. The obligations to notify all result in the victim, or suspected victim, being recorded in the NRM, a system that was originally set up pursuant to CoE THB Convention.[37] This Convention was ratified by the UK on 17 December 2008, and came into force on 1 April 2009, long before the current set of MS/THB laws. The NRM, in place since 2009, operates as a system for ensuring that potential victims can obtain support. It does not operate on a statutory basis, with some calling for this point to be reviewed, and to instigate a formal appeals system against its decisions.[38]

Entry into the NRM is via one of the recognised First Responder organisations, which include all police forces, and other law enforcement agencies, but also in England NGOs such as the Salvation Army, or in Scotland, TARA (Trafficking

34 See www.gov.uk/government/publications/modern-slavery-strategy.

35 The Scottish Government has its own human trafficking and exploitation strategy; see www.gov.scot/policies/human-trafficking/trafficking-and-exploitation-strategy/.

36 E&W Modern Slavery Act section 52 Obligation to notify the Secretary of State, Human Trafficking and Exploitation (Criminal Justice and Support for Victims) Act (Northern Ireland) 2015 section 13 Obligation to notify the National Crime Agency, and Human Trafficking and Exploitation (Scotland) Act 2015, section 38 obligation to notify Police Scotland.

37 CETS No. 197.

38 Home Office, Review of the National Referral Mechanism for victims of human trafficking, November 2014, p 9.

Awareness Raising Alliance), or Migrant Helpline. All adults need to consent to being entered onto the NRM. Child victims do not need to give consent. The 2014 Home Office Review of the NRM points out that "it is not in fact a single system" but a network of "a large group of dedicated people, professionals, immigration staff, police and others working alongside a vibrant and passionate voluntary sector".[39] The approach to the use of the NRM differs in the different UK jurisdictions.[40] All NRM forms should (E&W) or can (NI & Scotland) be referred to the police, but this does not require the potential victims to assist the police in their investigations. If the victim does not want to be recorded in the NRM then an alternative anonymised system of notification can be used, using a MS 1 form. In practice, in Scotland, people about to be entered into the NRM who have an associated unresolved UK immigration status, will be advised on their migration status by the NGO Migrant Helpline before being so recorded. Apparently did does not happen as standard practice in the rest of the UK.

A pilot project is operating in the UK called Victim Navigators, which involves specialists in "trauma informed and specialist support" being embedded with police forces and the Borders Agency which provide "support during the crucial post-rescue period and ongoing coordination between the victim and the officers investigating their case".[41] This is in line with similar initiatives where police in the UK are increasingly taking a more caring approach to vulnerable people in society, while also pursuing criminals.[42] The Victim Navigators pilot programme, in addition to assisting the victim, has led to substantial improvement for the law enforcement, with "89% of victims supported by Victim Navigators engage with police investigations compared with an UK average of 33% providing police with key evidence to pursue investigations and increase prosecutions".[43]

There are two decision points within the NRM system, a "reasonable grounds decision, which decides whether there are reasonable grounds to believe an individual is a potential victim", and a "conclusive grounds decision, which decides whether 'on the balance of probabilities' there is sufficient information to believe an individual is a victim".[44] These decisions are made by either the UK Human Trafficking Centre, UK Visas and Immigration or, for "a very small number of criminal cases",[45] Immigration Enforcement, with approximately 86% of referrals

39 Ibid., p 11.
40 Ibid.
41 Independent Anti-Slavery Commissioner Annual Report 2021–2022, op. cit., p 28, point 2.3.4.
42 For example, Police Scotland's Annual Policing Plan 21/22, pages 28–30, the co-location, and co-responses with the other Scottish Emergency Services, so that, for example, a mental health nurse is often on patrol in the police car.
43 Independent Anti-Slavery Commissioner Annual Report 2021–2022, op. cit., p 28, point 2.3.4.
44 Privacy information notice: national referral mechanism, Updated 24 May 2019, www.gov.uk/government/publications/human-trafficking-victims-referral-and-assessment-forms/privacy-information-notice-national-referral-mechanism.
45 Home Office, op. cit., p 13.

getting a positive decision based on reasonable grounds.[46] Issues have arisen with the internal processes in UK Visas and Immigration, of which more later. Usually a "reasonable grounds" decision is made within 5 to 10 days of referral.[47] The UK Human Trafficking Centre, based at the NCA, is the main collator of information on the NRM.[48]

If a negative decision is made that an individual is not in fact a victim, then support that is being given ceases, and the individual then may become subject to alternative processes, such as criminal prosecution for their own crimes, or immigration processes, if they are in the country illegally. As pointed out by the Independent Review, victims with a positive conclusive grounds' decision post-NRM options "differ according to their nationality and circumstances".[49]

The CPS view of "identification and referral" through the NRM is that it "should assist in the detection of victims of trafficking before they are arrested or charged". The NRM decides "on the balance of probabilities". This decision has "no official status in a criminal court", where decisions must be made "beyond criminal doubt".[50] The fact that an individual has been given "either ***a reasonable grounds decision*** or ***a conclusive grounds decision*** that they are a trafficked victim … should be taken into account when considering the decision to proceed with a Prosecution" against them (emphasis in the original).[51]

The Independent Anti-Slavery Commissioner

The role of the UK Anti-Slavery Commissioner was created by sections 40 to 44 of the Modern Slavery Act with a UK wide remit. He or she predominantly operates in the public domain, publishing reports and recommendations aimed at joining up the operation of different actors in combatting MS or THB. These actors could be law enforcement, public authorities, such as local government, charities or individuals who are active in this area. Public authorities are legally obliged to cooperate with the Commissioner.[52] The role, as specified in section 41 does require the holder to encourage good practice, and undertaking and supporting research, with the first two appointees to this role have been former senior police offices with experience with combatting MS/THB crimes. The role does not involve handling or being involved in individual MS/THB cases.[53]

Kevin Hyland, the first Independent Anti-Slavery Commissioner,[54] gave evidence in 2018 to the UK parliament. He stated that an individual could be up to 3 years in the NRM process. This was because of capacity issues, with there being

46 Ibid., p 8.
47 Ibid., p 23.
48 Ibid., p 54.
49 Independent Review, op. cit., p 19.
50 Ibid., p 18.
51 CPS Policy on Prosecuting Cases of Human Trafficking, May 2011, p 31.
52 Modern Slavery Act 2015, section 43.
53 Ibid., section 44.
54 A post set up by Part IV of the Modern Slavery Act 2015, with a UK wide remit.

a lack of staff fully skilled in making decisions as to whether the individual is in fact a victim of THB etc.[55] By 2021 it was being reported that a victim waited an average number of 586 days for a conclusive decision, with some had been waiting since 2016.[56] In addition, up to one third of the victims being processed in the NRM are from outside the UK.[57] GRETA's Third Evaluation Report, using data to the 8 July 2021,[58] confirms that UK nationals comprised the largest number of referrals (27% at 2,836 referrals), followed by "Albania (1,705 referrals), Vietnam (887 referrals), China and India".[59] Of the "possible victims referred to the NRM the majority (6,564) of the possible victims referred to the NRM claimed they were exploited in the UK only, 2,762 claimed to have been exploited overseas only, and 817 were exploited both in and out of the UK".[60]

Reports may be made to the NRM once the individual arrives in the UK, with a view to accessing the support measures, but the trafficking or MS offence occurred in another jurisdiction. Sometimes UK police can transfer intelligence to other jurisdictions, such as via Europol, even post-Brexit.[61] However, in many instances the UK Foreign Office actively prohibits UK police from sharing intelligence with other countries. This could be for many reasons, from political to security reasons. The conversion rates from the point of charging an individual with a THB offence to obtaining a conviction "have been comparable with other crimes", however bottle necks arise in the system with "only a small proportion of the modern slavery crimes recorded by police result in a charge".[62]

Part of the issues underpinning the above bottleneck may be the vulnerability of witnesses, and their unwillingness or inability to give evidence in court. Other reports to the NRM are of historic trafficking cases. However, there are also problems with the design of the NRM, which does not allow police to develop information into actionable intelligence in the traditional policing way. This includes police not being able to access intelligence already in the NRM, say by accessing historic material in order to assist in building up a current case, a matter raised by Kevin Hyland in evidence given to the UK Home Affairs Committee.[63] This point was also raised in the 2018 report of the House of Commons Committee of Public Accounts, which has called "the digitisation of the National Referral Mechanism (NRM) [to be made] a priority".[64] The NCA has informed

55 Kevin Hyland, former Independent anti-trafficking Independent Anti-Slavery Commissioner in evidence to the Home Affairs Committee Tuesday 23 October 2018 Meeting started 2.31 p.m., ended 4.52 p.m.

56 Independent Anti-Slavery Commissioner Annual Report 2021–2022, op. cit., p 6.

57 Kevin Hyland, op cit.

58 GRETA, op. cit., p 10.

59 Ibid., p 12, point 14.

60 Ibid.

61 Independent Anti-Slavery Commissioner Annual Report 2021–2022, op. cit., p 24, point 2.2.2.

62 House of Commons Committee of Public Accounts, Reducing modern slavery, Thirty Sixth Report of Session 2017–2019, 25 April 2018, p 15.

63 Kevin Hyland, op cit.

64 House of Commons, op. cit., p 3.

the Public Accounts Committee that a better system for developing intelligence in this crime area was required,[65] which allied to "improving police officers' understanding of the systems, legislation, paperwork and powers available to them",[66] should assist in this area. The Home Office has also had problems analysing NRM data in detail, as "the system it is stored in does not enable data to be analysed in a meaningful way".[67] The NRM is dealing with high volumes with, in 2021 "12,727 referrals were made into the NRM", a 20% increase on 2020,[68] of which 5,468 were children.[69] The House of Commons Committee on Public Accounts had recommended that the NRM system be reformed by January 2019 so that its data could be properly analysed, in order "understand the crime, the businesses and the sectors where prevalence is highest, and, where victims consent, to understand what happens to victims after they leave the NRM".[70] The Independent Review reported in May 2019 that the Home Office was "undertaking extensive reforms to the National Referral Mechanism",[71] and by August 2019 it was being reported that a new digital case-working system was being introduced. It is hoped that these issues will, *inter alia*, be addressed.

Exploitation as a Defence against Prosecution

One of the main protections for victims of slavery or THB is the use of their status as victims of these offences against prosecution for other criminal offences. The provisions in the three main UK jurisdictions are similar, but not the same.[72] The defence of slavery or trafficking victims is set out in section 45 of the Modern Slavery Act. This has been interpreted for E&W in the joint appeals case in the Court of Appeal of *MK v R*,[73] as requiring defendant victims to "raise evidence to show the ingredients of s.45 apply", but they do not have to "prove those ingredients", thereby lessening the evidentiary burden on already traumatised and vulnerable people. Section 45 of the Modern Slavery Act states that the accused "is not guilty of an offence" if they were under the age of 18 at the time of committing the offence, and they committed the offence "as a direct consequence" of being a slavery or THB victim. Required is that "a reasonable person in the same situation as the person and having the person's relevant characteristics would do that act", given the situation that they found themselves in. This defence does not operate in the case of offences listed in Schedule 4 of the Modern Slavery Act,

65 Ibid., p 15/16.
66 Ibid.
67 Ibid., p 12.
68 Independent Anti-Slavery Commissioner Annual Report 2021–2022, op. cit., p 12 point 1.2.1.
69 Ibid., p 20 point 1.5.1.
70 House of Commons, op. cit., p 6.
71 Independent Review, op. cit., p 8.
72 Modern Slavery Act 2015, Part 5, Human Trafficking and Exploitation (Scotland) Act 2015, Part 2, and Human Trafficking and Exploitation (Criminal Justice and Support for Victims) Act (Northern Ireland) 2015, Parts 3, 4, and 4A.
73 [2018] EWCA Crim 667.

which contains a very lengthy list of offences, putting into question the section 45 defence referred to above. How the section 45 defence was to operate was in point in the English case of *R v DS*,[74] a case involving county line drug dealing of class A drugs by someone who was initially underage. In this case a conclusive grounds decision by the competent authority under the NRM had been obtained. This decision needs to be considered when deciding if a defendant is a victim of THB, and whether the "offending has a very close nexus with the exploitation".[75] It was held that the prosecutor is then entitled to challenge a conclusive grounds decision before a jury, and to rebut the section 45 defence,[76] rather than having the prosecution stopped completely, as had happened in the initial trial court.

The NI act[77] sections 22–24 cover similar situations for NI. Under section 22.6 if the victim was under the age of 18 at the time of the offence, then they will not be guilty of an offence, if the "act was done as a direct consequence of the person being, or having been, a victim of" "slavery, servitude, forced or compulsory labour" or "human trafficking". NI also differentiates persons between the age of 18 and 21 for the purposes of guilt in committing an offence while a victim of THB or equivalent relevant exploitation.

Covering both E&W and NI, the CPS Policy on Prosecuting Cases of Human Trafficking, May 2011, is also relevant. This is predominantly detailed advice from the CPS to its prosecutors across the country as to how a MS/ THB case is to be prosecuted in court. It does provide however[78] that "there is a strong public interest to stop the prosecution" of victims of THB, in particular "where there is clear evidence that the [adult] suspect has a credible defence of duress". The issue of duress in law, and the "more subtle forms of coercion exercised by traffickers and exploiters" is also addressed.[79] Relying also on the E&W court's ruling in the case of *R v O*,[80] there is a requirement on both prosecution and defence lawyers "to take all reasonable steps to identify victims of trafficking and be pro-active in causing enquiries to be made". Prosecutors should be alert in the case of likely child victims of trafficking.[81] That said, the CPS Policy points out that there is no guarantee of immunity from prosecution for victims of THB,[82] with each case needing to be examined on its merits. The CPS in England lost a 2021 case at the ECtHR, *VCL and AN v The United Kingdom*,[83] for breach of Article 4

74 [2020] EWCA Crim 285.
75 *R v DS* [2020] EWCA Crim 285, paragraph 41.
76 Ibid., paragraph 42.
77 Human Trafficking and Exploitation (Criminal Justice and Support for Victims) Act (Northern Ireland) 2015.
78 CPS policy, op. cit., p 30.
79 Ibid.
80 *R v O* [2008] EWCA Crim 2835.
81 CPS policy, op. cit., p 31.
82 Ibid.
83 *VCL and AN v The United Kingdom*, Applications nos. 77587/12 and 74603/12, ECtHR, 5th July 2021, paragraph 219.

(Prohibition of slavery and forced labour) and/or Article 6 (Right to a fair trial) of ECHR, on the issue of failing to investigate the status of accused as potential THB victims (who had been under the age of 18 at the time), thereby affecting the overall fairness of criminal proceedings. Both applicants had been found to be credible victims of THB by the relevant competent authority for England,[84] but the CPS had chosen to ignore that finding, "without any significant evidence capable of displacing the conclusion of the Competent Authority".[85] The prosecution itself did not violate the provisions of Article 4, however the ruling now requires "police, prosecutors, defence and the courts to identify indicators of trafficking whether or not the suspect makes any disclosure that they are potential victims, and whether or not they make any admissions concerning the offence".[86] GRETA states, with regard to this case that the "criminalisation of victims contravenes the State's obligation to provide services and assistance to them, and discourages them from coming forward and co-operating with the investigation into those responsible for their trafficking".[87]

Scotland takes a different approach to legislating for non-prosecution of victims, requiring that the Lord Advocate (chief prosecutor, and so called even when staffed by a woman) will issue instructions[88] on the prosecution of both adult and child victims. The Lord Advocate's directions on prosecution in Scotland states, "the list of offences which victims of human trafficking or exploitation may commit is constantly evolving".[89] It states that there is a strong presumption against prosecuting both child[90] and adult[91] victims of trafficking. Given the requirement for "All cases of this nature must be reported to the National Lead Prosecutor for Human Trafficking and Exploitation for a final decision to be made",[92] and given the relative size of the jurisdiction, there is a very high likelihood that prosecution for these offences is more tightly coordinated in Scotland than in the rest of the UK.

84 Ibid., paragraph 116.
85 Ibid., paragraph 124.
86 Independent Anti-Slavery Commissioner Annual Report 2021–2022, op. cit., p 30, point 2.4.1.
87 GRETA, op. cit., p 50 point 174.
88 Human Trafficking and Exploitation (Scotland) Act 2015, section 8.
89 Lord Advocate's Instructions for Prosecutors when considering Prosecution of Victims of Human Trafficking and Exploitation, point 4.
90 If a child "(a) is a victim of human trafficking or exploitation and (b) the offending took place in the course of or as a consequence of being the victim of human trafficking or exploitation, then there is a strong presumption against prosecution of that child for that offence".
91 (a) is a victim of human trafficking or exploitation; (b) has been compelled to carry out the offence; and (c) the compulsion is directly attributable to being the victim of human trafficking or exploitation; then there is a strong presumption against prosecution of that person for that offence.
92 Lord Advocate's Instructions, op. cit., point 29.

Protection of Victims as Witnesses

Protection of victims of THB and MS in the context of criminal proceedings in E&W is provided for,[93] with similar provisions in the NI.[94] There are no comparable provisions in the counterpart Scottish act, although there is an amendment made to section 8.5 of the Victims and Witnesses (Scotland) Act 2014 for a THB (etc.) victim to specify the gender of the interviewer. There are provision of independent child trafficking advocates in E&W,[95] the appointment of Independent child trafficking guardians in Scotland,[96] and Independent Guardians in NI.[97] The E&W provisions had not yet been fully rolled out, with, by May 2021 children in one third of England "not yet able to access this provision".[98] In addition to recommending full use of these provisions, the Independent Review proposed extending the service "to young people who need the service over the age of 18 and up to 21 or 25".[99] Further, as the role is "more akin to a 'guardian'", going further than advocacy, but rather "developing a holistic understanding of [the young person's] needs and making decisions on their behalf in their best interests", it was recommended that the independent child trafficking advocates be more commonly known as "Independent Guardians".[100] In addition the Modern Slavery Act provides that victims of slavery be granted civil legal aid[101] in the case of immigration law, employment law and damages. This is done by amending the Legal Aid, Sentencing and Punishment of Offenders Act 2012, which predominantly only applies in E&W.

Non-THB/MS sexual offences related to children continues to be governed by Sexual Offences Act 2003, predominantly for E&W, the Sexual Offences (Northern Ireland) Order 2008/1769, and the Sexual Offences (Scotland) Act 2009. These cover a wide range of sexual offences and are drafted differently in the different jurisdictions. However, they all cover rape and sexual offences against children, to include incitement or causing children to engage in sexual activity,[102] and arranging or facilitating sexual offences with children.[103] Also covered is child prostitution and

93 Modern Slavery Act, section 46.
94 Human Trafficking and Exploitation (Criminal Justice and Support for Victims) Act (Northern Ireland) 2015, sections 23 and 24.
95 Modern Slavery Act, section 48.
96 Human Trafficking and Exploitation (Scotland) Act 2015, section 11.
97 Human Trafficking and Exploitation (Criminal Justice and Support for Victims) Act (Northern Ireland) 2015, section 21.
98 Independent Anti-Slavery Commissioner Annual Report 2021–2022, op. cit., p 21, point 1.5.6.
99 Independent Review, op. cit., p 16.
100 Ibid., p 56.
101 Modern Slavery Act, section 47.
102 Sexual Offences Act 2003, sections 5–29, Sexual Offences (Northern Ireland) Order 2008/1769, part 3, Sexual Offences (Scotland) Act 2009, part 4.
103 Sexual Offences Act 2003, section 50, Sexual Offences (Northern Ireland) Order 2008/1769, Article 21.

pornography.[104] Extra-territorial effect is established for these offences.[105] Legislative provisions are made for, *inter alia*, risk orders,[106] sexual offences prevention orders,[107] foreign travel orders,[108] and surrender of passports.[109]

General Assistance to Victims

There are new legal provisions, from 2023, dealing with assistance and support for victims of MS in E&W.[110] The initial guidance issued by the Secretary of State was clearly insufficient to meet international and EU obligations. It is argued therefore that the E&W provisions for the support of adult victims were "significantly weaker" than those in Scotland or NI,[111] with Scotland and NI going "beyond the minimum international standards".[112] The 2022 Nationality and Borders Act contains provisions for this to be covered by statutory instrument, however the 2022 act, which would have varying applicability across the UK, depending on context, now has provisions which provide for the withdrawal of "support from some victims on account of their criminal past and the requirement for victims to make disclosures to a deadline or a to risk undermining their credibility",[113] a matter of concern for the UK's Independent Anti-Slavery Commissioner.[114]

The NI legislation provides that assistance and support to adult victims of relevant offences is given,[115] as with E&W, for 45 days.[116] The NI legislation, post 2022, further provides that this assistance could be given for "such longer period as the Department thinks necessary",[117] with a similar provision to be found in the post 2022 version of the E&W Modern Slavery Act, providing for a possible

104 Sexual Offences Act 2003, section 47–51, Sexual Offences (Northern Ireland) Order 2008/1769, Articles 37 to 41, Criminal Law (Consolidation) (Scotland) Act 1995, sections 7–13, and Criminal Justice and Licencing (Scotland) Act 2010 section 41 (Indecent images of children).

105 *Inter alia*, for acts done by UK nationals or residents, Sexual Offences Act 2003 section 72, Sexual Offences (Northern Ireland) Order 2008/1769, Article 76, and Sexual Offences (Scotland) Act 2009 section 54. Also covered in Scotland, incitement in Scotland to commit certain sexual acts outside Scotland, Sexual Offences (Scotland) Act 2009 section 54A.

106 Sexual Offences Act 2003, sections 112A to 129.

107 Ibid., sections 103A to 113.

108 Ibid., sections 103D, 114–122.

109 Ibid., sections 103D, 117A and 117B.

110 Modern Slavery Act 2015, section 50.

111 C. Beddoe and V. Brotherton, *The Anti-Trafficking Monitoring Group; Class Acts? Examining Modern Slavery Legislation across the UK*, Anti-Slavery International for The Anti-Trafficking Monitoring Group, 2016, p 45.

112 Ibid., p 45.

113 Nationality and Borders Act 2022, sections 59 and 63.

114 Independent Anti-Slavery Commissioner Annual Report 2021–2022, op. cit., p 6.

115 Human Trafficking and Exploitation (Criminal Justice and Support for Victims) Act (Northern Ireland) 2015, section 18.

116 Ibid., section 18.4.

117 Ibid.

further 30 days of assistance and support.[118] Assistance and support is not conditional on the victim providing support for criminal proceedings.[119] This support can continue even if the victim has left NI,[120] or where a person is deemed to be no longer classified as a victim.[121]

In Scottish legislation,[122] at sections 9 and 10 address this issue, making provisions for support for adult victims of THB under the Scottish legislation for the two offences. This has been supplemented by the Human Trafficking and Exploitation (Scotland) Act 2015 (Support for Victims) Regulations 2018/90. This support continues for a period of 90 days,[123] a period which is to end either at the end of the 90 days, or on "the date on which there is a conclusive determination that the adult is or is not a victim" of a relevant offence. As victims are often highly traumatised, this period, up from CoE Convention requirement for 30 days,[124] and the standard E&W and NI current provisions of 45 days (which now post 2022 can be extended), is seen to be very important. In addition to the duty to support adult victims of THB there is a duty imposed on local authorities across the UK to provide supportive services to children.[125]

Human Trafficking and Border Control

The interaction of the THB/MS system with Border Control has been an issue of contention for some time. There are specific provisions in the Modern Slavery Act 2015 addressing the needs of overseas domestic workers,[126] which covers workers either domestic workers in private households or private servants in diplomatic households, who may be treated differently to other categories of victims. Assuming the individual had leave to enter the UK as a domestic worker, then if that individual has become a victim of MS or THB then UK immigration rules must provide leave to remain so that individual can change employer, with the specified maximum period being not less than six months.

The pre-Brexit position was that once the support period for any MS or THB victim has expired (for the relevant UK jurisdiction) both EEA and non-EEA nationals could "be granted discretionary leave to remain" if they are supporting

118 Modern Slavery Act 2015, section 50A, as inserted by the Nationality and Borders Act 2002, section 64.
119 Human Trafficking and Exploitation (Criminal Justice and Support for Victims) Act (Northern Ireland) 2015, section 18.5.
120 Ibid., section 18.8.
121 Ibid., section 18.9.
122 Human Trafficking and Exploitation (Scotland) Act 2015.
123 Human Trafficking and Exploitation (Scotland) Act 2015 (Support for Victims) Regulations 2018/90, section 2.
124 CoE Convention on Action against Trafficking in Human Beings 2005, CETS No. 197, Article 13.1.
125 This is under the Children's Act 1989 for E&W. Also relevant are the Children's Scotland Act 1995, as amended, including by the Children and Young Persons (Scotland) Act 2015, and in NI, the Children's (Northern Ireland) Order 1995.
126 Modern Slavery Act 2015, section 53.

an ongoing criminal investigation, are pursuing a civil claim against their abuser, or "their personal circumstances warrant a grant of leave to remain".[127] Both categories of victims were "also eligible for the Home Office-funded Voluntary Returns Service, which [provided] them with financial and material support to return to their home country".[128] In organising this repatriation, it is necessary, for the wellbeing of the victim, and for their personal security, for the organising agency to consider linking up UK and third country law enforcement and NGO/ health case support. Apparently, this did not always happen, with gaps appearing even in repatriation to the then other EU member states. Confirmed victims who were non-EEA nationals were "automatically ... considered for a grant of discretionary leave", unless they had "an outstanding asylum claim".[129] It has already been noted post Brexit that the UK "is no longer part of the European Return and Reintegration network", with a need to develop replacement processes to assist returning individuals from the UK to EU member states.[130] When a THB victim makes an asylum application there is an automatic reduction in subsistence, which in 2018 was from £65 per week to £35 per week.[131] This reduction has quite an impact on the individual concerned.

The lack of independence of the NRM process from the Home Office and UK Visas and Immigration is also a contentious issue.[132] All those with migration issues in Scotland get immigration advice before entering the NRM process, as all such NRM reports are handled by the NGO, Migrant Helpline. This process has not been replicated across the rest of the UK. NGOs involved in the NRM process are particularly concerned about the "conflation of asylum and trafficking, the timeliness of decisions and the use of arguments about credibility which focus on minor discrepancies".[133] UK Visas and Immigration are of the view that making two separate decisions arising from the one interview "streamlines the process for victims", and avoids "re-traumatising victims".[134] However, the Home Office Review stated that "it is difficult to maintain confidence in making two different decisions when using the same information and staff".[135] In addition, the type of accommodation provided for asylum applicants is not often suitable for highly traumatised victims of THB.[136] UK Visas and Immigration's processes were challenged and found wanting in the case of *R (Atamewan) v The Secretary of State for the Home Department*,[137] which addressed a historical THB case. UK Visa and Immigration decision-making processes has

127 Independent Review, op. cit., p 19.
128 Ibid.
129 Ibid.
130 Independent Anti-Slavery Commissioner Annual Report 2021–2022, op. cit., p 20, point 1.4.10.
131 Kevin Hyland, op cit.
132 Home Office, op. cit., p 9.
133 Ibid., p 43.
134 Ibid.
135 Ibid.
136 Ibid., p 34.
137 [2013] EWHC 2727 (Admin).

since changed.[138] A Migrant Victims Protocol was announced in December 2021 which aimed to "ensure that no immigration enforcement action will be taken against a victim of crime while their case is being investigated and prosecuted", with advice to be given to victims "about regularising their immigration status".[139]

The House of Commons Committee of Public Accounts found that the Home Office has not "set up its modern slavery activities as a coherent programme with an all-encompassing governance structure".[140] It has failed to "set measures or targets for what success looks like for the strategy across the system or identified clear roles and responsibilities for all organisations involved".[141] Of interest to the Committee on Public Accounts, there was also a lack of knowledge about "how much money is spent across government on tackling modern slavery", meaning that government could not prioritise or "assess how effective different elements of its strategy" were.[142] While the general objective of the Modern Slavery Act 2015 had been ambitious in many respects, the operationalisation of the strategic response clearly showed many failings.

Maritime Enforcement

Law enforcement provisions in UK territorial waters against THB and MS is provided for, for all three UK jurisdictions in the Modern Slavery Act 2015.[143] This power can only be exercised in foreign territorial waters where that other state consents to the exercise of those powers. The exercise of powers against a foreign registered ship can only be exercised either where the home state has requested assistance, the home state has authorised the UK to so act, or there is an international treaty in place authorising the UK to so act in those circumstances. There are also provisions on hot pursuit in UK territorial waters, which apply to all three UK jurisdictions.[144]

Extra-territorial Effect

All three UK pieces of legislation have considerable extra-territorial effect, using the active personality principle. The Modern Slavery Act 2015, section 1 offence of slavery, servitude, forced or compulsory labour has no restrictions as to where these offences are to be carried out for the provisions of this act are to apply. There is global territorial reach in section 2 of the Modern Slavery Act 2015

138 Home Office, op. cit., p 26/27.
139 Independent Anti-Slavery Commissioner Annual Report 2021–2022, op. cit. p 14, point 1.2.5.
140 House of Commons, op. cit., p 5.
141 Ibid.
142 Ibid.
143 E&W provisions being provided in section 35, Scotland, section 36 and NI, section 37, Modern Slavery Act 2015.
144 Modern Slavery Act 2015, section 38.

against UK nationals. Territorial reach against non-UK nationals under the Modern Slavery Act 2015 is established if "any part of the arranging or facilitating takes part in the United Kingdom" or if "the travel consists of arrival in or entry into, departure from, or travel within, the United Kingdom".[145] This extension of UK territorial reach would include any "aiding, abetting, counselling or procuring" with a view to committing a human trafficking offence.[146] Bothe the NI act[147] and the Scottish act[148] offences also have extra territorial effect.

Transnational Law Enforcement

The basic framework for transnational law enforcement is set out in the Crime (International Co-operation) Act 2003, which has UK wide application, with the NCA taking a lead role on behalf of the UK, operating a multilateral/international office. UK continues to engage with EU transnational law enforcement frameworks post Brexit. The UK Home Office operates an £11 million Modern Slavey Innovation Fund, with UK Aid funded programmes supporting THB and exploitation programmes.[149] GRETA reported that "as of December 2019, E&W were participating in 24 live Joint Investigation Teams (JITs) on THB with seven EU member states, including financial investigations".[150] Police Scotland, the national police force in Scotland, were involved in seven THB related JITs, and the Police Service of Northern Ireland (PSNI) had also been involved in THB JITs with EU member states.[151] The CPS, as prosecutors, were involved in 18 live JITs during the same time period.[152] With a view to developing long term relationships with countries along trafficking supply chains leading to the UK, police officers from Romania and Poland had been "seconded to work in policing in the Met Police Unit dealing with modern slavery and human trafficking".[153] It has also been reported in the media that Police Scotland have hosted officers from Vietnam.

The NCA maintains a "network of International Liaison Officers (including in Albania, Romania, Nigeria, China, Vietnam) who provide support in investigations",[154] and they have "established an office in Manila in October 2018 which aims to tackle child sexual abuse".[155] GRETA has also reported that "the UK had signed bilateral treaties with Nigeria and Vietnam on asset tracing and recovery".[156] In Scotland both TARA, one the key NGOs in THB/ exploitation, has

145 Ibid., section 2.7.
146 Ibid., section 4, extending the provisions of section 2.
147 Human Trafficking and Exploitation (Criminal Justice and Support for Victims) Act (Northern Ireland) 2015.
148 Human Trafficking and Exploitation (Scotland) Act 2015, section 1.4.
149 GRETA, op. cit., p 55, point 203.
150 Ibid., p 55, point 204.
151 Ibid.
152 Ibid., p 55, point 205.
153 Ibid.
154 Ibid., p 54, point 197.
155 Ibid., p 41, point 139.
156 Ibid., p 55, point 207.

visited Romania with Police Scotland in 2018 with a view to ensuring "survivors are supported on their return and reduces their risk of being re-trafficked".[157]

Conclusion

The UK has taken a gold-plated approach to meeting most of its EU and international THB commitments, with all three UK jurisdictions having two distinct offences of THB and "slavery, servitude, forced and compulsory labour" on their statute books. All three jurisdictions have considerably increased the EU THB punishment requirements from five years, or in aggravated circumstances, 10 years, to a possibility of life imprisonment. The difference in approach in the UK is probably leading to the substantially higher numbers of forced labour and male victims than is common across Europe. This difference in reporting is also probably affected by greater understanding among practitioners, leading to a greater number of UK nationals being recorded, to include the substantial UK children being "identified as being involved in county lines".[158] While other countries of origin vary from year to year, trafficking of nationals from Albania, Vietnam, Nigeria, and Romania into the UK remains substantial.

An interesting development in the UK that of the Victim Navigators pilot project, providing specialists in "trauma informed and specialist support" being embedded with police forces and the Borders Agency is also seen as having been very beneficial, not only for the victims, but also for law enforcement. Of interest to law enforcement has been the increase of prosecutions.[159] However, the use of NRM data for intelligence purposes is still a problem for UK law enforcement, with the Home Office also having problems processing the data. The ongoing prioritisation of the digitisation of NRM data should assist.[160]

Also noteworthy from the UK is the support provisions for possible victims which is substantially up on the CoE Convention requirements for 30 days.[161] Both E&W[162] and NI[163] are providing for 45 days support, with post 2022 optional further periods of support.[164] Scotland is more generous in its support period of 90 days[165] or earlier if the determination is that adult is not a victim of a

157 Ibid., p 69, point 276.
158 Independent Review, op. cit., p 8.
159 Independent Anti-Slavery Commissioner Annual Report 2021–2022, op. cit. p 28, point 2.3.4.
160 House of Commons, op. cit., p 3.
161 CoE Convention on Action against Trafficking in Human Beings, op. cit., Article 13.1.
162 Human Trafficking and Exploitation (Criminal Justice and Support for Victims) Act (Northern Ireland) 2015, section 18.4.
163 Ibid., section 18.
164 Modern Slavery Act 2015, section 50A, as inserted by the Nationality and Borders Act 2002, section 64, and Human Trafficking and Exploitation (Criminal Justice and Support for Victims) Act (Northern Ireland) 2015, section 18.4.
165 Human Trafficking and Exploitation (Scotland) Act 2015 (Support for Victims) Regulations 2018/90, section 2.

relevant offence. None of this assistance and support is conditional on the victim providing support for criminal proceedings.[166] However, support for child potential victims in E&W, in particular the independent child trafficking advocates,[167] was not by May 2021 fully rolled out, with children in one third of England "not yet able to access this provision".[168]

Both the CoE Convention and the THB directive ask states to examine making provisions on the non-punishment of victims involved in unlawful activities if they are found to be victims of THB.[169] While this option exists for prosecutors in all three UK jurisdictions, the lack of an automatic defence due to having been exploited has been highly contentious. As GRETA argues the "criminalisation of victims contravenes the State's obligation to provide services and assistance to them and discourages them from coming forward and co-operating with the investigation into those responsible for their trafficking".[170]

An emerging issue is that the Nationality and Borders Act 2022 provides for the withdrawal of "support from some victims on account of their criminal past and the requirement for victims to make disclosures to a deadline or a to risk undermining their credibility",[171] provisions which would have varied applicability, depending on context, across the UK. Presumably, these will be issues which will be raised in the subsequent court case and would be for the judge or jury to decide on. It will be interesting to see how these new provisions interact with the ECtHR ruling in *VCL and AN v The United Kingdom*,[172] which issued in 2021. The UK lost the case which was argued based on breach of either/ or Article 4 ECHR Prohibition of slavery and forced labour, and Article 6 ECHR - Right to a fair trial, on the issue of failing to investigate the status of accused as potential THB victims (who had been under the age of 18 at the time), thereby affecting the overall fairness of criminal proceedings. The ruling requires "police, prosecutors, defence and the courts to identify indicators of trafficking whether or not the suspect makes any disclosure that they are potential victims, and whether or not they make any admissions concerning the offence".[173]

Bibliography

Beddoe C. and Brotherton, V., *The Anti-Trafficking Monitoring Group; Class Acts? Examining Modern Slavery Legislation across the UK*, Anti-Slavery International for The Anti-Trafficking Monitoring Group, 2016.

166 Human Trafficking and Exploitation (Criminal Justice and Support for Victims) Act (Northern Ireland) 2015, section 18.5.
167 Modern Slavery Act, section 48.
168 Independent Anti-Slavery Commissioner Annual Report 2021–2022, op. cit., p 21, point 1.5.6.
169 CoE Convention, Article 26, Directive 2011/36/EU, Article 8.
170 GRETA, op. cit., p 50 point 174.
171 Nationality and Borders Act 2022, sections 59 and 63.
172 Case of *VCL and AN v The United Kingdom*, op. cit., paragraph 219.
173 Independent Anti-Slavery Commissioner Annual Report 2021–2022, op. cit., p 30, point 2.4.1.

CPS, *Policy on Prosecuting Cases of Human Trafficking*, May 2011.

GRETA, *Evaluation Report United Kingdom Third Evaluation Round Access to Justice and Effective Remedies for Victims of Trafficking in Human Beings*, GRETA (2021)12, Council of Europe, 2021.

HM Government, *Modern Slavery Strategy*, 2014, Crown Copyright.

Home Office, *Review of the National Referral Mechanism for Victims of Human Trafficking*, November 2014.

House of Commons Committee of Public Accounts, *Reducing Modern Slavery*, Thirty Sixth Report of Session 2017–2019, 25 April 2018.

Hyland, K., former Independent anti-trafficking Independent Anti-Slavery Commissioner in evidence to the Home Affairs Committee Tuesday 23 October2018 Meeting started 2.31 p.m., ended 4.52 p.m.

Independent Anti-Slavery Commissioner, *Annual Report 2021–2022 Presented to Parliament pursuant to Section 42(10)(b) of the Modern Slavery Act 2015*, (2022), Crown Copyright.

Independent Review of the Modern Slavery Act 2015, *Final Report Presented to Parliament by the Secretary of State for the Home Department by Command of Her Majesty*, May 2019, CP 100.

Lord Advocate's Instructions for Prosecutors when considering Prosecution of Victims of Human Trafficking and Exploitation, 2016, as updated, 2021.

NCA, *National Strategic Assessment of Serious and Organised Crime 2021*, Crown Copyright, 2021.

Police Scotland, *Annual Policing Plan 21/22*, Scottish Police Authority.

Scottish Government, *Human Trafficking and Exploitation Strategy*, Crown Copyright, 2017.

Stoyanova, V. *Human Trafficking and Slavery Reconsidered: Conceptual Limits and States' Positive Obligations in European Law*, Cambridge University Press, 2017.

Legislation

Children's Act 1989

Children's Scotland Act 1995.

Children and Young Persons (Scotland) Act 2015.

Children's (Northern Ireland) Order 1995.

CoE Convention on Action against Trafficking in Human Beings 2005, CETS No. 197.

CoE Convention for the Protection of Human Rights and Fundamental Freedoms, Rome, 4 November 1950, CETS No. 5.

Criminal Law (Consolidation) (Scotland) Act 1995.

Criminal Justice and Licencing (Scotland) Act 2010.

Directive 2011/36/EU of the European Parliament and of the Council of 5 April 2011 on preventing and combating trafficking in human beings and protecting its victims, and replacing Council Framework Decision 2002/629/JHA, OJ L 101/1.

Gangmasters (Licencing) Act 2004.

Human Trafficking and Exploitation (Scotland) Act 2015.

Human Trafficking and Exploitation (Scotland) Act 2015 (Support for Victims) Regulations 2018/90.

Human Trafficking and Exploitation (Criminal Justice and Support for Victims) Act (Northern Ireland) 2015.

Justice (Sexual Offences and Trafficking Victims) Act (Northern Ireland) 2022.
Modern Slavery Act 2015.
Nationality and Borders Act 2002.
Sexual Offences Act 2003,
Sexual Offences (Northern Ireland) Order 2008/1769.
Sexual Offences (Scotland) Act 2009.

Cases

MK v R [2018] EWCA Crim 667.
R (Atamewan) v The Secretary of State for the Home Department, [2013] EWHC 2727 (Admin).
R (on the application of A) v London Borough of Croydon, R *(M) v London Borough of Lambeth* [2009] EWHC 939 (Admin); [2009] 5 WLUK 178; [2010] 1 F.L.R. 193; [2009] Fam. Law 659; (2009) 153(20) S.J.L.B. 40.
R v DS [2020] EWCA Crim 285.
R v O [2008] EWCA Crim2835.
VCL and AN v The United Kingdom, Applications nos. 77587/12 and 74603/12, ECtHR, 5 July 2021.

Website

www.gov.uk/government/publications/human-trafficking-victims-referral-and-assessment-forms/privacy-information-notice-national-referral-mechanism.

8 Conclusion

Introduction

Neglected in academic debate to date has been the legal obligation to develop, operationalise and deepen existing transnational criminal law provisions to combat THB along the trafficking supply chains. Transnational THB, the focus of this book, is caused by poverty, the drive to better oneself, and the limited range of options available in an individual's home country. It is exacerbated by migration control, particularly in destination countries, and the classification of THB as a national security issue. As stated by von Tigerstrom, "many people are relatively insulated from the effects of insecurity in other countries, while others are extremely vulnerable".[1] The full picture requires the Japanese approach to human security, and a "freedom from want" analysis to be developed, as mentioned in Chapter 1. It is closely connected with smuggling of migrants, however THB involving "the person as a commodity whereas smuggling involves the person as consumer".[2] It is often, but not exclusively, facilitated by organised crime gangs, predominantly driven by the need to make money, but also often for other personal reasons, such as sexual exploitation, which cannot be obtained by legitimate means.

The broader picture of THB, or the profiting from another's misery is vast, and cannot be adequately addressed within the confines of one book. However, the enactment of legislation for, and operationalisation of a response to the transnational crime of THB is a question of laws, law enforcement networks, and transnational evidence and prosecution. The Canadian conceptualisation of human security as "freedom from fear", as advocated by Glasius and Kaldor,[3] should be adopted to deal with THB. This would require further development of International and European THB law and practice, to include using several other legal provisions, many of which already exist. Practitioners tasked with

1 B. von Tigerstrom, *Human Security and International Law: Prospects and Problems*, Hart Publishing, 2007, p 56.

2 H. Cullen, *The Role of International Law in the Elimination of Child Labour*, Martinus Nijhoff Publishers, 2007, p 49.

3 M. Glasius, and M. Kaldor, *A Human Security Doctrine for Europe: Project, Principles, Practicalities*, Routledge, 2006.

DOI: 10.4324/9781003429791-8

operationalisation of, what is for them, multi-layered legal frameworks transnationally would need to adopt Onuf style constructivism[4] in order to develop the necessary transnational law enforcement and prosecution frameworks, and thereby both better protect victims of THB and related exploitation, and better combat transnational organised crime, a requirement of state security.

THB can and often does occur within one state and can occur in an increasing range of circumstances. Transnational law, however, is an appropriate framing of THB as it crosses state boundaries. Transnational criminal law aims to globalise but not internationalise criminal law.[5] It is reliant on "state action and is fundamentally horizontal in nature".[6] As Boister points out, transnational criminal law is functional in nature, and is "an appropriate descriptive term to encapsulate offences spanning – "transcending" – two or more national jurisdictions".[7] Related exploitation must also be brought into the frame under the human security – freedom from fear lens, with resulting global regulatory gaps, to include for children, need to be examined and addressed. The lack of the fully operationalisation of the provisions on the Palermo Convention along THB, and related exploitation, supply chains, is also of concern, and needs to be addressed.

As stated by von Tigerstrom, "the way security is defined reflects and has profound implications for our view of society, including law as part of society".[8] This book argues that a human security approach should be taken to the interpretation of legal text, and an understanding of the crime of THB. This approach should prioritise the security of individuals, wherever they come from, whatever their nationality, and whatever their immigration status in that state. UN General Assembly has held that human security "is based on national ownership", and "requires greater collaboration and partnership among Governments, international and regional organizations and civil society".[9] The human security approach takes the view that "the security of all individuals everywhere is the common concern of all".[10] It requires "making individuals the primary referent objects of security instead of states", requiring a focus on the threat to individual's "lives, safety, and rights".[11] The concept of "'mutual vulnerability' is an important element of one understanding of human security".[12] The human security concept is not seen as having a legal definition itself, but rather the "notion is both an operational and a

4 N. Onuf, *World of Our Making*, University of South Carolina Press, 1989.
5 N. Boister, *An Introduction to Transnational Criminal Law*, Oxford University Press, 2012, p 275.
6 Ibid.
7 N. Boister, 'Transnational Criminal Law?', (2003), 14 *European Journal of International Law* 5. p 975.
8 von Tigerstrom, op. cit., p 3.
9 UN General Assembly Resolution, 10 September 2012, 127th plenary meeting, A/RES/66/290, paragraph 3.
10 von Tigerstrom, op. cit., p 194.
11 Ibid., p 193.
12 Ibid., p 19.

policy framework".[13] It is a concept that should be operationalised in a number of areas, to include "taking action against human traffickers".[14]

Human rights law, often used to discuss THB, "contains a well-developed body of norms to address the potential for states to threaten or fail to protect individuals within their jurisdiction".[15] Human rights are focused on the relationship between a state and its citizens and residents, those "subject to its jurisdiction".[16] A state rarely has legal obligations to those outside its jurisdiction, "even if those individuals are affected by its actions".[17] A human security approach, therefore, would be broader than the traditional human rights approach, which prioritises those who can get a legal system to work to their benefit, whether that be through their legal status in that jurisdiction, or through access to necessary legal advice. In the absence of international criminal law formally recognising THB as an international crime – and *ius cogens* under Article 53 of the Vienna Convention, or even a clearer understanding of the emerging *ius cogens* under Article 64, we are left with needing to develop the transnational legal framework to combat THB.

If the traditional national security approach is taken to dealing with the victims of THB this will be at the expense of tackling the underlying organised crime, then a state is weakening its own national security from within. If organised crime is allowed to flourish within any one state it leads to internal serous national security risks. The human security prism highlights the "ways in which states and the pursuit of national security may negatively affect individuals' security in ways that do not amount to human rights violations".[18] A human security approach needs to be taken to the victims of THB, while the resources of the state are used to combat the traffickers, seize their proceeds of crime, which is often used to fund further transnational or national criminality. The full range of anti-money laundering tools, of which there are many transnationally, need to be fully deployed, and as organised crime move their operations online, national law enforcement, and transnational law enforcement networks and operations also need to move online to detect and disrupt organised crime's operations. Despite extensive global provisions combatting anti-money laundering and proceeds of crime, some jurisdictions still "face domestic procedural barriers to freezing, seizing and confiscating assets in foreign jurisdictions".[19] The OSCE is reporting that "investigators and prosecutors often must wait long periods of time (up to years)

13 M. Noortmann and C. Ryngaert, 'Towards a (New) Human Security-Based Agenda for International Law and Non-state Actors?' in C. Ryngaert and M. Noorthmann, *Human Security and International Law*, 2014 Intersentia, p 196.

14 Ibid.

15 von Tigerstrom, op. cit., p 205.

16 Ibid., p 74.

17 Ibid.

18 Ibid., p 205/6.

19 OSCE, *Leveraging Anti-Money Laundering Regimes to Combat Trafficking in Human Beings*, OSCE 2014, p 21.

to obtain financial information, witness testimony and evidence from foreign jurisdictions".[20] This seriously prejudices ongoing transnational operations.

The need for states to effectively cooperate with each other to protect their own citizens, citizens from other states and stateless persons, prioritising human security over national security, requires the development of transnational law enforcement frameworks. This is the approach taken in the EU, with the development of the concept of shared national sovereignty, where EU directives also benefits from the principles of supremacy and direct effect in its relationship with the legal systems of the EU member states. Rijken argues that the "traditional concept of state sovereignty … must be abandoned" to properly address the transnational crime of THB.[21] State sovereignty "is closely connected to the traditional conception of security".[22] As pointed out by Noorthmann, "human security and territorial sovereignty are different paradigms based on mutually exclusive security concepts".[23]

The development of transnational legal frameworks needs to negotiate the interlegality of different THB and related texts, coming from a variety of regulatory actors. Taking a Eurocentric approach, these vary from the UN Convention on Transnational Organised Crime 2000 (Palermo) and its allied protocol on THB (Palermo protocol), to a variety of UN Conventions, relevant ILO conventions and at a European regional level, the CoE THB convention (THB convention), and relevant rulings of the ECtHR. In addition, for EU member states, the EU is also an important regulatory actor.

The interpretation of these legal texts therefore needs to be done in a way in which practitioners, whether they be law enforcement officials, investigators where these are different to law enforcement, as is the case in some legal jurisdictions, and prosecutors can operationalise the legal frameworks in a way that allows them to effectively interact with their counterparts in another legal jurisdiction along the THB supply chain, as discussed in Chapters 1 and 4. The priority should be, at all stages of the interpretation, development, and operation of the transnational legal framework for THB is to effectively combat this transnational crime and provide the freedom from fear for potential victims as is required by the Canadian approach to human security. Practitioners, whether they be law enforcement, investigating or prosecuting officials, must be able to make the emerging transnational law enforcement structure work in a way that safe convictions of those engaged in the transnational crime of THB can be obtained, while providing the victims, or suspected victims, with the required human security response. There is, however, a problem with definitions when examining both the key texts, and national implementation of international legal obligations.

20 Ibid.
21 C. Rijken, *Trafficking in Persons Prosecution from a European Perspective*, TMC Asser Press, 2003, p 271.
22 von Tigerstrom, op. cit., p 64.
23 M. Noorthmann, 'Human Securities, International Laws and Non-state actors: Bringing Complexity Back', in C. Ryngaert and M. Noorthmann, *Human Security and International Law*, Intersentia, 2014, p 18.

In negotiating the interlegality resulting from the different regulatory actors in THB and related crimes, the question arises whether the criminal definition of THB is greater than the sum of its parts, slavery, servitude, forced labour and compulsory labour, and the related definition of exploitation. While analysing the relevant texts and case law it is necessary to be aware of the distinction of interpreting a legal text through the lens of human rights law and the lens of criminal law, with criminal law requiring full respect of the principle of legality, which was examined in Chapter 4. The EU sees "legality as a multilevel concept that integrates multiple legal actors and layers of legal sources today",[24] with the principle of legality within the EU being "a shared responsibility".[25] This process requires regard to be and to "national constitutions and to international instruments" when the CJEU develops its case law.[26] The EU, when developing its own legal jurisdiction, uses the concepts of harmonisation, predominantly in commercial law, approximation, and mutual recognition. Bantekas has pointed out that the EU is "thus moving towards a treaty-less regime in the field of criminal justice, where relevant EU legal instruments help create a hybrid, regional set of general principles of criminal law and regional customary law, in at least the definition of particular transnational offences".[27]

Forced and Compulsory Labour

The THB Protocol utilises the terms forced and compulsory labour, and these need to be interpreted considering the use of these terms under the ILO conventions. At the same time, it is necessary to acknowledge that, as with the UN human rights treaties relevant to this area, the UN transnational criminal law provisions are drafted and are intended to be used in a very different context to those being used in an ILO context, with its tripartite structure and use not just of criminal law but also civil and administrative law remedies. In addition, the ECtHR, for CoE member states, has also relied on the ILO Conventions to assist in developing its own laws relevant to slavery, servitude, forced and compulsory labour, as discussed in Chapter 2. From the above analysis the focus of the ILO in the context of forced and compulsory labour is much broader than that which is taken under the THB Protocol.

ILO law in the area of forced and compulsory labour was adopted with the understanding that "states were seen as key actors", however even from the

24 F. Meyer, 'C-387/02 Berlusconi and Others. The Berlusconi Judgment: A Cornerstone of European Legality', in V. Mitsilegas, A. di Martiona and L. Mancano, *The Court of Justice and European Criminal Law: Leading Cases in a Contextual Analysis*, Hart Publishing, 2019, p 43.

25 Ibid., p 47.

26 P. O'Higgins, 'The Interaction of the ILO, the Council of Europe and European Union Labour Standards', in B. Hepple, *Social and Labour Rights in a Global Context: International and Comparative Perspectives*, Cambridge, 2002, p 62/3.

27 I Bantekas, 'The Principle of Mutual Recognition in EU Criminal Law' (2007) 32 *European Law Review* 3, p 384.

beginning of ILO law on forced and compulsory labour there have been references to "non-state actors".[28] As pointed out by Kaufmann, Article 5(1) of ILO Convention No 29 refers to private individuals, companies and associations.[29] The ILO obligations on forced and compulsory labour therefore "have a horizontal effect" requiring "states to impose respective legal obligations on private actors, such as multinational enterprises".[30] Kaufmann points out that given that slavery and slavery like practices "are peremptory norms of international law (*ius cogens*)", as discussed in detail in Chapter 2, and therefore are "binding on the international community as a whole", this has led to ILO Conventions Nos 29 and 105 being "the most highly ratified" of the ILO "fundamental conventions".[31] The EU, for its part, "has shown an increasing willingness to embrace ILO standards".[32] The OECD has also been invoking the aid of ILO declarations in developing its policies.[33]

To complete the picture, the UK approach to legislating separately for forced and compulsory labour as well as THB, under *inter alia*, the Modern Slavery Act 2015, and the consequences of this approach was analysed in Chapter 7. This approach is likely to have had a significant impact on the higher numbers of male and forced labour numbers being reported from the UK, as discussed in Chapter 1. The UK's Gangmasters and Labour Abuse Authority is possible counterpart to the EU's European Labour Authority (ELA),[34] which started operating from 1 August 2021,[35] and has yet to become fully involved in the forced labour aspect of THB. In due the ELA should assist in strengthening the EU's response to this issue, as THB for forced labour is substantially less reported in the EU in comparison to the UK, as discussed in Chapter 1.

Further complexity arises with the additional enactment of THB provisions in individual EU member states, as discussed in Chapter 2, leading to diversity in approaches, and academic criticism, given that the EU has only adopted minimum rules in defining the criminal offence.[36] This diversity in national implementation, could give rise to issues for transnational cooperation,[37] both inside the EU,

28 C. Kaufmann, *Globalisation and Labour Rights; The Conflict between Core Labour Rights and International Economic Law*, Hart Publishing, 2007, p 54.
29 Ibid.
30 Ibid., p 43.
31 Ibid., p 54.
32 O'Higgins, op. cit., p 67.
33 Ibid., p 66.
34 See www.ela.europa.eu/en.
35 Regulation (EU) 2019/1149 of the European Parliament and of the Council of 20 June 2019 establishing a European Labour Authority, amending Regulations (EC) No 883/2004, (EU) No 492/2011, and (EU) 2016/589 and repealing Decision (EU) 2016/344, OJ L 186, 2019/07/11, p 21.
36 Directive 2011/36/EU of the European Parliament and of the Council of 5 April 2011 on preventing and combating trafficking in human beings and protecting its victims, and replacing Council Framework Decision 2002/629/JHA, OJ L 101/1, Article 2.3.
37 V. Stoyanova, *Human Trafficking and Slavery Reconsidered: Conceptual Limits and States' Positive Obligations in European Law*, Cambridge University Press, 2017, p 32.

where the European Arrest Warrant does not always require the double criminality test to be met,[38] but also in the EU's surrender provisions with third countries, to include the post Brexit UK, where the double criminality test may need to be met.[39] In addition, some states, in their implementation of THB legislation, have omitted one or other of the constituent elements of the THB crime,[40] leading to substantial differences in domestic legislation. This will lead to negative consequences for the operationalisation of those legal provisions.[41]

As pointed out by Stoyanova "human trafficking is not a form of exploitation" itself,[42] focusing rather on activities preparing for or anticipating exploitation.[43] Facts underpinning the crime of THB can but does not have to overlap with the facts underpinning "slavery, servitude, forced or compulsory labour".[44] THB includes "the recruitment, transportation, transfer, harbouring or receipt of persons".[45] Therefore there is a need for states to prohibit both THB and "slavery, servitude, forced and compulsory labour". However, Stoyanova reports that this is not the case outside the context of THB in many CoE member states, with other states only criminalising slavery as a crime against humanity, and not as a standard domestic crime.[46] With some jurisdictions copying into domestic legislation international law definitions for THB international law "definitional ambiguities"[47] become part of national criminal law, lacking the necessary clarity and precision for effective investigation and prosecutions.[48]

The gaps in domestic legal frameworks have led to efforts in some jurisdictions to draft domestic THB legislation to cover more behaviour than was anticipated in the international texts, leading to academic criticism.[49] If the freedom from fear approach to human security is adopted, as advocated in this book, this should sharpen the domestic definitions of THB, and this situation would be avoided. Other laws are, or should be, on national statute books to address exploitative situations short of either THB or slavery, servitude, forced or compulsory labour.

38 Council Framework Decision 2002/584/JHA on the European Arrest Warrant, OJ L 190, 18/07/2002, p 1, Article 2.2.
39 UK EU Trade and Cooperation Agreement, OJ L 149/10, Articles 599.4.
40 R. Haverkamp, E. Herlin-Karnell and C. Lernested, 'Introduction', in R. Haverkamp, E. Herlin-Karnell and C. Lernestedt, *What is Wrong with Human Trafficking? Critical Perspectives on the Law*, Hart Publishing, 2018, p 5.
41 Stoyanova (2017), op. cit., p 181.
42 Ibid., p 42.
43 Ibid.
44 Ibid., p 292.
45 THB Protocol, Article 3(a.).
46 Stoyanova (2017), op. cit., p 343/4.
47 Ibid., p 73.
48 Ibid., p 345.
49 P. H. Van Kempen and S. Lestrade, 'Limiting the Criminalisation of Human Trafficking; Protection Against Exploitative Labour versus Individual Liberty and Economic Development', in R. Haverkamp, E. Herlin-Karnell and C. Lernestedt, *What is Wrong with Human Trafficking? Critical Perspectives on the Law*, Hart Publishing, 2018, p 236.

Then an understanding needs to develop that there is a continuum of exploitation, from the standard contract law issues, to be resolved at domestic employment law tribunals, through the state legal provisions on abusive labour law practices, which are the concern of labour inspectors, who normally issue administrative penalties, but there may also be provision for criminal penalties, through then to the more severe offences entailing, depending on the facts of the case, either the THB provisions or the slavery, servitude, forced or compulsory labour provisions. If any of the required legal provisions, or relevant law enforcement capacity is missing from national legislative provisions, or lacking in some way, then there will be gaps in the human security framework, and human beings will continue to be exploited without an effective legislative or law enforcement response.

Problems continue with regard to the terms "exploitation" and "consent". Only exemplars for the term "exploitation" are provided in international and EU legal texts.[50] States need to "exercise their discretion" within their own legal systems in order to develop this concept.[51] At the same time states need to develop the concept of exploitation in a way that not only addresses their needs in domestic criminal law, but also in a way that facilitates transnational criminal law.[52] The issue of consent, and the impact of consent in the context of THB is also unclear. This replicates the issue of consent in the context of forced labour, with the ECtHR case of *Chowdury and Others v Greece*[53] holding that a victim's prior consent "is not sufficient to exclude the characterisation of work as forced labour", and that the facts need to be examined in each case.[54] The same approach will have to be taking in the context of THB.

Across European legal systems the *mens rea* for THB offences can vary from intentional to reckless.[55] The UK has enacted domestic legislation on THB and "slavery, servitude, forced and compulsory labour" with its possibility of life imprisonment, adopting the *mens rea* of "intention" or "knows or ought to have known".[56] These offences are classified as being at the most serious of the criminal scale in the three main UK jurisdictions. An issue also arises about the dividing line between THB and other domestic crimes such as fraud, deception, abduction, pimping and procurement, which also needs to be addressed in domestic jurisdictions,[57] and for the benefit of transnational law enforcement. While the above definitional issues have the potential to impact not just domestic criminal legal

50 F. Viganò, 'Introduction: An Unfortunate State of the Law', in R. Haverkamp, E. Herlin-Karnell and C. Lernestedt, *What is Wrong with Human Trafficking? Critical Perspectives on the Law*, Hart Publishing, 2018, p 241.
51 Ibid.
52 Stoyanova (2017), op. cit., p 68.
53 *Chowdury and Others v Greece*, Application no. 21884/15, ECtHR, 30 March 2017.
54 Ibid., paragraph 96.
55 Stoyanova (2017), op. cit., p 46.
56 Modern Slavery Act 2015, section 1.1a and section 2.4, Human Trafficking and Exploitation (Scotland) Act 2015, section 1 and section 4.1 (knew or ought to have known), Human Trafficking and Exploitation (Criminal Justice and Support for Victims) Act (Northern Ireland) 2015, section 4.1 (intention).
57 Stoyanova (2017), op. cit., p 41.

systems, but also the development of transnational law enforcement of THB, law enforcement, particularly in Europe, are finding that the volume of serious THB is such that law enforcement is only going over the lowest hanging fruit.[58] Core THB offences are sufficiently clear enough in practice, that transnational law enforcement's concerns are predominantly around prioritisation and resourcing of these criminal investigations.

As can be seen from the above, THB beings is a "highly complex" area of law.[59] When examining the issue of THB from a human security lens, there is a need also to look beyond the key texts to see where the gaps are in the current national, regional and transnational legal frameworks, and what other documents can be used to fill those legal gaps in order to increase human security. While the main international document, the Palermo protocol talks about "especially women and children", THB is increasingly been seen as covering all people, and for a wider range of purposes. Forced labour is increasingly accounting for male victims, with forced criminality, particularly in the UK, accounting for high child victim numbers. Equally, exploitation of human beings in global supply chains, where wealthy countries outsource misery to poorer countries also needs to be addressed.

Children

The issue of child trafficking is one of those areas where there are clear gaps in the international and EU THB legal frameworks. It would have benefited from further consideration during the drafting of the THB Protocol. The lack of detail in the protocol requires the examination of other documents, to include the UN Convention on the Rights of the Child 1989 (CRC) and its two optional protocols. Also required to fill the gaps are the ILO Convention on the World Forms of Child Labour 1999 (No 182) and ILO Recommendation 190 – Worst Forms of Child Labour Recommendation 1999. There are, however, weaknesses in both the UN CRC documents and the ILO Convention No 182 (WFCL) when it comes to the definition of a child, with the THB Protocol being much clearer in stating that it is anyone under the age of 18 years. Consent, whether that be from the parent or the child itself, also muddies the waters when it comes to the operation of both the CRC and its protocols and ILO Convention No 182 (WFCL) for all forms of exploitation. In addition, the ILO Convention No 182 (WFCL) does not cover all possible instances of exploitation, as family and small-scale agricultural holdings[60] and domestic service are not expressly provided for.[61] There is clarity in under the THB Protocol that a child cannot consent to exploitation.[62]

58 Europol presentation at the IALS, London on the 3 October 2017.
59 T. Obokata, *Trafficking of Human Beings from a Human Rights Perspective: Towards a Holistic Approach*, Martinus Nijhoff Publishers, 2006, p 38.
60 ILO Minimum Age Convention, 1973 (No. 138), Article 5.3.
61 Cullen, op. cit., p 140/1.
62 UN Protocol to Prevent, Suppress and Punish Trafficking in Persons, Especially Women and Children, supplementing the United Nations Convention against Transnational Organized Crime 2000, UNTS 2237, Article 3.c.

Not covered in ILO Convention No 182 (WFCL), however, is "adoption or child victims of organ transplants".[63] The CRC Optional Protocol to the Convention on the Rights of the Child on the sale of children, child prostitution and child pornography does refer at Article 2 to the "sale of children ... for remuneration, or any other consideration". When the issue trafficking of children for inter country adoption is addressed the Hague Convention on Intercountry Adoption 1993, the lack of provisions in this convention to combat transnational sale of children for adoption also needs to be addressed. The CRC Optional Protocol to the Convention on the Rights of the Child on the sale of children, child prostitution and child pornography does refer, at Article 3.b, to the "transfer of organs of the child in for profit". Child organ trafficking is a serious issue, needing to be addressed along with adult organ trafficking. A problem also arises regarding the sale of foetuses, as reported from Vietnam.[64] No doubt this is also happening in other countries globally, and both national and transnational legal frameworks, and law enforcement needs to be developed to combat the organised crime groups involved. Thyu *et al.* discuss the issues of embryo and foetuses trafficking,[65] which leads to the question where exactly the boundary line between THB and trafficking in organs, tissues and cells is. Presumably, different jurisdictions will draw the line at different places depending on their view of when exactly life starts from the point of view of their criminal laws, and which will be reflected in their laws on abortion. Nevertheless, the further legal thought needs to be given to this issue.

Reflecting the weaknesses in the global frameworks in addressing the issue of children in the context of THB, as discussed in Chapter 5, there continues to be some notable child related gaps in the EU directive on THB. It still does not cover the crime areas of child sex tourism (discussed in Chapter 5) or online paedophilia activity. Further EU, and CoE documents need to be examined to find relevant provisions, which arguably should have been covered, at least additionally, in the THB legislation. The CoE operates the Convention on the Protection of Children against Sexual Exploitation and Sexual Abuse (Lanzarote Convention),[66] while the EU operates Directive 2011/93/EU on combatting the sexual abuse and sexual exploitation of children and child pornography.[67] The CoE Convention on Cyber Crime 2001,[68] (discussed in Chapter 5) and the EU's Council

63 D. Rishikesh, 'The Worst Forms of Child Labour: A Guide to the ILO Convention 182 and Recommendation 190', in G. Nesil, L. Nogler, and M. Pertile, *Child Labour in a Globalized World A legal analysis of ILO Action*, Ashgate, 2008, p 85/86.

64 H. L. Thyu, H. T. H. Yen, and N. Q. Bao, 'Fetus Trafficking in Viet Nam – the New Criminal method of Human Trafficking' (2021) 10 *International Journal of Criminology and Sociology*.

65 Ibid.

66 CoE Convention on the Protection of Children against Sexual Exploitation and Sexual Abuse 2007, CETS No. 201.

67 Directive 2011/93/EU of the European Parliament and of the Council of 13 December 2011 on combating the sexual abuse and sexual exploitation of children and child pornography, and replacing Council Framework Decision 2004/68/JHA, OJ L 335, 2011/12/18, p 1.

68 Budapest, CETS No. 185.

Decision to combat child pornography on the internet[69] are also required to complete this picture.

Operationalising Transnational Legal Frameworks

The THB Protocol is optional but has been widely ratified. Once ratified, the THB Protocol and its associated Palermo Convention, with which it should be read, "suffers from the fact that the treaty provisions for enforcement are weak and hardly ever used".[70] This is despite the fact that THB is now estimated to be "the fasted growing form of organized crime and ranks as the third largest source of illicit profit after narcotics and arms trafficking".[71] This is a problem as "criminal networks have learned to exploit differences between various countries in terms of judicial systems, taxation, technological advances, and law enforcement".[72] As stated by the OSCE, "the pace of international co-operation in criminal matters has not kept up with the pace of the movement of people and goods across national borders".[73] From the perspective of CoE states though, the ECtHR case of *Rantsev v Cyprus and Russia*,[74] requires its states to "to take operational measures to protect victims, or potential victims, of trafficking", in circumstances where "[s]tate authorities were aware, or ought to have been aware, of the circumstances giving rise to a credible suspicion that an identified individual had been, or was at real and immediate risk of being trafficked or exploited",[75] as discussed in Chapter 4. In the view of the ECtHR rights arise under both Article 4 (Prohibition of slavery and forced labour), also relevant to Article 5 ECtHR (Right to liberty and security), included the need for effective policing. An entire paragraph of the *Rantsev* judgment was devoted to the "difficulties involved in policing modern societies" and the need for law enforcement to make "operational choices… in terms of priorities and resources".[76]

There is a need for most states to negotiate and implement agreements at a bilateral or multi-lateral level to effectively operationalise the provisions of the THB Protocol. These negotiations would be best done along specific THB supply chains, which are increasingly being identified by law enforcement working in this area. Bi- or multi-lateral treaties signed by governments, building on the provisions of the Palermo Convention and its THB Protocol, can provide the legal framework within which practitioners, lawyers, law enforcement, investigators for those jurisdictions where these are different to law enforcement, and prosecutors, can work to operationalise the legal framework in order to effectively combat the

69 Council Decision 2000/375/JHA of 29 May 2000 to combat child pornography on the Internet, OJ L 138, 09/06/2000 p 1.

70 N. Boister, (2003), op. cit., p 960.

71 OSCE, (2014), op. cit., p 12.

72 S. E. Cornell, 'The Interaction of Drug Smuggling, Human Trafficking, and Terrorism', in A. Jonsson, *Human Trafficking and Human Security*, Routledge, 2009, p 55.

73 OSCE, (2014), op. cit., p 21.

74 *Rantsev v Cyprus and Russia*, Application no. 25965/04, ECtHR, 7 January 2010.

75 Ibid., paragraph 285.

76 Ibid., paragraph 286.

particular THB supply chain that has been identified, taking a human security approach. This operationalisation will be following Onuf's approach to constructivism,[77] where practitioners from different jurisdictions will be bringing their own socialised understandings of how to operate within their own jurisdictions to the developing transnational legal framework. The EU has and advantage of having developed a transnational law enforcement and prosecution framework within its Area of Freedom Security and Justice (AFSJ).

The effective operationalisation of the provisions on the THB Protocol will require many levels of engagement of practitioners along the identified THB supply chain, with a lot of detailed work required to build effective investigations/ law enforcement frameworks, leading to effective prosecutions of the criminals and the securing of the safety of the victims or potential victims. Different designs of states, and the allocation of the roles of prosecution, investigation and law enforcement can differ considerably from one state to the next, issues which have been addressed for the benefit of EU member states in developing of their AFSJ. While this AFSJ has its own flaws, and needs further development, it can still act as a model which can be developed by other states to address the transnational crime of THB.

National differences can be overcome, and should not "necessarily pose any threat to coexistence and co-operation", as at the EU level.[78] Andreadakis, in the context of the EU project, states that "when different cultures, nationalities and traditions manage to co-exist and create a harmonised legal system, such system combines all the virtues and values of them".[79] Both the active and passive personality principle have been adopted by both the CoE Convention and the EU directive in the criminalisation of THB offences,[80] with the passive personality principle remaining missing from the UK legal framework.

With a positive legal obligation to enact and operate transnational law enforcement and justice frameworks to combat THB, and complying with the principle of legality discussed above, for most legal jurisdictions' treaty-based networks need to be developed between states to address the issues which arise, both from a law enforcement and victim protection perspective. Obokata has called for a framework that "unifies ... responses at the national, regional and international level" so as to "promote effective global action against trafficking".[81] Boister points out that states are reluctant to sign transnational organised crime bilateral treaties with "non-parties of the ICCPR [International Covenant on Civil and Political Rights] because of wariness of harsh penalty regimes".[82] This is also the situation for the UK, as the UK

77 Onuf, op. cit.
78 S. Andreadakis, 'Regulatory Competition or Harmonisation: The Dilemma, the Alternatives and the Prospect of Reflexive Harmonisation', in M. Andenas and C. Baasch Andersen, *Theory and Practice of Harmonisation*, Edward Elgar, 2011, p 58.
79 Ibid.
80 CoE Convention, Article 31, Directive 2011/36/EU, Article 10.
81 Obokata, op. cit., p 38.
82 N. Boister, 'The Cooperation Provisions of the UN Convention against Transnational Organised Crime: a "Toolbox" Rarely Used?', (2016), 16 *International Criminal Law Review* p 64.

Foreign Office actively prohibits UK police from sharing intelligence with other countries, for a wide variety of reasons, to include political and security reasons.

This issue needs to be expressly addressed by states in their negotiations with other countries, under their obligations, under both the Palermo Convention, and for contracting parties, the ECHR, as highlighted in *Rantsev*, regardless of which other third country they need to work with to combat THB, as discussed above. Traditional reluctance to deal with a country with a poor human rights record needs to be reconciled with European human rights requirements to proceed against human traffickers and protect their victims in a transnational context. A human security approach to THB requires that victims of THB, regardless of where they come from, are protected. International treaty drafters will have to put a lot of thought into the relevant treaty provisions, law enforcement practice manuals and internal prosecution and victim practice provisions to effectively address these issues in a transnational context.

At the level of practice however, law enforcement agencies have been "concentrating more on arrest and deportation of illegal migrants", a significant number of whom would be classified as victims in a THB context.[83] This has allowed the organisers of THB to remain free to recruit more victims and to arrange for more irregular crossing of borders. A high level of resourcing is required to combat THB, together with considerable effort to effectively tackle the underlying organised crime gang, both domestically and transnationally.[84] Consent to being "trafficked" or more accurately to be smuggled, or exploited, remains a complex legal issue in many jurisdictions. However, once coercion, deception, abuse of authority etc. is established, this should nullify the issue of consent.[85]

The THB Protocol frames the transnational crime of THB in the context of organised crime. The EU, for its part, in its directive on THB,[86] and in its earlier THB legislation,[87] has disaggregated the crime of THB from the concept of organised crime, with the presence of organised crime being an aggravating factor for the purposes of punishment. The CoE has taken a similar approach,[88] as has the UK. As pointed out by Shelly, "much of human trafficking is committed by smaller crime networks rather than large scale organisations".[89] Movement of people for the purpose of their exploitation "necessitates a degree of flexibility and

83 Obokata, op. cit., p 80.

84 Ibid.

85 A. Gallagher, *The International Law of Human Trafficking*, Cambridge University Press, 2010, p 28.

86 Directive 2011/36/EU, op. cit.

87 Council Framework Decision 2002/629/JHA on combating trafficking in human beings, OJ L 203, 01/08/2002 p. 1, which replaced Joint Action 97/154/JHA of 24 February 1997 adopted by the Council on the basis of Article K.3 of the Treaty on European Union concerning action to combat trafficking in human beings and sexual exploitation of children, OJ L 63, 04/03/1997, p 2.

88 CoE Convention Articles 2 and 24.

89 L. Shelly, 'Human Security and Human Trafficking', in A. Jonsson, *Human Trafficking and Human Security*, Routledge, 2009, p 13.

fluidity that is not always essential when trafficking inanimate commodities such as narcotics or counterfeit goods".[90] Both the EU and the CoE also legislate for national THB. There has also been an important change of focus in the CoE and EU provisions, with the context of the CoE Convention being is on the rights agenda[91] and gender equality.[92] The EU directive's approach to combatting THB is to take an "integrated, holistic, and human rights approach".[93] A problem does arise, however with the EU directive stating that THB is a "gender specific phenomenon", with men and women being trafficked for "different purposes".[94] This could be too rigid an approach, leading to gender blindness, as all types of people are found by law enforcement officers, in all THB categories.

The UK has taken a gold-plated approach to meeting most of its EU and international commitments to THB. In addition to all three UK jurisdictions (E&W, Scotland, and Northern Ireland) having two distinct offences of THB and "slavery, servitude, forced and compulsory labour" on their statute book. All three jurisdictions have considerably increased the EU THB punishment requirements from five years, or in aggravated circumstances, 10 years, to a possibility of life imprisonment. Reliance is made in the criminal law of all three UK jurisdictions to definitions developed in European Human Rights law, leading to the need to negotiate the interlegality discussed in Chapter 2. Both the police and the Gangmasters and Labour Abuse Authority, originally set up in 2004, investigate offences in this area. The UK has been reporting substantially higher numbers of forced labour and male victims than is common across Europe, with the National Crime Agency reporting for 2021 that "coerced criminality" is now the most common reported form of exploitation in the UK.[95] As understandings among practitioners of the UK legislation has developed, UK nationals "now represent by far the highest proportion of potential victims identified at almost a quarter of all those recorded".[96] A substantial number of UK children are being "identified as being involved in county lines".[97] While countries vary from year to year, transnational trafficking of nationals from Albania, Vietnam, Nigeria, and Romania into the UK remains substantial.

Prosecution of individuals and companies under UK law is based on an extensive active personality principle, therefore not adopting the passive personality principle as advocated by both the CoE Convention and the EU directive,[98] as

90 T. Makareno, 'Organized Crime or Crimes Organized? Isolating and Identifying Actors in the Human Trafficking Chain' in A. Jonsson, *Human Trafficking and Human Security*, Routledge, 2009, p 29.
91 CoE Convention, Article 5.3.
92 Ibid., Article 1.1.
93 Directive 2011/36/EU, preamble, paragraph 7.
94 Ibid., paragraph 3.
95 NCA, National Strategic Assessment of Serious and Organised Crime 2021, Crown Copyright, 2021.
96 Independent Review of the Modern Slavery Act 2015: Final Report Presented to Parliament by the Secretary of State for the Home Department by Command of Her Majesty May 2019, CP 100, p 8.
97 Ibid.
98 CoE Convention, Article 31, Directive 2011/36/EU, Article 10.

discussed in Chapter 6. If the UK is not going to prosecute based on an offence committed against one of its nationals, particularly if the other state in question remains unwilling or unable to resource effective investigations and prosecutions within their jurisdictions and is a potential gap if the human security approach is to be properly adopted. In addition to standard punishments such as fines and imprisonment, prevention orders, risk orders and in E&W, trafficking reparation orders are all available to the courts. Prevention orders can include a prohibition of foreign travel, and the surrender of a passport.

Victims

Making a national or transnational legal system work to the benefit of a victim is always problematic. However, with THB, victims "are in the weakest position and least able to speak out and demand their rights".[99] As pointed out by the OSCE, even in countries which maintain "strong legal standards on the protection of victims' rights" effective implementation of THB laws remain "elusive".[100] When investigating the THB offence, both the CoE[101] and the EU[102] emphasise the need for law enforcement and prosecution not to be reliant on victims' testimony, as by the very nature of the crime, victims are already highly vulnerable. In addition, the issue of secondary victimisation of victims during the investigation or prosecution process has been addressed in the EU directive.[103] Alternative methods of evidence gathering need to be used. In addition, the UK pilot project of Victim Navigators, providing specialists in "trauma informed and specialist support" being embedded with police forces and the Borders Agency, who provide "support during the crucial post-rescue period and ongoing coordination between the victim and the officers investigating their case",[104] has proven to be very beneficial, not only for the victims, but also for law enforcement. Victims, having been given the necessary support, are more likely to assist and support police investigations, and thereby increase prosecutions.[105]

The CoE Convention requires that support for possible victims should be for 30 days.[106] The UK in implementing its provisions under this convention, has substantially increased on this provisions, with 45 days support being provided in

99 S. Kirchner and V. M. Frese, 'Slavery under the European Convention on Human Rights and the Jus Cogens Prohibition of Human Trafficking' (2015) 27 *Denning Law Journal*, p 134.
100 OSCE, (2014), op. cit., p 17.
101 CoE Convention, Article 27.1.
102 Directive 2011/36/EU, Article 9.1.
103 Ibid., Article 12.4.
104 Independent Anti-Slavery Commissioner Annual Report 2021–2022, Presented to Parliament pursuant to Section 42(10)(b) of the Modern Slavery Act 2015, (2022), Crown Copyright, p 28, point 2.3.4.
105 Ibid.
106 CoE Convention on Action against Trafficking in Human Beings 2005, CETS No. 197, Article 13.1.

both E&W[107] and Northern Ireland,[108] with both jurisdictions post 2022 providing for optional further periods of support.[109] None of this assistance and support is conditional on the victim providing support for criminal proceedings.[110] However, support for child potential victims in E&W, in particular the independent child trafficking advocates,[111] was not by May 2021 fully rolled out, with children in one third of England "not yet able to access this provision".[112] Scotland provides support for a period of 90 days[113] or earlier if the determination is that adult is not a victim of a relevant offence.

A discussed in Chapter 6, both the CoE and EU documents ask states to examine making provisions on the non-punishment of victims involved in unlawful activities if they are found to be victims of THB.[114] While this option exists for prosecutors in all three UK jurisdictions, the lack of an automatic defence due to having been exploited has been highly contentious. As GRETA states the "criminalisation of victims contravenes the State's obligation to provide services and assistance to them and discourages them from coming forward and co-operating with the investigation into those responsible for their trafficking".[115]

Conclusion

Many gaps remain in the transnational and European regional legal framework, which need to be addressed, to complete a human security approach to THB and related exploitation. These gaps arise at all levels, at the transnational, European regional and, as in the case of the UK, examined in Chapter 7, the individual state. One of the main challenges identified in the UK, and for which the UK has been highly criticised by the House of Commons Committee of Public Accounts, was the finding that there had not been "a coherent programme with an all-encompassing governance structure".[116] There had been a lack of measurable targets, and no clear understanding of what success

107 Human Trafficking and Exploitation (Criminal Justice and Support for Victims) Act (Northern Ireland) 2015, section 18.4.
108 Ibid., section 18.
109 Modern Slavery Act 2015, section 50A, as inserted by the Nationality and Borders Act 2002, section 64, and Human Trafficking and Exploitation (Criminal Justice and Support for Victims) Act (Northern Ireland) 2015, section 18.4.
110 Human Trafficking and Exploitation (Criminal Justice and Support for Victims) Act (Northern Ireland) 2015, section 18.5.
111 Modern Slavery Act, section 48.
112 Independent Anti-Slavery Commissioner Annual Report 2021–2022, op. cit., p 21, point 1.5.6.
113 Human Trafficking and Exploitation (Scotland) Act 2015 (Support for Victims) Regulations 2018/90, section 2.
114 CoE Convention, Article 26, Directive 2011/36/EU, Article 8.
115 GRETA Evaluation Report United Kingdom third evaluation round Access to justice and effective remedies for victims of trafficking in human beings, GRETA (2021)12, Council of Europe, 2021, p 50, point 174.
116 House of Commons Committee of Public Accounts, Reducing modern slavery, Thirty Sixth Report of Session 2017–2019, 25 April 2018, p 5.

would look like.[117] In addition there had been a lack of "clear roles and responsibilities for all organisations involved".[118] UK has problems with how the National Referral Mechanism operates, the large numbers of potential victims it is processing, and the length of time it takes to be processed, with substantial delays having been reported for a number of years, and by 2021 the average number of 586 days being taken for a conclusive decision, with some having been waiting since 2016.[119] One-third of the victims being processed in the NRM are from outside the UK.[120]

The EU, for its part, has now identified the "challenges created by the digital age for law enforcement and judicial bodies in the fight against trafficking" "related to the modern law enforcement response to technological developments"[121] and the need for "dialogue with relevant internet and technology companies to reduce the use of online platforms for the recruitment and exploitation of victims".[122] This in line with the OSCE findings in its 2020 report on the use of technology tools to combat THB.[123] The EU is also seeking to "enhance actions to improve victims' support and referral in the cross-border context, towards the objective of setting up a European referral cooperation mechanism",[124] which might be worth examining formally, with a treaty base, by other countries in the context of high volume THB global supply chains.

Work is ongoing at many levels to examine the national and transnational crime of THB, to see if new approaches will assist in combatting this crime. For example, discouraging demand, is seen as part of the prevent approach to the problem. Increasing capacity in many states is seen to be another. This contribution advocates the full development and operationalisation of the transnational legal framework to combat the transnational crime of THB, adopting a human security approach.

Bibliography

Andreadakis, S., 'Regulatory Competition or Harmonisation: The Dilemma, the Alternatives and the Prospect of Reflexive Harmonisation', in Andenas, M. and Baasch Andersen, C., *Theory and Practice of Harmonisation*, Edward Elgar, 2011, 52–64.

117 Ibid.
118 Ibid.
119 Independent Anti-Slavery Commissioner Annual Report 2021–2022, op. cit., p 6.
120 Kevin Hyland, former Independent anti-trafficking Independent Anti-Slavery Commissioner in evidence to the Home Affairs Committee Tuesday 23 October 2018 Meeting started 2.31pm, ended 4.52pm.
121 Communication from the Commission to the European Parliament, the Council, the European Economic and Social Committee and the Committee of the Regions on the EU Strategy on Combatting Trafficking in Human Beings 2021–2025, Brussels, 14.4.2021, COM (2021) 171 final, p 11.
122 Ibid.
123 OSCE, Leveraging innovation to fight trafficking in human beings: A comprehensive analysis of technology tools, OSCE/ Office of the Special Representative and Co-ordinator for combating Trafficking in Human Beings, 2020.
124 Communication from the Commission, op. cit., p 14.

Bantekas, I., 'The Principle of Mutual Recognition in EU Criminal Law' (2007) 32 *European Law Review* 3, 365–385.

Boister, N., *An Introduction to Transnational Criminal Law*, Oxford University Press, 2012.

Boister, N., 'The Cooperation Provisions of the UN Convention against Transnational Organised Crime: a "Toolbox" Rarely Used?' (2016) 16 *International Criminal Law Review*, 39–70.

Boister, N., 'Transnational Criminal Law?' (2003) 14 *European Journal of International Law* 5, 953–976.

Communication from the Commission to the European Parliament, the Council, the European Economic and Social Committee and the Committee of the Regions on the EU Strategy on Combatting Trafficking in Human Beings 2021–2025, Brussels, 14 April 2021, COM (2021) 171 final.

Cullen, H., *The Role of International Law in the Elimination of Child Labour*, Martinus Nijhoff Publishers, 2007.

Europol presentation at the IALS, London, 3 October 2017.

Gallagher, A., *The International Law of Human Trafficking*, Cambridge University Press, 2010.

Glasius, M., and Kaldor, M., *A Human Security Doctrine for Europe: Project, Principles, Practicalities*, Routledge, 2006.

GRETA, *Evaluation Report: United Kingdom Third Evaluation Round; Access to Justice and Effective Remedies for Victims of Trafficking in Human Beings*, GRETA (2021)12, Council of Europe, 2021.

Haverkamp, R., Herlin-Karnell, E., and Lernestedt, C. *What is Wrong with Human Trafficking? Critical Perspectives on the Law*, Hart Publishing, 2018.

House of Commons Committee of Public Accounts, *Reducing Modern Slavery*, Thirty Sixth Report of Session 2017–2019, 25 April 2018.

Hyland, K., former Independent anti-trafficking Independent Anti-Slavery Commissioner in evidence to the Home Affairs Committee Tuesday 23 October 2018 Meeting started 2.31pm, ended 4.52pm.

Independent Review of the Modern Slavery Act 2015: Final Report Presented to Parliament by the Secretary of State for the Home Department by Command of Her Majesty, May 2019, CP 100.

Independent Anti-Slavery Commissioner, *Annual Report 2021–2022 Presented to Parliament pursuant to Section 42(10)(b) of the Modern Slavery Act 2015*, (2022), Crown Copyright.

Jonsson, A., *Human Trafficking and Human Security*, Routledge, 2009.

Kaufmann, C., *Globalisation and Labour Rights; The Conflict between Core Labour Rights and International Economic Law*, Hart Publishing, 2007.

Kirchner, S. and Frese, V. M., 'Slavery under the European Convention on Human Rights and the Jus Cogens Prohibition of Human Trafficking' (2015) 27 Denning Law Journal, 130–145.

Meyer, F., 'C-387/02 Berlusconi and Others. The Berlusconi Judgment: A Corner stone of European Legality', in Mitsilegas, V., di Martiona V., and Mancano, L., *The Court of Justice and European Criminal Law: Leading Cases in a Contextual Analysis*, Hart Publishing, 2019, 37–54.

Makareno, T., 'Organized Crime or Crimes Organized? Isolating and Identifying Actors in the Human Trafficking Chain' in Jonsson, A., *Human Trafficking and Human Security*, Routledge, 2009.

NCA, *National Strategic Assessment of Serious and Organised Crime 2021*, Crown Copyright, 2021.
Obokata, T., *Trafficking of Human Beings from a Human Rights Perspective: Towards a Holistic Approach*, Martinus Nijhoff Publishers, 2006.
O'Higgins, P., 'The Interaction of the ILO, the Council of Europe and European Union Labour Standards', in Hepple, B., *Social and Labour Rights in a Global Context: International and Comparative Perspectives*, Cambridge University Press, 2002, 55–69.
Onuf, N. *World of Our Making*, University of South Carolina Press, 1989.
OSCE, *Leveraging Anti-Money Laundering Regimes to Combat Trafficking in Human Beings*, OSCE, 2014.
OSCE, *Leveraging Innovation to Fight Trafficking in Human Beings: A Comprehensive Analysis of Technology Tools*, OSCE/ Office of the Special Representative and Co-ordinator for combating Trafficking in Human Beings, 2020.
Rijken, C., *Trafficking in Persons Prosecution from a European Perspective*, TMC Asser Press, 2003.
Rishikesh, D., 'The Worst Forms of Child Labour: A Guide to the ILO Convention 182 and Recommendation 190', in Nesil G., Nogler, L., and Pertile, M., *Child Labour in a Globalized World: A Legal Analysis of ILO Action*, Ashgate, 2008, 83–99.
Ryngaert, C. and Noorthmann, M., *Human Security and International Law*, 2014, Intersentia.
Stoyanova, V., *Human Trafficking and Slavery Reconsidered: Conceptual Limits and States' Positive Obligations in European Law*, Cambridge University Press, 2017.
Thyu, H. L., Yen, H. T. H., and Bao, N. Q., 'Fetus Trafficking in Viet Nam – the New Criminal method of Human Trafficking' (2021) 10 *International Journal of Criminology and Sociology*, 1594–1603.
UN General Assembly Resolution, 10 September 2012, 127th plenary meeting, A/RES/ 66/290.
von Tigerstrom, B., *Human Security and International Law: Prospects and Problems*, Hart Publishing, 2007.

Legislation

CoE Convention on Action against Trafficking in Human Beings 2005, CETS No. 197.
CoE Convention on Cybercrime 2001, CETS No. 185.
CoE Convention on the Protection of Children against Sexual Exploitation and Sexual Abuse, 2007, CETS No. 201.
Council Decision 2000/375/JHA of 29 May 2000 to Combat Child Pornography on the Internet, OJ L 138, 09/06/2000 p 1.
Council Framework Decision 2002/584/JHA on the European Arrest Warrant, OJ L 190, 18/07/2002, p 1.
Council Framework Decision 2002/629/JHA on Combating Trafficking in Human Beings, OJ L 203, 01/08/2002 p 1.
Directive 2011/93/EU of the European Parliament and of the Council of 13 December 2011 on Combating the Sexual Abuse and Sexual Exploitation of Children and Child Pornography, and replacing Council Framework Decision 2004/68/JHA, OJ L 335, 2011/12/18, p 1.
Directive 2011/36/EU of the European Parliament and of the Council of 5 April 2011 on Preventing and Combating Trafficking in Human Beings and Protecting its Victims, and replacing Council Framework Decision 2002/629/JHA, OJ L 101/1.

Human Trafficking and Exploitation (Criminal Justice and Support for Victims) Act (Northern Ireland) 2015.
Human Trafficking and Exploitation (Scotland) Act 2015.
Human Trafficking and Exploitation (Scotland) Act 2015 (Support for Victims) Regulations 2018/90.
ILO Minimum Age Convention, 1973 (No. 138).
Joint Action 97/154/JHA of 24 February 1997 adopted by the Council on the basis of Article K.3 of the Treaty on European Union concerning action to combat trafficking in human beings and sexual exploitation of children, OJ L 63, 04/03/1997, p 2.
Modern Slavery Act 2015.
Nationality and Borders Act 2002.
Regulation (EU) 2019/1149 of the European Parliament and of the Council of 20 June 2019 establishing a European Labour Authority, amending Regulations (EC) No 883/2004, (EU) No 492/2011, and (EU) 2016/589 and repealing Decision (EU) 2016/344, OJ L 186, 2019/07/11, p 21.
UN Protocol to Prevent, Suppress and Punish Trafficking in Persons, Especially Women and Children, supplementing the United Nations Convention against Transnational Organized Crime 2000, UNTS 2237, p 319.
UK EU Trade and Cooperation Agreement, OJ L 149/10.

Cases

Chowdury and Others v Greece, Application no. 21884/15, ECtHR, 30 March 2017.
Rantsev v Cyprus and Russia, Application no. 25965/04, ECtHR, 7 January 2010.

Website

www.ela.europa.eu/en

Index